TOP ROCK GIRLY JOCK

TOP ROCK GIRLY JOCK

A Chicago Radio First!

CONNIE SZERSZEN

STARBRIGHT PUBLISHING
Barrington, IL

TOP ROCK GIRLY JOCK

COPYRIGHT © 2008 BY CONNIE SZERSZEN

All rights reserved. No part of this book may be reproduced, stored in a retrieval system, or transmitted in any form or by any means electronic, mechanical, photocopying, recording, or otherwise, except in the case of brief quotations in critical articles or reviews, without prior permission in writing from Starbright Publishing.

10 9 8 7 6 5 4 3 2 1

ISBN: 978-0-615-30718-3
Library of Congress Control Number: 2009907823

Published by
Starbright Publishing
PO Box 3141
Barrington, IL 60010

www.StarbrightPublishing.com
www.TopRockGirlyJock.com

Fine Art Information at
www.PortraitArtChicago.com
www.portraitartist.com/szerszen

Cover Design by Kathryn Marcellino
www.MarcellinoDesign.com

Printed in the United States of America

With Love and Thanksgiving to the Holy Spirit

Dedicated to the Ones I Love

Mary, my mother—my inspiration and best friend—
The dearest part of me
Stanley, my father—proudly served in WWII—
And shared fun & laughter at home
Jerry, my brother—proudly served in Viet Nam—
Our family enjoyed his wit and wisdom

To all my listeners
Who showed me such kindness and loyalty

And especially to
Penny Lane
Who led me to the microphone

Hang on to your "Lucky Hat"—

Reach for the Stars—

And always

Treasure the Stardust within you!

Contents

ONE	When You Wish Upon a Star	11
TWO	Nine to Five	49
THREE	She Loves You—Yeah Yeah, Yeah!	61
FOUR	Cherry, Cherry	67
FIVE	Dawn—Go Away, You're No Good for Me	87
SIX	All Shook Up	101
SEVEN	Over the Rainbow	119
EIGHT	Rock and Roll All Night	143
NINE	I'm Not in Love	227
TEN	Another One Bites the Dust	239
ELEVEN	Stayin' Alive	259
TWELVE	Catch Us If You Can	275
THIRTEEN	The Wind Beneath My Wings	279
FOURTEEN	Alone Again, Naturally	293
FIFTEEN	Ring My Bell	305
SIXTEEN	Heaven Knows	309
SEVENTEEN	Ball of Confusion	323
EIGHTEEN	Rock On	333
NINETEEN	Hit the Road Jack!	343

Someone once said—

"Disc jockeys are too lazy to work—
Or too dumb to get another job"

Here are just a few who have proven that wrong—
And found success far beyond the "DJ" stage

>Johnny Carson
>George Carlin
>Paul Harvey
>Rush Limbaugh
>Jimmy Kimmel
>Glenn Beck

But then, I never planned on becoming a disc jockey

 **ONE**

When You Wish Upon a Star

Twirling around the kitchen to "Dance, Ballerina, Dance," wearing my cute Baby-Doll black patent leather shoes with the little ankle straps, I danced and danced—sometimes going barefoot—doing my version of ballet, actually standing on the very tips of my toes, without toe-shoes! The radio was almost always on in our apartment. In my bedroom, I would lie across the bed, on the bedspread that my mother had made–bluer than blue, with pretty pink rosebuds. As I looked out at the neighbor's yard, cluttered with junk and disheveled stacks of old lumber, I'd daydream to the songs, all alone on my own little musical island. Decades later, all grown up, I'd be doing the same thing—only the musical island would be a radio station's soundproof studio. Big girls love to daydream just as much as little girls do.

This is how I remember my first home at 1316 West Chestnut Street in Chicago. It was in the old Polish neighborhood—Chicago and Ashland. "Constance Estelle Szerszen" was my full name. "Estelle" was my mom's choice for a female version of my dad's name, "Stanley." My brother Jerry's middle name is "Marion" (just like John Wayne's real name) and a male version of my mom's name, "Mary."

TOP ROCK GIRLY JOCK

Dad's family lived on Huron Street near Noble. He came from a large family of eleven children. I remember hearing about how hard it was for his mom to get dinner ready. Almost everyone wanted something different. So Grandma would prepare several dishes so that each kid would find something he or she liked. Poor Grandma. Also, their apartment was only a three-bedroom—so the kids really had to bunk with each other. Probably a good thing—kept away the bogeyman—mainly because there wasn't any room left for the bogeyman.

The Szerszen ancestors hail from the part of Poland that is now a part of Austria. The word *"Szerszen,"* by the way, is a Polish word for *hornet*. The legend says that *"if it bites you seven times, you'll die."* Not sure where that legend got started. I don't think Mom knew that before she married Dad. Anyhow, I'm sure he never bit her—maybe just nibbled a bit—Hah!

Mom's family was smaller—only seven children. All the kids were born in the U.S., except for little Janka. She was born in Poland, and died there from a ruptured appendix when she was only ten years old.

The family had moved to Poland when Mom was about five. Well, actually, my grandmother and the kids moved; my grandfather stayed in Chicago and worked in the stockyards (where, coincidentally, I would have my first speaking role in a movie that was filmed there). When he had saved enough money, Grandpa moved back to Poland and bought their home and some acreage where they grew their own vegetables and raised chickens.

My grandmother had always wanted the family to move back to the States, thinking that life would be easier in America. So, when Grandma Anna died, Mom returned to the U.S. She moved in with her brother Joe and his family, on 21st Street near Damen Avenue, and took a job at Pixley & Ehlers restaurant. This is where she learned yummy recipes and unusual dishes which we got to enjoy later. In her spare time, Mom loved going to the movies. She was rediscovering America and refreshing her English. In Poland they had called her an American; in America they called her Polish.

When You Wish Upon a Star

Mom and Dad met at a dance. Music-Dance-Romance! Both my parents loved music. Dad would play the concertina and sing, sing, sing. Mom was more into dancing, and in those days it was the *Polish Hop*—the polka! Not only were they into music, but they were both very creative.

When Dad was in the Army Air Force, he hand-carved an oak picture frame for my baby picture—it sits on the mantle 'til today. While he was stationed in the islands, Dad would deep-dive for shells which he used to make necklaces for Mom and me. Later he'd build decorative bookcases—and other custom items for our home. Dad became a highly skilled sheet metal worker and was great with the precision needed for that job. Dad just *loved* stainless steel. Eventually, he made all sorts of utensils for Mom, saying how they would never rust. My Mom would laugh about how heavy they all were—but they never did rust.

TOP ROCK GIRLY JOCK

Mom became a "couturier" in Poland (not sure how to say a French word in Polish) and she would design and tailor clothes for her clients. By the time she was home again in the U.S., she was creating gowns for entire bridal parties—not only the gowns, but the bridal crown, the veil, the ring pillow—even the dress for the mother of the bride. I can still see her sitting at her White sewing machine, working late into the night to meet deadlines for fittings. She could also sketch and paint and her works were always admired by her teachers. Actually, she could do almost anything! She made the best kolaczki—she gardened—she knit—she crocheted—and taught me how to do all that too. I think she may have been the original *Martha Stewart*.

We lived on the top floor of a three-story apartment building, and later moved to the middle floor. There were two bedrooms, a kitchen, dining room, and living room. There was an old oil stove that Mom had to start up each morning, because by the time we got up, Dad had already left for work. My brother and I would huddle around the stove, snuggling up to Mom to keep warm as we waited for the heat to come on.

The attic was where all the tenants hung their laundry on wash day. I can still smell that fresh dampness from the clothes as I followed Mom, climbing up the treacherous, curving, worn wooden steps to the top, where she would stretch and hang the lace curtains, pinning them inch by inch along the stretcher bars.

There was always something fun to do at home. The backyard flooded with each heavy rainfall. In the middle of the yard was a 4x4 foot cement square with a drain in the center. My brother would take 2x4's, and line them up to make a path to the square where he would claim his territory. I, of course, was too afraid to try walking those narrow planks. So, it became his own little island where only he and God knew what pretend-games went on in his mind.

My brother was always full of fun. Except for that one time when he was just a baby, lying on the table, waiting for Mom to change his diapers.

"Mommy, it's raining." I whimpered, as Mom came rushing back with the diapers, shooing me out of range. I don't remember it, but my Mom sure did—because she then had a double clean up on her hands.

She also told me about that shopping day, when I was just a toddler. Mom was putting away some groceries as I sat on the table with the rest of the bag and, when she turned to put away the butter, all she found was an empty wrapper and my gooey fingers on my lips—"Mmmmmm—yummmmm." Yup, I ate the whole stick of butter before she even turned around, slippery kid that I was. And I still love butter—artery clogger that it is. You'd think it'd just slide *off* those arteries—but noooooo. Mom was so worried I'd be sick—but I think butter agrees with me.

And who could forget the rats from the alley. When I was younger, I thought they were so cute—so did my brother. My mom was terrified as we ran off trying to play with them. She had her hands full with only two of us.

There was almost always music playing in our home. If the radio wasn't on, then my folks would play some of their fave 78 rpm records—the kind that broke if you dropped them (I found out).

One Christmas, my parents gave me a record player with a great collection of records made especially for children. They were unbreakable plastic with cute colorful pictures on them. My favorites hum in my head 'til today—"A tisket, a tasket, a green and yellow basket"—"Brush your teeth, brush your teeth every single day—" but my favorite song was *"Green for Go, Red for Stop, be your own little traffic cop!"* (More about *"Green for Go"* later—and more about the *traffic cop* too!) I was barely five years old when this foreshadowing appeared.

When I was about six, I was surprised one day to hear my mom sounding all excited on the telephone in our dining room. She hung up the phone and turned to me, all smiles!

"Guess what, Connie! *You're* going to be on the *Mary Hartline Show*!"

TOP ROCK GIRLY JOCK

I wasn't exactly sure what that meant—but I had seen the show. Television was brand new and we were all watching every one of the few shows that there were. We especially loved the kiddie shows, like *Mary Hartline* and *Howdy Doody*. Of course, we also tuned in to *Milton Berle*, *The Lone Ranger*, *Flash Gordon*, and stuff like that. Looking back on it now, I guess they'd call my mom a *stage mom*. She encouraged me to try anything that might be fun for me.

When we got to the *Mary Hartline Show*, they showed us kids the contest games we'd have to play. We were told that as soon as we knew the right answer to a question, to take a step forward to a marked spot on the contest floor. Since I was so shy, I waited for the other kids to move before I did, even though I knew the answer immediately. At the end of the show, they gave us all prizes. A staff member asked what my hobby was. I said, "Reading," (which I loved to do). But I didn't love reading as much as I loved dolls. So the little girl next to me got a pretty doll (probably the Mary Hartline doll that is so collectible today) while I got a Tru-View Master thing—not nearly as lovable as the doll. I was a little disappointed, but even more disappointed was my brother Jerry, who had had a secret crush on Mary Hartline, even at the age of five. He was so excited when he heard he'd finally get to see her in person. He adored her long, flowing blond hair. But on the day we were scheduled to be at the studio, that long blond hair was neatly coiled in a tight little bun at the back of her head.

"What happened to your hair?" Jerry bluntly demanded in true Sagittarius fashion, totally crushed.

Mary Hartline just gave him the sweetest smile, but his life would never be the same.

One of my brother's fave memories is the day he spotted a pony out on the sidewalk, and some guy asked him if he wanted to sit on the pony! He gave Jerry a cowboy hat and some neat little chaps—just like a real cowboy. Then they went to find Mom so she could see how cute he looked—and so she could *buy* some pictures of Jerry. Naturally, when I saw him, I cried 'til I got *my* picture on the pony too.

When You Wish Upon a Star

Dale Evans would've done the same. I mean, it wasn't often you'd see a pony on Chestnut Street. The only time a horse went by was either in the alley, hitched to the wagon of the *rag-man*, or out front, pulling the peddler's cart, as he shouted out his wares—selling fresh produce to the neighborhood. (Mom—does he also sell butter?)

Right across the street from our apartment was Eckhart Park, where Mom and Jerry and I would watch Dad do daring high dives into the pool. He was a great swimmer, and it was amazing to me, how he would disappear under the water and, as we anxiously watched and waited, holding our breath, he'd finally resurface. The blue chlorinated water splashed over the edges of the pool and sparkled in the sunlight. It's as fresh in my memory as if it were yesterday. Life was all "Sunshine and Lollipops."

TOP ROCK GIRLY JOCK

School was interesting. One day someone came to our class and asked to test two students. The nun sent me and George, who was smart and cute; and I was glad to be teamed up with him. We were tested separately in a private room—must've been some sort of I.Q. test. They gave us numbers to memorize and then repeat, forwards, and backwards—stuff like that. I liked school—it was fun; and sometimes even fun on the long walk home. It was then that I got my first kiss—near my ear. I think he missed 'cause he came at me so fast; I never saw him coming. But it wasn't George—it was Ronald.

In first grade, at St. John Cantius school, (now the Chicago Academy of the Arts), I was asked to sing the lead in the year end concert. Mom sewed all the costumes—the girls were in blue flower headdress and fairy wings of baby blue netting. In the '90s, St. John's was also featured in some major films. It had a theatrical destiny!

A couple years later, at St. Francis of Assisi, Mom outfitted the class in a "Dutch" theme. (Later I found many boyfriends with the same theme—but that's another story.) We were decked out in wooden shoes (made of cardboard) and Dutch costumes, which she created for the entire group. Mom loved to design and sew and this was great extra income for our family.

Back in the first grade show, I had to sing the only solo, as the rest of the class backed me up. I sang "Cruising Down the River," and remember looking for my folks in the audience as I stood out front on stage, prim and proper, with my hands folded just as the nun had instructed. (I can't remember anyone ever asking me if I *could* sing. I was just told to do so.)

In later years, to hear me sing, all you had to do was look in the back seat of the family car, where I'd perform all the new songs in the latest *Hit Parade,* while my brother, also in the back seat, pleaded for me to shut up! There was always a good selection of song magazines at the Montgomery Wards on Chicago Avenue and I'd be sure to make enough of a fuss to get my folks to buy me one before we left the store. "Hey there, you with the stars in your eyes"—"Cross over the bridge"—I'd sing, as we drove back home, crossing over the Chicago River.

Second grade found me to be the youngest actor in the school play. My character even had to cry in one scene. It was easy. All I had to do was think of the worst thing that could happen in my life—which would be my mom dying—and the tears would come. I didn't like thinking about that, but it did make me cry. It was probably method acting before I even knew what that was. And my middle name was now also starting to make some sense. *Estell*e is the Latin word for *a star*—shooting, or falling, would remain to be seen.

I remember sitting on the little white cabinet next to the kitchen sink, rehearsing my lines with Mom. Seven lines, all in Polish. Mom made sure I pronounced my words correctly. Although I spoke Polish before I ever spoke English, it was more like baby-talk. Even Polish lessons in school didn't add much to my vocabulary. Daj mi buzi!

But I had no trouble memorizing. In those days, I could recite an entire page of textbook from memory. I was always called on to read and recite to the class. It was a snap for me and I got tons of gold stars. You'd get a gold star for each book you took out and read, and I loved to read! We had a table at the back of the classroom stacked with books that we could check out—kind of a mini-library. But when we had a chance to go to the real library, it was absolutely mind-boggling. So many books, so little time.

Near the end of my second grade, we moved to a new apartment, where my cousin Irene lived, at 4252 West Cortez, which later became part of the old Orr school grounds. (To think there might be a parking lot where my bedroom once was is kind of weird.)

My room was at the very end of the hall, past the living room. I felt a little isolated from the rest of the family, but it did have a cute little balcony that I just loved—kind of like a castle would have. It was all mine to look out at and fantasize about castles and princes!

Mom and Dad decorated. Dad had talked Mom into putting up this really ugly wallpaper—deep purple with huge white lilies and green vines connecting them. When you walked into the living room it about knocked you back into the kitchen.

My brother Jerry and I now attended St. Francis of Assisi Catholic School on the northwest side of Chicago. In third grade, I again found myself at the front of the class, reciting and performing.

One day, the nun chose me to be the narrator for a skit on Christopher Columbus. My best friend, Esther, was supposed to play Columbus. While we were rehearsing our little skit, I suggested how we should play out the scene.

"You know, Esther, when Columbus landed in America, he kissed the ground!" I reminded her.

Esther made it real clear to me, "No way am I kissing the ground!"

I said, "Aw, come on, Esther, just bend down and pretend to kiss the floor. They'll get the idea. You don't really have to *kiss* it. Just pretend!"

She refused. So I gave in—even though I thought this was *"a Kodak moment"* in the discovery of America!

I said, "OK, we'll skip it."

When it came time for the actual scene in front of the class, I don't know what came over me, but I heard these words come out of my mouth—"And then, Christopher Columbus kissed the ground!"

I looked over at Esther. She gave me such a look! After a few moments, I realized she wasn't going to kiss the ground, so I continued on.

It wasn't until fourth grade that the *Quiz Kids* radio show came around—sponsored by the *Chicago Sun-Times*. Esther was very bright and she and I were chosen by the nun to be quiz kids—(my first radio performance, but at the time, I didn't know it would *not* be my last). It was at the Conrad Hilton Hotel, in the same room where they used to have ice shows. The floor had wooden panels that covered the ice when the show was not on. I was on the radio—on ice, but the ice was covered—so symbolic, I often thought later, since I would have loved to have been a professional ice skater. I just wasn't any good at it—and lessons were too expensive—but I loved to skate!

I was about seven, when I got my first skates. I was thrilled! They had double blades, so I wouldn't fall as easily. This was back when we lived on Chestnut Street right across from Eckhart Park, where they prepared an ice skating rink every winter. One day, an older friend of mine came over. She loved my skates and wanted to try them out. Something inside told me this was not a good idea. She took one glide on my brand new little skates, and, *SPLAT!!!* The double blades had flattened out like a thin crust pizza! They were totally smashed! These skates were made to hold a kid, not a teenager. I was as crushed as my skates! I cried right in front of her—I didn't care. My mom told me they could be fixed, but I don't remember ever skating on them again.

So, as I sat there at the quiz show, on the radio, with an ice rink beneath me, I was having the time of my life—such fun. It wasn't 'til later that my mom said,

"Why were you swinging your legs back and forth like that? All the other kids were sitting still in their seats, but you kept swinging your legs!"

(Now that I look back on it, it was another foreshadowing of all the radio critiques I'd go through later in life with program directors. "Why did you say that? Do this, don't do *that!* Do that, don't do *this!*")

But, really, the other kids probably just weren't having as much fun as I was! Being on the radio was so exciting! So the first question was asked. I knew the answer, but again, I was so shy, and just like on the *Mary Hartline Show,* I waited for someone else to make the first move. My friend Esther did. And I noticed she didn't even wait until the end of the question to raise her hand. (Doesn't take me long to catch on.)

From then on, I raised my hand before the quizmaster finished the sentence. Esther and I were in a dead heat (enough to melt the ice beneath us). But since I had hesitated on that first question, she won the round by one point. We all got medals and Esther and the other round winners got their pictures in the *Chicago Sun-Times*. I was a little disappointed not to be included. (I had no way of knowing then that one day my picture would make the cover of the *Chicago Sun-Times* Sunday "Midwest" magazine.)

This quiz show added to the lesson I learned way back in kindergarten. I used to love the swing in the playroom, as did all the other kids. When recess was called, everyone would run to the swing first. I had always waited for the others to make the first move, and by the time I got there, the swing was full and there was no room for me.

Another odd thing I remember from kindergarten is that I felt older than the other kids. They were five-year-olds like me, but somehow I felt older. I had unusual reflections on life. I remember walking home from school one day and, as I passed a wrought-iron fence, I stopped and looked up into the sky, and was suddenly struck with this feeling of *confinement*. I remember thinking, here I am, on this sidewalk, next to this fence, and stuck here in this limited space—so far away and so isolated from everything grand and bigger out there in the heavens. Perhaps kids today have a different view of things, what with all the shuttles to space. But for that brief moment, I felt so small and helpless in this grand universe.

Later, when I studied Nietzsche, I wondered what thoughts struck him in that walk, the day he lost his mind. He claimed that "All great thoughts are conceived while walking." Did he also contemplate the heavens? Maybe if he'd had more faith in God, he wouldn't have gone insane trying to figure it all out.

"My genius is in my nostrils," he once said. (*Hmmm*—one good sneeze could've done him in.) But he did have great insight into music—"Without music, life would be a mistake." So true. "Only sick music makes money today." (Now, how many times have you heard your parents say *that*—must be true.)

TOP ROCK GIRLY JOCK

It was while we lived in the apartment on Cortez Street that I had my first close brush with death—simply a bad case of the measles. It was almost my First Holy Communion day and I was so sick. The doc made a house call and told my mother to keep the room dark. My fever was extremely high. He said I had a fifty-fifty chance of living through this. I was devastated—not so much because I might be dying—but because I might miss my First Holy Communion day! Again I cried. (I cry a lot.) I wanted to be there with my classmates. My mom had sewn this beautiful, white dress for me, with ruffles, bows, beading, and a lace apron—she even made the veil. Just gorgeous! I got even more delirious thinking that I might miss this special day. It must have been my tantrums that finally made the doc say to my mom, "OK, she can go to the church—but only at Communion time—and then back home to bed right after—and don't let her get close to anyone else!"

So I made it! I then went on to the photo studio (since it had been all prearranged), but my pictures had to be re-done, because my locks were all wilted from the perspiration of my fever. I now have two sets of Communion Day pictures—a sick and a healthy version.

When You Wish Upon a Star

Hey, check those *locks*. (I actually like the first one (the sick one) better; and why was that flower arrangement in my second picture? (Weren't those supposed to be for funerals?)

Anyway, my parents had gone all-out for this special occasion, and even booked a banquet hall to celebrate. It was our first big family party. I stopped in to say hello to everyone, and then went back home, where cousins Mary and Jeannette took turns playing nurse. The fun went on without me; my folks kept everyone entertained and fed. I slept through it all and survived. Of course—I had received Jesus that day.

TOP ROCK GIRLY JOCK

Art, music, and movies were my pleasures! Even as a little girl, I *loved* the movies! My earliest memories are of hearing Bing Crosby singing, "In the Cool, Cool, Cool, of the Evening." What a fun, uplifting song it was for me. I sang it all the way back home as we walked down *the avenue*—Chicago Avenue—stopping, on the way, to pick up some *bunch* tamales from the hot dog vendor. These tamales were square-shaped, and folded over—so yummy. But they don't sell those anymore because someone in government somewhere claimed there wasn't enough meat in them to call them *tamales*—so, these days you can only buy the rolled tamales.

The River of No Return, a Marilyn Monroe movie, also stashed beautiful melodies and river-rafting scenes in my head. Oddly, I remember the songs or certain scenes from movies more than the stories themselves. When I was growing up, musicals were hot—*The Unsinkable Molly Brown, Gigi, West Side Story, Flower Drum Song, South Pacific*—("Once you have found her—ne—ver—let—her—goooooo!"). At the end of those movies, with the music still playing through the credits, I'd walk up the sloping floor of the dark theater towards the exit doors—and I'd be hit with this *feeling!* I'd feel like I had been *in* that movie—the music—the happy ending—the heroine—was *me!* I floated out with the music and only got snapped back to reality when I hit the daylight outdoors.

And while I was pretending to be those famous heroines, decades later, I'd learn that people were pretending to be me. Some loyal kid listeners would "play DJ"—Doug in Indiana imitated Larry Lujack, and his girl cousin pretended to be me. (Who would've thought?)

And that caller at the radio station—when the guy said how he loved meeting me at the club last night and was looking forward to our date—he thought I was *beautiful*. I hated to tell him I was working on the air that night—that he must have met someone else who claimed to be me. Well, at least she was beautiful.

I loved art just as much as the movies. There used to be an advertisement in magazines titled, *"Draw Me"* above a woman's profile. And if you could successfully draw this woman, you might win an art scholarship or art supplies. Since I had already won a tennis racket in a local newspaper art contest by coloring Easter bunnies, I felt encouraged. I won, I think, not only because of my coloring skills, but because something in the back of my mind told me to place these bunnies on a hill, add some flowers and trees, etc.; in other words, embellish their scanty scene with an environment. (You kids might wanna try that in your next coloring contest.)

But when it came to drawing the woman's profile, I couldn't do it. I struggled. My mom, who was very artistically gifted, came to the rescue. She drew it freehand, and then told me to trace over her drawing, over and over again, until I felt I could do it myself. She then told me to try and do it freehand. And so I did. And I won! But I didn't win a prize—only a pitch to take their art courses—which I never did.

Soon afterward, a big contest came along in *The Chicago American* newspaper, co-sponsored with the theater company, Balaban & Katz. It was to promote the new movie, *The Beginning of the End*. Children were invited to color scenes from the movie. A new scene was printed in the paper each day for seven days. First prize was a trip to Hollywood and Disneyland. Second prize was a movie camera! It was just what our family wanted, needed, and couldn't afford. So, I entered the contest, hoping to snatch that second prize!

I spent the week carefully coloring the scenes the best I could and finished three or four of them. One day my cousin invited me over. We didn't get together too often, and this sounded like way more fun than sitting home alone, coloring. But there was Mom, reminding me,

"You'd better take those cartoons with you and finish them while you're over there; they've got to be done by this week-end."

I thought, what? I'm gonna be busy playing! Besides, I never thought I had a chance at winning anyway. It was just wishful thinking—like wishing on a star.

But rather than disappoint my mom, I took along the pictures from the newspaper and told my cousins I could play board games with them just as soon as I finished painting these in. (By now I was using watercolors.) So I sat at their table (while they played) and whipped them out. The girl with the skirt got a polka dot skirt—the boy got a striped shirt in bright colors. I ran with my imagination, coloring them in whatever fun way struck me at the moment. I was in a playing state of mind, after all! Finally! They were done! Now I could play! Mom sent them in.

One day the phone rang and the voice at the other end explained she was from the newspaper and wanted to speak with Connie. When my mom handed me the phone, I held my breath. Could it be? In my mind I already had my finger on that zoom lens. Could it be that I had won the movie camera? The voice on the phone said,

"Congratulations, Connie! You've won first prize in *The Chicago American* coloring contest!"

I was stunned! I never expected *first* prize! (Or *any* prize for that matter.) And, as I listened to her description of all the wonderful things I had just won with first prize, I thought, what about the movie camera? What I really wanted was *second* prize! I didn't say anything as she explained the all-expense-paid-trip for two to Hollywood and Disneyland for a week, and $100 fun money. She said that they had already picked a first prize winner, but my entry came in at the very last minute, and was far better than what they had picked, so that contestant got second prize (*my* movie camera) and I became the first prize winner. I finally started to enjoy it for what it was—that old "gift horse in the mouth" thing. I looked at Mom and said,

"Mom, remember when I gave you that really fancy nightgown for Christmas, and you said, 'Where am I gonna wear this? I'm gonna have to go to Hollywood!'"

My mom was always super-psychic. She always sensed what was coming, even though she may not have known it at the time.

"Well, Mom—we're going to Hollywood!" I shouted.

When You Wish Upon a Star

Girl, 14, Wins Big Coloring Contest, Trip

BY MORT EDELSTEIN

Three years ago when Connie Szerszen was only 11, she tried to draw the outline of a face she saw in a magazine, and because it looked so bad she cried.

Her mother, Mrs. Mary Szerszen, understanding her daughter's plight, told her:

"Darling, you just can't do something well the first time you try it. You must keep practicing until you become skilled at whatever you want to do."

Connie never forgot her mother's advice. She devoted all her free time to drawing.

TOP COLORING WINNER

Today, at 14, Connie is the happiest youngster in Chicago.

She was adjudged the winner in THE CHICAGO AMERICAN's Coloring Contest, and she will be given a five-day, round-trip dream vacation to Hollywood and Disneyland.

As part of her prize, she will be allowed to take a guest. Connie didn't hesitate in announcing who that will be. She said:

"Mother will go with me. We've always dreamed of going to Hollywood, and now we can."

DEPICT MOVIE SCENES

The contest required each youngster to draw six scenes from the movie, "Beginning of the End," which had its world premiere at the B & K Roosevelt Theater.

The movie, a science-fiction thriller with a Chicago locale, will soon appear in neighborhood B & K theaters.

Connie, who lives at 4906 W. Byron st., recently graduated at the top of her class at St. Bartholomew Catholic School. In the fall, she will attend Alvarnia Catholic High School.

SHE'LL STUDY ART

About her future, the pretty, brown-haired youngster says:

"I'll take art courses in high school, and keep up my daily practice of drawing. I hope someday to become a martist."

Her father, Stanley, 40, is a sheetmetal worker, and her brother, Jerry, 12, is a sixth grade student at St. Bartholomew.

CONNIE SZERSZEN
Wins Hollywood trip.

We laughed at how the article put words in our mouth when they paraphrased us. Everything happened so quickly. *The Chicago American* sent photographers to capture our departure. They snapped shots of Mom and me waving good-bye as we boarded the plane. I was starting to get that *heroine-movie-star* feeling that I had had walking out at the end of all those movies! But now it was *real*! I was being honored by this newspaper! They were making me a celebrity! The headline in the paper read—

She's a Very 'Colorful' Girl!

(Cute play on words—for the winner of the coloring contest!)

TOP ROCK GIRLY JOCK

She's a Very 'Colorful' Girl

"GOODBY CHICAGO" waves pretty Connie Szerszen, 14 (left) and her mother, Mrs. Mary Szerszen, as they leave Midway Airport on Continental Airlines' DC-7B for a, five-day all-expense-paid trip to Hollywood and Disneyland. Connie won trip by submitting top entry in The Chicago American's "Beginning of the End" Coloring Contest.

This was the first airplane ride for both Mom and me. TWA—one of the best in those days. It was a four-engine propeller, not a jet. We took off and were miraculously airborne. It was thrilling; and everything was going fine until we hit a huge air pocket and a sharp pain stabbed between my eyes as we dropped a thousand feet or so! I thought I was gonna die (never fly in a propeller plane with a cold). The stewardess said to chew gum, but nothing seemed to help the pain. Mom was worried—there went her daughter again—always victim to some odd malady. Then, dinner-time came. Mom and I prepared our tea—a dash of cream, a little spoonful of sugar. We each took a sip at the same time—no chance to warn each other—it wasn't tea—it was *bouillon soup!* We must have been a pretty sight, spitting and sputtering all over our trays. *Beverly Hillbillies* before their time!

When You Wish Upon a Star

But we had a wonderful week in Hollywood! They made me the honored guest at "The Marineland of the Pacific" and I was asked to feed the porpoises. I had to walk out on a long, narrow ramp over a three-story tank of water where the porpoises, hopefully, would jump to grab the slimy, dead fish I held in the tongs. When the first porpoise jumped, I jerked back in fright! He was almost as big as me! Of course, he missed. So I grit my teeth and thought I'd better hold this yucky bait out farther so this starving porpoise could grab it or I'll be out here all day in front of all these people looking like a fool. Worse yet, he might even yank me into the tank with him. I'm afraid of deep water and can't swim. (Of course, I smiled at the crowd while I thought all this.) The next time around, it worked! The porpoise grabbed the fish and I was out of there!

Then our tour guide arranged a complimentary boat ride for Mom and me on the Pacific Ocean. Oh, great—like the three-story fish tank wasn't enough deep water on this trip! I thought—for sure—we were going to drown! The waves were wicked. The *one* thing my mom could *not* do was swim. Mom pretended not to be afraid, but I could see it in her eyes (and white knuckles). She hated drowning as much as I did. The next day we read in the *L.A. Times* that one of those boats had overturned, tossing tourists into the Pacific. Mom probably saw that coming—she just didn't know exactly when.

Winning that trip to Hollywood/Disneyland made me feel so blessed. We visited Paramount Studios where I met Anthony Perkins, who would soon be a star in *Psycho*. (Just as strange as some of his movies, were his real life events. He died on September 12th of 1992 and his wife died almost to the date, nine years later. She was one of the 911 victims whose flight crashed into the World Trade Center.) Anthony was sweet and signed my grade school autograph book, as I interrupted his lunch. (I was getting bolder.)

We then went on to the *Lawrence Welk Show* where I got more autographs—from Lawrence and the Lennon Sisters. The next stop was to guest on the *Queen for a Day* show with Jack Bailey. We got there late (a Szerszen trait) so were never televised, but had our pictures taken on stage with Jack and the queen.

When You Wish Upon a Star

We ate at Farmer's Market, shopped for souvenirs, and kept our eyes peeled for movie stars. Then it was off to Disneyland! Our hotel was beautiful, with real orange trees growing in our private little patio. As we enjoyed the luxurious suite, I went to take a bath first and came out raving about the plush towels they had. Mom went next, and when she came out laughing, she told me—that the real plush one wasn't a towel—it was a bath mat. Well, excuuuuuse me, I had never seen a bath mat. At home we just had towels and a little rug on the floor.

At the park, we went on all the tame rides since Mom had a heart condition and wild rides could cause her heart to beat irregularly. I was always a chicken when it came to roller coasters, anyway, so I was fine with that. As a kid, I had gone on "The Comet" a couple times at Riverview and thought I was gonna die. Twice was enough.

We had fun at Disneyland. So much to see! We got wrapped up in the *fantasy* of it all. Because after all, we were in the very place where sometimes—*when you wish upon a star*—dreams really *do come true.*

TOP ROCK GIRLY JOCK

After winning that wonderfully dreamy trip, my next first prize came as a sophomore at Alvernia High School—with *The New World* poster contest. Besides creating original artwork for the poster, you had to also come up with a little slogan of sorts that would pitch *The New World*—a Catholic newspaper.

One night while trying to drift off to sleep, the words came to me. (This would be the first time a great idea would come to me just as I was hoping to fall asleep. Since then I have learned to keep a pad and pencil within arm's reach—and a little light source, because the *best* ideas came just when I really wanted to go to sleep! And if I didn't jot them down, they'd be totally gone by morning—lost in the netherworld of my mind.)

"HEAR THE CHIME—NOW'S THE TIME—DON'T DELAY—SUBSCRIBE TODAY!"

I drew a cartoon of a little girl standing by a clock that was as big as she was. (Not sure how original this part was since I had seen this in a magazine and just altered it to suit my poster.)

I won $100 cash and a wardrobe from Goldblatt's that still begs an explanation. (Maybe they had read that *Chicago American* newspaper caption—"She's a Very 'Colorful' Girl"?) Part of my gift wardrobe was a blue-orange-green-yellow-red-purple (did I leave out any color?) tweed winter coat. I also won an amber-colored rhinestone necklace with two dozen, four-inch strands of rhinestones that covered most of my chest—(move over, Cleopatra). It looked great with my navy blue Alvernia high school uniform (just kidding). But if I were to try wearing all these items at once, people might think there was something wrong with me. Circus clowns showed more fashion sense than that! There were more clothes to the prize, but none were as memorable as those two items.

I felt so honored, though, actually meeting Mr. Louis Goldblatt (we shopped at Goldblatt's often—but I guess not often enough, since they eventually folded) and now *The New World* would print my picture with him and the other contest winners.

When You Wish Upon a Star

The following year I won first prize again! This poster showed two elves putting up a huge billboard sign that read—

"MY NEWS IS TRUE—NOT EDITOR'S FICTION—DON'T PASS ME UP—GET YOUR SUBSCRIPTION!"

How this popped into my head, I can't recall, but I enjoyed rhyming words! This time I asked if *I* could pick out the wardrobe. They agreed. So Mom and I went to the Goldblatt's store and chose

TOP ROCK GIRLY JOCK

$100 worth of sweaters, skirts, and slacks. What fun! We picked out things I would find useful to wear—not clothes headed for the next clearance sale. Again, I got my picture in *The New World*—and this time with the other owner of the store, Mr. Joel Goldblatt, who also seemed like a real nice guy.

When You Wish Upon a Star

CONNIE SZERSEN, Alvernia High school junior, receives award from Cardinal-Elect Meyer for winning first place in THE NEW WORLD poster contest, high school division.

We went to another wonderful banquet at the Blackstone Hotel, with many clergy guests and dignitaries of *The New World*, where all the winners received award bonds from Cardinal Meyer.

My mom sewed a cobalt blue, woolen sheath dress for me to wear. I notice now, after all these years, that none of the other girls wore hats. I loved to wear hats—and still do. Other than being born in July, it was the one thing Princess Diana and I had in common.

Oh, I forgot—we were also both princesses. Of course, *she* was a *real princess*—whereas *I* only became the *"Polish Princess"* on the radio—Hah! But even then, I wore my "lucky hat" behind the microphone—partly because the brim blocked my view of the engineers who would always make me laugh when I didn't want to— and partly because it *was*—my "lucky hat."

TOP ROCK GIRLY JOCK

But my art teacher was astonished! I was the first student ever in the entire Catholic Archdiocese of Chicago to win first prize in two consecutive years. She wasn't usually pleased with me because I never volunteered to wash the windows at school. We were all supposed to do clean-up duty, but I told her my parents were paying for me to get an education, not to wash windows. I could do that at home for free, and never did. Actually, I didn't even know *how* to wash windows. So why even ask me.

Besides my art studies, I also took drama classes. I liked acting but was petrified at having to speak in front of a class—yet totally encouraged by my speech and drama teacher, Sr. Vitalis, (who is now over 100 years old). One of our assignments was to give a presentation to the class. I agonized over those public spectacles. I wouldn't sleep the whole night before and imagined everything going wrong that could go wrong. I kept reminding myself of Shakespeare's quote, "Present fears are less than horrible imaginings," and hoped he was right. Maybe it would be less scary than I imagined. The night seemed to go on forever, but as the sun blasted out the moon, the dreaded day dawned.

When You Wish Upon a Star

My first presentation centered on hors d'oeuvres. I thought if I could present something visual and enticing—like food—perhaps no one would look at *me*! So I quickly gave instructions on preparing unique appetizers—a slice of bread, trimmed of crust, slathered with cream cheese, and a thin sliver of carrot in the center. Folded on the diagonal, they looked like calla lilies! They were so cute! No one paid attention to me, as I handed one out to each hungry student. *It worked!* This was another of my mom's creations. Her adorable appetizers saved my day.

Our next presentation was to read a script taken from a written ad. We were to look through magazines and papers 'til we found something that interested us, and then read it as a commercial. I will never forget this. The class was asked to critique each other. One of the students said,

"When Connie reads into the microphone, her voice sounds so different than when she's just talking. It sounds so professional—so good!"

I thought, whaaaaaat? Where's that coming from? I didn't really think I sounded any better than anyone else. It was a bit surprising to hear how my voice sounded deeper through the microphone, but I thought everyone's did. Looking back on it now, I guess my mom and some of her family did have unusual timbres to their voices. Whether mine was deeper, or just somehow different, it was probably hereditary. Years later I would be told by a program director that my voice sounded really good on the air, as most women's voices tended to sound nasal. I sort of had this natural advantage.

High school days, and all that went with it, were finally coming to an end. I was still excruciatingly shy. I had studied drama, art, French—anything I truly loved. I excelled in algebra, and got my worst grades in geometry. Biology was a snap, except for the earthworm project. My lab partner refused to touch a dead earthworm. I hate earthworms, but had no choice; so I did it—no problem, as long as it's not slithering around. I never have, nor ever will, touch a *live* earthworm. So *I* dissected the slimy, dead creature. "When the going gets slimy—"

But I really enjoyed doing biological illustrations—creating works of art—my amoebae and paramecium were museum quality—Hah! Art seemed to sneak into every class.

Even back in third and fourth grades, I would sketch little fashion figures, decking them out in ballerina skirts or big floppy hats. My classmates just loved them; and I'd quickly and quietly draw them out. One after another, they got passed around—everyone wanted one. Meanwhile the nun was teaching us something up there at the front of the class. It's helpful to sit at the back of the room if you're gonna fool around during classes; anyway, that's where I usually got assigned to sit since my last name began with an *"S."*

Some nuns went out of their way to encourage a student's artistic gifts. One *artsy* student and I were quite often pulled out of regular classes and asked to draw colored chalk scenes on the blackboard, to decorate the classroom. So we drew and colored, while the other kids had regular lessons. This was probably some kids' first hint that life isn't always fair.

School days, however, always held some challenges for me. I wasn't happy unless I got the very best grades. At St. Bartholomew grade school, I graduated at the very top of my class—first place out of three classes of ninety students. I was amazed; I thought for sure some of the kids were way smarter than me. But I may have been a better guesser!

TGFMC (for you texting addicts)—*Thank God For Multiple Choice*—(or did I mis-Tweet?) I don't text—I'm still learning Pig-Latin.

At the graduation ceremony, they presented me with a beautiful leather-bound Catholic Missal. (At Alvernia High School I slipped a bit and only made the upper ten per-cent of my class of three-hundred-plus students.)

But a secret, torturous, incident would long linger on my mind. In my last year of grade school, a classmate who sat next to me, said,

"You say the word *'the'* funny."

She told me this just before I was called on to recite. She looked at me intensely and accusingly and said I didn't pronounce the word *"the"* as clearly as others. (I suppose it was more like the pronunciation of the coach of *"Da"* Bears or *"Da"* Mayor of our city.) Mine might have been a *Chicago-Polish* kind of pronunciation. I was shattered! All these years, I had excelled in reciting and reading to the class and loved doing it. No one had ever mentioned anything like this to me before. The thought that I had not been pronouncing words correctly, horrified me. I always wanted to do things right—to be perfect!

And so, when the teacher called on me, I stood up and started to read. Suddenly my heart started racing; I was getting short of breath. And that classmate was sitting right there watching. I had no idea what was happening to me! I thought I was going to faint, so I just stopped. Everyone looked at me. I excused myself and left the room. I ran to the bathroom where I could be alone and just waited 'til I could breathe normally again. The nun was confused—I had always been so good. Was I sick, she later asked me. She said I got very pale. I didn't know how to answer her. I had never experienced anything like this before. It was probably a panic attack, although I didn't know it at the time.

From that day on, I went out of my way to avoid reciting or performing in front of anyone. My shyness was now saddled with a self-consciousness that hung with me throughout high school. I was never part of *the in crowd* and that was fine with me.

Years later, during one of my radio shows, I got a call from a former classmate.

"You *can't* be the same Connie Szerszen I went to high school with! Are you? You were always so *quiet!*"

"Yes, I am," I answered, "that's me—the *Top Rock Girly Jock of WIND!*"

I've come to believe that shyness can sometimes be part of one's appeal. Shy folks are not so *in your face*—stealing your thunder. Some of the most gifted entertainers are/were shy and suffer from stage fright. Barbara Streisand and Carly Simon both cringed at live performances. Some entertainers scheduled to perform for the Queen have been known to back out the day before. Lucille Ball was turned away from an acting school because of her shyness. Legendary actor, Laurence Olivier, had bouts of stage fright—and even Elvis had said on stage, "If you think I'm nervous, you're right." More recently, performance snafus by Jessica Simpson and her sister, Ashlee, probably resulted from shyness.

I'm no psychologist and can only analyze this from my own experience. It seems shyness, self-confidence, and stage fright can all get jumbled up together—part of the same package. Maybe shyness starts from a fear of not being good enough in other people's eyes—a worry about not presenting your *best self*. If shy people are so concerned with others' opinions, then they are more apt to be easily liked—because they are *people-pleasers* at heart—and who doesn't love a people-pleaser. Shy people may simply have a heightened sense of awareness of others, and so, strive to *please* more.

But Rick Nelson's "Garden Party" gave the best advice of all—

"You can't please everyone—so you got to please yourself—"

Anyway, considering the long list of shy entertainers, I feel like I'm in pretty good company.

When You Wish Upon a Star

Above— Mom's Parents,
　　　　Anna & Ignace
Right— Dad's Folks,
　　　　Catherine & Albert

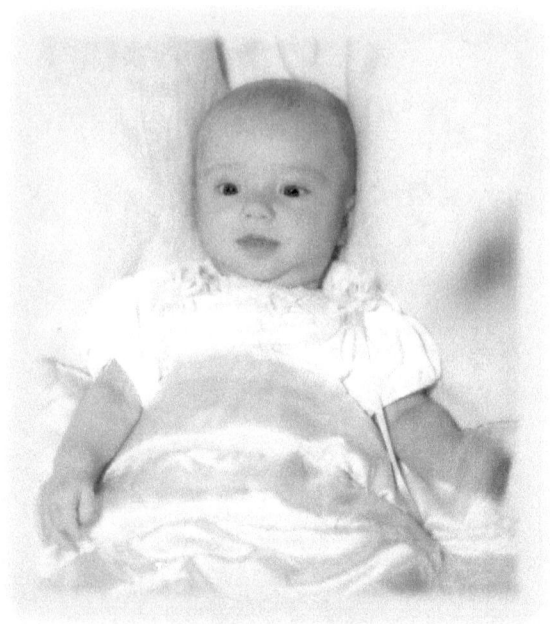

At 3 months

Later with Mom and Dad on leave from the Army Air Force

When You Wish Upon a Star

Jerry was born
into the
Szerszen
family
just before my
second
Christmas

TOP ROCK GIRLY JOCK

Top left to right—
Age 3 with first doll—Jerry fights off rats—I'm on *Jer's* island
Mom sewed our Easter outfits & my first Flower Girl gown

When You Wish Upon a Star

Top left to right—
Dad, me & Jer on the bridge at Olson Rug Co. (Cheap day trip)
Dad, Jer, Mom—our 1st house, 4908 W. Byron St. (Cute hat, Jer)
Jerry the photographer — Our first dog, Lassie
Backyard ice rink Mom would freeze for us each winter
(And freeze, she did!)

 TWO

Nine to Five

My very first job was as a *candy girl* at the Portage Park Theater on Milwaukee Avenue on Chicago's northwest side. We were now living at our first house –on Byron Street—so it was easy walking distance to *Six Corners* as it was called (the intersection where Irving Park Road, Milwaukee, and Cicero Avenues met).

Other than padlocking a co-worker in our storage room, I did pretty well. Near the back side of the theatre was a combination storage-locker-dressing room. This was where we kept popcorn, and butter in the cooler; and where we changed from our street clothes to the yellow cotton uniforms that all the candy girls wore. I never noticed that a senior candy girl had come in to change clothes on the other side of the lockers, as I changed into my uniform, walked out, slammed and padlocked the door on the outside. We always kept it locked to prevent theft of supplies. Of course, being padlocked on the outside, no one would ever expect anyone to be on the inside. It wasn't until six hours later, when the next shift started, that an employee went in to change clothes, and found this hysterical, screaming-mad woman ready to kill me. Good thing for me she was locked in. Really, though—if she would've screamed that loud before, maybe someone would've heard her over the movie—then again, maybe she did, and just sounded like part of the movie. I was reprimanded, but not fired. If the sneaky, quiet, little lady would've at least said *hello* to me, this never would have happened. Not my fault.

It was fun working at the Portage. I had crushes on two of the ushers—both named Andy—(which made things simpler). One was blond—the other dark haired. (Anything's *my type*.) Neither one ever asked me out. I was a pimply, skinny, waiting-to-blossom teenager—and let's not forget—shy. But I loved my first job! It paid ninety cents an hour and we often got overtime—I sometimes worked twelve hours a day. (We Polish girls work hard.)

South Pacific was playing at the time. At the candy counter, fully stocked and ready, we waited for those memorable lines,

"*Ring the bell again! Ring the bell again!*"

That was our cue. This meant intermission time, when all the folks would explode out the theater doors—like human popcorn. We could hardly keep up with everyone wanting their extra butter—no butter—Milk Duds—Good & Plenty—and make that good and plenty fast! After all, they had to hurry back to their seats before the movie started. Then just as quickly as it began, it would be empty and quiet again.

Such fun! I loved every minute of it! But I was still in high school, and this was just a summer job. Later I read that Elvis' first job was also at a movie theatre, as an usher. I fantasized about him being an usher at the Portage—we had so much in common. (*Sigh!—whimper—sigh!*)

After high school, my mom suggested I take a break and try working for a while. She felt that school was getting to be too much of a strain for me since I wasn't happy unless I could get straight A's—which I usually did. So I took a job as a secretary. I had excelled at Gregg shorthand, and even won a medal for 120 wpm. So, while my brother went off to college, I started my business career.

We were now living in our brand new home at 4344 N. Nordica in Norridge. I checked the local Help Wanted ads hoping to find something in the neighborhood; and applied for a job at Bankers Life

& Casualty Company, an insurance company about fifteen minutes from home.

Because of my great secretarial skills, I was hired in the General Systems & Operations/Methods Department comprised of twelve men. When I left, they had to hire two girls to replace me—I was such a workhorse. I also worked for the vice president of the department, approving expense reports, designing forms, and typing tons of operational material for the computer programs—big breaking news in those days. Since I had an art background, they commissioned me to do some free-lance calligraphy for their award certificates; eventually I transferred to their ad agency as a production assistant.

Some of my former high school classmates also took secretarial positions at Bankers Life, so it became a kind of extended school atmosphere. My friend Mary was secretary to Rod MacArthur, one of the vice presidents, who was also the son of the owner, John D. MacArthur.

This insurance-business-family also had an interesting connection with the movie industry. One of their family members was the son of actress Helen Hayes—James MacArthur—who had a steady role in *Hawaii Five-O*.

Mary loved working for Rod—he was fun, kind, and generous. He brought Mary and me unique perfumes from Paris, where he often traveled with his French wife. In those days, you couldn't find such special items here. These perfumes were made with wax which filled little plastic balls or baskets—only about 1" high—with hand-painted flowers on them to match the scent. In later years, Marshall Field's sold them; but eventually the entire line was discontinued. They were so precious—and, of course, I still have some—because I save everything. (Anybody want some fruitcake?)

Mary and I took our first vacation together to Ft. Lauderdale. Somehow our picture got in the neighborhood paper—*The Times*—like why, I have no idea. Maybe the motel sent it in for publicity.

TOP ROCK GIRLY JOCK

(*Hmmmm*, seems the sun bleached out my hair—y'think?)

We checked out the clubs and beaches and one day decided to go deep-sea fishing. Someone said we'd get a faster tan on the water as the sun reflected off the waves.

And so I caught my first fish ever—a 4'2" barracuda. All I really wanted was a sun-tan, but this monster bit my line and I was as hooked as it was. The crew said I had to reel it in myself—those were the rules. The way it flipped in and out of the water, it was like something out of a movie (a scary movie). Later I had bruises on my legs from the pole as I fought for that fish. After all that hard work I wished it had been a pretty sailfish instead of a boring barracuda. Dad made me stuff it.

Nine to Five

"Barracuda"—Betcha Heart writes a song about this some day

I made many great friends at Bankers. Sue and I modeled for a hairstyle fashion show which made us feel so glamorous!

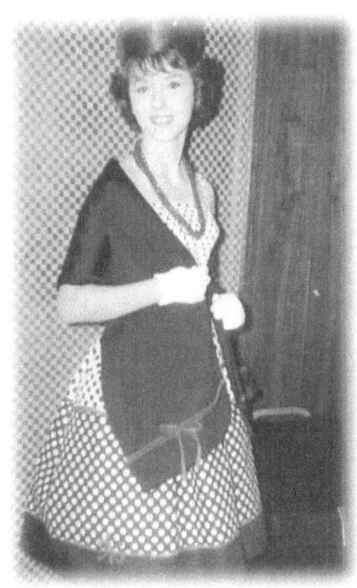 

Me—With Auburn Hairpiece   Sue—A *REAL* Blonde

We always had lots of laughs in the lunch room—with Florence, and Marion, who also worked for one of the vice presidents, as most of us girls did. There sure were a bunch of vice presidents there.

Left—Secretarial Me, and Marion

But soon the challenges were gone. The job was getting to be too routine. I didn't want to stay there my whole life and end up a Banker-Vet with a medal. Not exactly my cup of Lipton. It was time to move on. The whole world was out there! Downtown Chicago was waiting—just a short ride down the Kennedy. There *had* to be something more exciting! Or at least, something more artsy!

Ever since high school, I had been taking part-time art classes. My first was at the Art Institute of Chicago, where I studied fashion design. Since Mom was such an excellent designer, she was an inspiration to me. All the ladies sought her out to design and sew dresses for them because she *fit* them so perfectly. A tuck here and a tuck there, and they were *Cinderella*.

So, since this art course combined fashion with art, it covered everything that both my mom and I loved doing. I would first draw out my fashions and then create them with actual pieces of fabric. But even as much as I loved designing clothes, I felt there was a lot more I wanted to know about art. I wanted to learn about color, different mediums and painting techniques.

Nine to Five

That came from the American Academy of Art, where I continued studying part-time. *Life* class found me sketching nudes in charcoal. (My dad would always ask to see what I had done in class that day—he carefully studied my drawings of the women models with an appreciative eye—Hah!) I passed through the obligatory color wheel-fundamentals stage, and started to learn about illustration, typesetting and layout for ads. I was so honored when Mr. Stake, my teacher at the Academy, sent a note to my folks. He told them he found me so gifted that they should consider sending me full-time (Mom and Dad's artsy genes at play). Although I did fairly well at the projects assigned to me, I had no real interest in typography and layout design. I just liked to paint and draw—the *fine art* aspect of it all. My mom worried that there was no stability or future in an art career—and I agreed. Poor Mom had no way of knowing at the time, that I was avoiding the instability of a career in art; only to one day replace it with the instability of a career in radio.

So I started searching out other jobs. Something had to be more exciting than working for the insurance company. Again, I scoured the Help Wanted ads—this time in *The Chicago Tribune*—and I found a position at the University of Illinois, Circle Campus. They were looking for a secretary in the Department of Engineering. It was intriguing to me because it would be in a university atmosphere. Although I wouldn't be a student, I'd get to experience some college life!

In those days we used typewriters instead of computers. My IBM typewriter had different language balls that could be switched, from English to Greek. Most documents I had to type were *not* in English, but in Greek. There was no way of knowing if I had a *typo*. It was (pardon the expression) all "Greek to me."

After a couple months, it was a boring routine again. The only fun we had as secretaries, was finding our boss's love letters to his girlfriend. My co-worker would call me into the ladies room where she'd show me what she found in his wastebasket after tidying up the office; we giggled as we read the intimate details, wondering what his wife would say if she only knew. Ahhh, *l'amour*.

But he could be something to deal with. (Maybe this was why this secretarial position had been so available.) One of my duties was to open all his mail, and have it on his desk ready for him to read when he arrived in the morning. One day he started screaming at me!

"Who opened this box?!!!" he ranted and raved.

I did, of course. It was what he had assigned.

"Can't you read," he yelled, "this can't be opened by anyone but *ME!* And even *I* am not allowed to open this unless I am behind *locked doors!*" he howled.

Picturing him behind locked doors was a pleasant thought at the moment. Little did he know he was talking to a girl who knew how to padlock someone in a room. I looked at him closely to see if his eye-teeth were getting longer or if hair was starting to sprout on his face and neck. Might be time for the "Monster Mash." Well, this particular mail was some silly top-secret thing from NASA. How was I to know? I was just following his orders. He should've warned me.

One day he had to fly out of town on business. He asked an aide to drive *my* car, using *my* gas, while he dictated to me in the back seat. How important was this letter—or this job—I was starting to think. It seemed like my secretarial positions had gone from *boring* to *weird*.

Before long I applied for a transfer to another department. At the University of Illinois Research and Educational Hospitals, I became secretary to the brilliant Dr. Cotsonas, Head of the Department of Medicine. Now instead of typing in Greek, I was transcribing my shorthand notes of medical terms—words I never even knew existed. There were regular meetings in the conference room where the university doctors convened to discuss student courses for the upcoming semester. I took the *minutes* in shorthand during the three hour sessions. Yes, they had tape recorders in those days; what was wrong with this picture? I had to write down every word they said—there was endocrinology, cardiology, pathology, and gynecology. It was *crazyology*! I figured out pretty quickly that I had to devise my own shorthand—especially for the *-ology* part of the word, which was everywhere! Roberta, another secretary, suggested I take a course in medical transcription, but I didn't plan on staying there that long.

Above—Years later—At Doc Cotsonas' retirement party

Above—Roberta Nelson, who always remembered my B-day!

TOP ROCK GIRLY JOCK

I did manage to find a way to sneak some art into this job too, though, by entering two of my oil paintings into the employee art show. A couple wanted to buy my oil of a little boy in blue; but I told them I couldn't sell it because my folks hung that one in their living room and it matched their décor. So then, they asked to buy the oil of the little girls in the field; I was sorry to tell them that that rose-colored one matched my bedroom décor. So I didn't sell anything, but was so honored they asked. They even doubled the offer from $100 to $200; as tempting as that was, I said no, because I really didn't have much time for painting and didn't know when I'd have a chance to do more. (Stupid move on my part, I know.)

Nine to Five

One thing that made me decide to quit this job was the fact that since I was working in a research hospital, many of the patients never made it out of there. One day I overheard one of the doctors happily and proudly proclaim, as he headed into the conference room at the end of the hall,

"Hey, we sent one home alive today!"

I remember seeing a little boy in the elevator; his skin was all yellowed. I thought, poor thing—so young—and would he be one of the lucky ones to make it out of here alive? Down the hall from my office, cardiac catheterizations were performed almost daily. In those days, this was a new and delicate procedure. How many were dying down the hall while I sat typing? Then, when the horrible news hit, of the Richard Speck student nurse killings on campus, one of whom was a sister of one of our doctors—well, that was it for me. It was all just too depressing. The only fun there was dating some of the medical students, who usually dropped me when they met nursing students. Nurses were always more desirable than secretaries. (Probably because of those pristine white uniforms—white is a sign of purity—probably a turn-on.)

But before I bailed out, another secretary and I decided to tour the medical school during our lunch hour. Our first stop was the medical library where we saw unusual embryos in sealed jars. I saw a Cyclops. Never thought such a thing ever existed. Our second stop was the anatomy classroom. It was lunchtime, so no students were there—only cadaver after cadaver—laid out on open tables. Some looked like they might have been human at one time. Others looked like something out of a horror movie. My knees buckled. I thought I was gonna pass out! Now I was absolutely sure I had to find a happier place to work. There was too much sickness and death here. There had to be better ways to spend a lunch hour.

Not long after, I found what sounded like a great job—*downtown Chicago!*—with the Wrigley Company. "Double Your Pleasure, Double Your Fun!" Naturally, it was in the historical Wrigley building. I felt so important walking in to work there. It was so big time. One of my duties was to balance the checkbook of one of the Wrigley heiresses—her trips to Catalina Island, her shopping, her luxurious lifestyle—*BORING!*—when it's her life and not yours. Hah! I lasted two weeks! They offered me more money to stay on—but not enough to make my checkbook look like that of the heiress.

So I started scanning the *Trib* again and spotted an ad for a secretary for a radio station. I had no idea what station—it didn't say. I called. It paid $20 a week less than what I was making at Wrigley. My friend Sharon said,

"Go for it! It sounds like so much fun!"

I hesitated. They were very interested; partly because of my skills, but mainly because I was not a *groupie*. I had no idea who was on the air or what they were doing. I was just a well-qualified secretary. Well, *yeahhhhhhh*—how many secretaries are they gonna find who have typed in Greek and transcribed medical terminology! And although I didn't know much about radio, I *was* really into music.

THREE

She Loves You—
Yeah, Yeah, Yeah!

The Beatles were hot—and cute. What normal American girl wouldn't scream her head off for them. Like Elvis déjà-vu.

I thought back to my exciting trip to Hollywood just a few years ago. My friend Nancy and I had taken a silly-girl-vacation together. We were young adults, acting like kids. My cousin Joey was a Marine and stationed in Anaheim, California. He and his wife were expecting their first child and they invited us over for dinner. Joey showed us the Marine base and a warehouse full of Chatty Cathy dolls that were going to be shipped to an orphanage in Asia—the dolls were defective—they didn't talk. (Didn't really matter, though, since Chatty Cathy only spoke English anyway.) He saw I loved the dolls, and asked if I wanted one, so Nancy and I each picked one out (probably depriving some poor orphans of a couple of dolls).

Later, we rented a convertible and took our Chatty Cathy dolls for a ride. We played with our dolls and drove through Hollywood and people looked at us funny. No, we weren't drunk and did not do drugs. We were just young girls caught in that twilight between adulthood and the little girls we once were—it was silly girl fun!

But, that fun wore off quickly. So one night we decided to go have some grown-up fun. Johnny Rivers was playing at the Whiskey-A-Go-Go on Sunset Boulevard. We were gonna rock-n-roll! We put on our *"Don't-I-look-cute?"* clothes and headed out to party.

Johnny was just finishing a set as we walked in and as we were trying to figure out where to get a drink, the security guys started to corral all the patrons up the stairs to the second level. Everyone was being pushed and shoved and crunched away from the main floor. Since we had never been there before, we couldn't figure out if this was normal activity, or if there was a fire or bomb scare! Then we heard the whispered rumors in the crowd.

"I heard the BEATLES are coming here tonight!"

"Are they gonna play here tonight?"

What! Was it true? **THE BEATLES**!!! Here!!! Tonight!!!

Well, I didn't need to hear much more to decide that I had to be *downstairs—not upstairs!* It was every silly girl for herself (good luck, Nancy!) as I shoved my way back down to the main floor, somehow getting past security, but still crushed in by people everywhere. Sardine City (with hot sauce). I didn't know which way to turn or where to go for the best view. But I didn't have to try hard for very long. The next thing I knew, there was John Lennon—and then George Harrison! Walking right past me! I was a part of that "human wall of flesh" the papers later reported. I reached out and *touched* them! *They were right next to me*! Never saw where they came from, but they headed past me towards a back booth; and as I looked for the next Beatle, there was Ringo! (Did he know we had a Chihuahua named after him?)

"Ringo, Ringo! Show me your rings!" I screamed with delight!

He gave me kind of a weird look, but he *did* look at me. Beatle-beggars can't be choosers. I quickly ran my hand over his ringed fingers—each one adorned with unique bands of gold and silver—just "Too Much" to take in with one glance. Right there! I touched him too! And, so *who* was left! My favorite Beatle—Paul McCartney!

She Loves You—Yeah, Yeah, Yeah!

(Paul—*"I Want to Touch Your Haaaaaand!"*) I stood my ground—but there was no Paul! Some people who came in with the Beatles joined them in their booth. But no Paul! Well, yeah! He was so cute; he probably had a hot date that night! I was a little disappointed, but the excitement of seeing the rest of them took over. Now we were getting shoved aside again. I aimed for a back wall, close to the booth with the Beatles. Later I learned that actress Lana Turner's daughter, Cheryl Crane, was in the booth next to the Beatles, and they were also joined by a beautiful buxom blonde—Jayne Mansfield. It seemed that one of the Beatles wanted to meet her, so this all had been prearranged.

Jayne Mansfield would later be killed in a car accident. Rumor had it that she belonged to some satanic cult and that her lawyer/manager/boyfriend was warned not to travel with her. Supposedly, she was on the list to be doomed because of her attempts to cut herself off from the cult. He died with her in that car crash. I remember driving that road from Biloxi, Mississippi, to New Orleans when we visited my brother. Jerry was in the Air Force then, stationed in Biloxi, and he knew from the local papers exactly where and how the accident happened. The car had gone under the back end of a truck. Some say she was decapitated; others say just the top of her head was cut off.

So, as I leaned on the back bar wall taking it all in, there stood another *Hollywood-Looking-Blonde* watching the Beatle booth too! We talked a bit about how exciting all this was and I could tell by looking more closely at her that she was definitely *"Hollywood"*—perfect hair and face. I asked her name—she said, "Mamie Van Doren!" Oh my goodness! The place was crawling with celebrities! How did I luck into this! Never did get to see much of Johnny Rivers—but by now I had forgotten all about him. Because—

ON THAT HOLLYWOOD NIGHT, I TOUCHED THREE OF THE BEATLES!

Nancy and I finally found each other in the crowd and left in delirium. Neither one of us could sleep at all that night; just knowing they were in the same town we were. The next day there were photos of the Beatles at the Whiskey-A-Go-Go on the front page of the *L.A. Herald-Examiner*. The headline read—

Beatles Go 'Frantic'

One shot showed George throwing a drink (scotch) at a UPI photographer ("While his—*camera*—gently weeps"). Supposedly, George had warned him not to take any more pictures, but he didn't listen (Tsk, Tsk!) George's drink was a slam dunk on the photographer, a deputy sheriff, and Mamie Van Doren. (I ducked.) (I could see "the drinks were on the house.") The papers reported that Ringo explained, "Paul just stayed home." I still wonder why poor Paul stayed home all alone—while there was all this action going on here. I mean, didn't he want to see Jayne Mansfield in the flesh? Or Mamie Van Doren? Or me?

I still couldn't believe that I had actually been standing right next to it all—a part of Beatle history! How Nancy and I happened to be there that night—at that club—and at that moment—is still remarkable. It's as if we knew when to show up. The article said—

> The Beatles had to be lifted bodily to get into the Whiskey-A-Go-Go, because of the crowds. When they left, it was to their rented mansion at No. 356 to get some rest after their Hollywood Bowl appearance. Estimated property damage was $5,000 and more than 50 juveniles were taken into police custody and later released. A newspaperwoman for 17 years, said, "It was frantic, impossible, ridiculous—but fun!"

#

That tattered, yellowed, clipping is still in my scrapbook—my special memory of the night I touched three Beatles. Have a peek—

She Loves You—Yeah, Yeah, Yeah!

LOS ANGELES EVENING AND SUNDAY
'RALD EXAMINER — Del Mar RACES Late Scratches
EST EVENING CIRCULATION IN AMERICA
WEDNESDAY, AUGUST 26, 1964 — 10 CENTS — NO. 153

Beatles Go 'Frantic'

The Beatles, Britain's anti-barbershop quartet, headed for Denver today after a Los Angeles visit in which property damage was estimated at $3000.

Appraisal of havoc wrought around Beatle Manor in Bel Air came early today as shaggy George Harrison was tossing a highball at a photographer in a Sunset Strip night club, and the last of more than 50 juveniles was being released from police custody.

Even so, authorities who worked overtime during the millionaire recording artists' three-day stay were inclined to agree with night club operator Shelly Davis' conclusions as he mopped thrown Scotch from a Beatle fan, Mamie Van Doren, who got between George and the photographer.

"It was frantic," said Shelly, 17 years a newspaperman, flack and showman. "It was frantic, impossible, ridiculous...but fun."

BOOTH JAMMED

The fun started about 12:45 a.m when about 200 patrons jamming Davis' Whisky A-Go-Go at 8901 Sunset Blvd., and 100 or so crowding the street outside discovered John Lennon had been slipped into a corner booth by Sheriff's deputies.

Within a few minutes the wall of human flesh around the booth was so solid that Harrison and Ringo Starr, also slipped in by deputies, had to be lifted bodily and passed over heads, where they joined seven others, including Jayne Mansfield, in a booth upholstered for four.

A few lucky fans got Beatle autographs on cocktail napkins smuggled through the wall by a waitress, as Davis announced over the loud speaker: "We have honored guests from England here tonight. Give 'em air or I'll have to close the place."

Paul McCartney missed the

(Continued on Page 4, Col. 4)

TODAY'S Top Features

—United Press International Photo by BOB FLORA
RINGO STARR, GEORGE HARRISON, JOHN LENNON (FROM LEFT)
Beatle Harrison points finger, orders photographer not to take picture

BEATLE HARRISON THROWS HIS DRINK AT THE PHOTOGRAPHER
Drink hit the photographer, a deputy sheriff, and actress Mamie Van Doren

Aftermath Of Beatles --$5000

(Continued from Page 1)

group's first visit to an American night club as patrons. "Paul just stayed home," Ringo told The Herald-Examiner, breaking off a conversation with two girls in an adjoining booth — Cheryl Crane, 21, Lana Turner's daughter, and her roommate, Andrea Luby, also 21.

50 WARNED

Robert Flora, United Press International photographer, got the highball treatment after Harrison warned him not to take any more pictures and Flora snapped one more which showed George tossing the drink.

Earlier, West Los Angeles police took more than 50 adolescents into technical custody—for violating a 10 p.m. curfew—as some 400 persons milled about the intersection of Bel-Air Road and Sunset Boulevard, hoping over several hours to catch a glimpse of a Beatle.

St. Pierre Roads, where the singers disappeared into a rented mansion at No. 356 for some rest after their Hollywood Bowl appearance Sunday, was blocked off by police, who estimated damage to flowers, shrubs and other residential property at $5000.

SPRINKLERS ON

Many residents turned on lawn sprinklers to discourage trespassing, but teenagers by the dozens ignored a drenching in order to penetrate barricades, only to be caught by officers in extra force and returned.

The scores of teenagers taken off in squad cars to West Los Angeles station did not have the sympathy of Judy Clampit, 19, of Long Beach.

"I think the Beatles are just sickening, funny-looking and horrible," she confided. "I wouldn't be here at all, but I had to bring several girls who are real Beatle fans."

Little did I know then, that in just a few years, I'd be working at a radio station with one of the disc jockeys who had actually traveled with the Beatles on their American tour—Jim Stagg. He, too, may have been there that Hollywood night; I just hadn't met him yet.

# FOUR

Cherry, Cherry

So I started to consider my friend Sharon's advice. Maybe the job at WCFL would be more fun. The position was for a combination talent coordinator/secretary. My duties would be to book the on-air personalities for personal appearances at local clubs, answer their fan-mail, and do any other necessary secretarial duties, such as taking their calls, getting them coffee, or running errands. I told them I would take the job, but asked if they were satisfied with me in six months, would they then pay me the extra $20 a week I was giving up from my old job. They agreed.

On my first day, I noticed how strangely all these middle-aged men dressed! Bell bottoms, flower-power shirts, Beatle hairstyles. It was like stepping onto London's Carnaby Street. So cool. This was a world apart from the medical center where the men, in the same age range, dressed stuffy and drab. But the doctors probably had no time nor reason for fashion trends—their focus was on trying to kick-start a heart somewhere.

And, when asked their age, many of the disc jockeys said they were twenty-five years old, when they were more like thirty-five. This was where I started to lie about my age. I learned that in radio, it was best to be the age listeners wanted you to be in order for them to truly enjoy you. It was supposed to be a fun, musical, fantasy-land.

Things went on wonderfully with my new job. There were no windows in the ugly green talent office. But it was in this very same office that tons of talented singers and bands would stop in to say hello, hoping to sway some disc jockey to play their record. One day they were merely talented; the next, they were famous.

I worked with some of the greatest names in Chicago radio—Jerry G. Bishop, Joel Sebastian, Dick Williamson, Jim Stagg, Ron Britain, Barney Pip, Dick Biondi, Bob Dearborn, Clark Weber, Howard Miller, and more. Many more—too many to remember—'cause disc jockeys don't usually last too long in any one job.

The work *was* exciting! The "Chicken-Man" series was taped at the station, and, when they occasionally needed a female voice, they'd ask me to do a line or two. Sometimes I was asked to record a line for a station promo. I was thrilled. This was my first *on-air* work since fourth grade, when I had been a quiz kid. (I was experienced—Hah!)

Other fringe benefits were the tons of promotional stuff we often got, as record promoters made their rounds and dropped off new albums for the DJs to experience. They also brought extras for them to hand out at their appearances, which helped promote new bands. Of course, they'd give the secretaries new LP's too, as they thought we might have some influence on the DJs. Sometimes we got to keep some of the prizes that the station offered in contests. The best one ever, was an original cell from the Beatles movie, *Yellow Submarine*. I only got one—from the tuba playing scene—but some girls at the station lucked out with a nice collection.

It was also easy to meet all sorts of famous people who came to the station for interviews.

One day I filled in for Patti, our receptionist in the main lobby.

This was the best place to be in the whole station because all the celebrities would step off the elevator and be right there at the front desk.

Left—Me, and Patti (nicknamed "WCFL's Julie Christie")

So there I sat, when a good looking blond-haired guy walked up to me. So cute, but kind of young to be walking with a cane, I thought. I asked whom he was here to see, and whom should I say was calling.

He answered, "Evil Knievel."

I laughed. I thought he was teasing me. Nobody has a name like that. So I asked again, and again he said, "Evil Knievel." Now I was starting to wonder, thinking that maybe the name just *sounded* funny, so I asked him to spell it. And he did—and it still didn't sound right. I phoned the person he came to see and said, rather cautiously, that "Evil Knievel" was here to see him. He didn't laugh. He said he'd be right out to meet him. While we waited, I tried to be sociable and started talking to Mr. Knievel.

"So—" I politely asked, "Why are you visiting us today?"

He told me they were going to do a radio interview with him. I asked him what he did. He said he jumped motorcycles. (By now he had to be wondering what planet I was from.) I then tried to compliment him and said,

"Oh, really! You know, you could probably get some great work out in Hollywood as a stuntman. I'll bet they'd love to have someone like you!"

He looked at me sadly serious and said, "Hollywood's filming the story of my life. George Hamilton is going to play me. That's why I'm here today—to talk about the movie."

"Oh, uh-huh," I said, as the importance of this celebrity started to sink in. Obviously, you couldn't live under a rock if you were gonna do this *reception* thing. It was trickier than I thought.

Famous entertainers were always coming to the station for interviews. We posed for pictures with them and got their autographs. I met many rock bands like—the Buckinghams, who were having hit after hit. One day someone took our picture in the talent office—

Left—Jerry G. Bishop, me upfront with Carl Giammarese—
those Bucks are sooooooo cute!
(Catch their new book—a great rock n' roll read!)

Cherry, Cherry

I met Noel Harrison, Glen Campbell, Minnie Ripperton, Tommy Boyce & Bobby Hart, Tiny Tim—and tons more. One day all the secretaries started buzzing excitedly around the station—that Neil Diamond was coming in for a live on-air interview.

He was scheduled to be on with Joel Sebastian. Joel was so cool, always a gentleman, and a *Moonchild* like me. He often asked me to bring him back something from the deli when I went to lunch—and almost always ordered an avocado salad and a corned beef sandwich on an onion roll with Swiss cheese. I never liked avocados until he offered me a taste of his salad. (Want some avocado, little girl?) It tasted odd to me, but now I have come to love avocado salads and corned beef sandwiches just as he did.

So, as Joel and Neil were on the air, while the songs were playing, Joel phoned the talent office and asked if I'd bring Neil a cup of coffee. Wow! Would I! Here, every girl at the station was dying to get close to him, and I was being asked to bring him coffee. I remember the moment I saw him. He smiled. He was so nice to me.

I was glad I wore my new green dress that day—the one my mom made for me. She was the best designer in the world! She changed the pattern to make this dress totally unique. It had long sleeves and a scoop neck, with slits in the shoulder seams, where a little skin would peek through (that Connie, such a vixen)—and there were green string bows at the top of the sleeves. So there I was, in my new little dress, serving coffee to *NEIL DIAMOND*!

Later that day, after Neil had left the station, his record promoter called me. He wanted to know if I would show Neil around Chicago. *WhooooooooMeeeeeee?????* I couldn't believe this! Of all the cute girls at the station, way more seductive-looking, why would he ask mousy me to show him around. I thought that was a huge mistake on his part; I told him he really must have meant one of the other girls. But then he said that Neil asked him to ask the girl in the green dress. *Whaaaaaaaat??????* That *was* me! Well, now, I was totally stunned. However, I was never a big Neil Diamond fan. I was more into Elvis.

But since Elvis wasn't here, Neil would have to do. (Oh, ain't she getting cocky!)

Then suddenly, there it was—my *hot Chicago night.* Neil was staying at the Holiday Inn on Lake Shore Drive. It was arranged that I would pick him up there and we'd go to Rush Street, where all the action was, and eat at one of the fancy restaurants.

In those days I was driving a little Corvair. It was my very first car—used, but it was all mine. I parked the car and walked into the lobby of the Holiday Inn. I asked the front desk to call him. He came downstairs and off we went. Neil Diamond and me—in my ugly little green Corvair! Wonder what he thought. He was very nice, not acting like a superstar, but just a guy out on the town for a nice time in Chicago.

So I drove down to Rush Street—still finding it hard to believe that I, a girl who didn't date all that much, was out with *NEIL DIAMOND!!!* I circled around until I found a parking spot on the street; it was a week-night and not real crowded. (Now that I think about it, he probably could have popped for a parking garage.)

We walked into this fancy restaurant (can't remember the name, but it's gone now anyway); we had no reservations, but were seated immediately since there was no one in the place. (Connie sure knows how to pick a hot spot when a superstar comes to town.) It seemed that none of the restaurant staff recognized him, but I kept waiting for that to happen.

(WCFL's Barbara Sternig, who later became Senior Reporter for *The National Enquirer,* might have loved this scoop; though she had tons of her own—they're in her book—*Secrets of a Tabloid Reporter.*)

So now, I started thinking *food!* Wow, am I gonna have a feast! I mean, this is Neil Diamond! What will it be? Chateaubriand? Lobster? Surf and Turf? Got to cost a fortune in this place, but that's how superstars live, I'm sure. I studied the menu, not wanting to make the first move. Not that I eat that much, but this was a big deal to me, not having to be considerate about ordering anything too expensive, as

I did on a normal date. I could probably have my pick and it wouldn't faze him in the least!

After a little while of checking the menu, Neil looked at me and said in his soft, ballad voice,

"I think I'm just gonna have soup."

You could've knocked me over with a paper napkin—if they'd had one. *Soup?!?* So what did *that* mean? My mind raced. Can he have soup, while I have Chateaubriand—for two—by myself? Was I supposed to sit here and chow down long after he's slurped up his soup? Should I have three courses while he watches me eat—and listens to me chew—or worse yet, tries to carry on a conversation with me while my mouth is stuffed like a Polish gołąbki. Maybe, he's fallen on hard times and has to budget his dinners. Maybe it's stomach or digestive problems? Acid reflux? All this flew through my head as I heard myself say,

"Yeah, me too—I'll have soup."

Pulllleeeeeezzzzzz! Would that be a cup, or a whole bowl? *Oooohhhh!* A whole bowl! Now, we're talkin,' big spender! I vaguely remember him saying I could order anything I wanted, but it was too late for that. It didn't take long to finish our soup, and off we went. He said he was getting kind of tired and would just like to go back to the hotel. Yeah, I know. All that soup-slurping can sure wear you out.

"Me too, I'm exhausted!" I chimed in.

All this excitement *was* wearing me down. Of course, had I been able to eat a decent meal, I might have gotten some of my energy back. So, a little hungry, but even more disappointed, I drove us back to the Holiday Inn. I was somewhat surprised when he asked if I'd like to come up to his room. I mean, after all, he was tired—and I was exhausted. So, Ms. Naiveté said, "Sure!"

Now, you're not gonna believe that I went up to his room because I sincerely thought I could learn something from a superstar about writing music, but that's what was really on my mind.

TOP ROCK GIRLY JOCK

I'd been taking guitar lessons at the local high school's night classes. I loved to experiment with music and lyrics. I thought this was a great opportunity to learn from a real talent. I started talking music with him,

"So, Neil, do you write the lyrics first, and then the melody—or the other way around?"

He studied me quietly for a moment.

"Why?" he said, "If I told you, you think you could do it?"

Hmmm, I wondered. Was that a put-down?—or was he thinking of co-writing with me?—or merely encouraging me? Well, it didn't take long to figure out he was encouraging me—but it wasn't about music. (Boys will be toys.) I remember what I wore that evening—not the green dress that my mom had made, but some clingy knit dress in white, lavender and baby blue. ("Lavender blue, dilly-dilly—")

He made himself comfortable, lying down on the bed, half-propped up on the cushy pillows. (Well, yeah, the guy said he was tired.) I thought this was my cue to leave, so the star could get some shut-eye. I turned towards the door, when suddenly he reached for my hand and pulled me towards him.

Cherry, Cherry

"Holly Holy!" One surprise after another! This night was full of surprises. I wasn't *that* tired! I didn't know what to say—what to do! Starting to worry that maybe he'd end up sharing more than a nap with me, I blurted out,

"Nooooooo! I'm a strict Catholic girl."

(It would be years before the Billy Joel song would explain all that—"Catholic girls start much too late.")

I always heard Neil was a great performer—but I wasn't gonna stick around to find out. Maybe I overreacted. He only may have wanted to sing to me ("Play Me?")—to think, I might have inspired his next hit—it could have been "Cracklin' *Connie*" instead of "*Rosie*." Then again, maybe I did inspire the—"Holiday Inn Blues."

Suddenly, things got very awkward. He didn't look too happy. On the other hand, he didn't look much like he cared one way or the other. Looking back on it now, he really had been a gentleman. Poor guy—had his pick of all the girls at the station, and he had picked a dud. He should've asked for someone in a red dress, not green. But maybe he, too, had plastic records when he was little, just like I did—*"Green for Go, Red for Stop."* Perhaps he thought I expected a little attention; I didn't. I had just wanted a full dinner—with dessert. So I left him there—"Forever in Blue Jeans,"—a "Solitary Man,"—hoping he'd still "Thank the Lord for the Nighttime."

Years later, I was interviewed for a cover story for the *Chicago Sun-Times* Sunday "Midwest" magazine, and saw in print, the story of my *date* with Neil Diamond. Because it was so memorable, I told a reporter off the record—but there it was for all of metropolitan Chicago to read—and it was paraphrased and twisted. (Sorry, Neil.) (How's that saying go?—"Don't kiss and don't tell?")

WCFL Radio was a mainstream 50,000 watt AM station in the heyday of rock & roll. It was "Top 40." It was big time and cool! I felt so lucky to be a part of it all.

TOP ROCK GIRLY JOCK

By now I had changed the station's answering machine that announced the DJ appearances. I called it *The Connie-Line*. Since I was the one recording the information, if a listener had more questions, they could call and ask for Connie. Anyway, it was kind of a kick, because now the DJs were announcing it on the air.

"Find out where the DJs will be appearing this week. Call *The Connie-Line!*" It also ended up in a flyer that promoted the DJs.

Soon, I started booking myself with the DJs, billing myself as *The Girl from Ten* (our slogan was *The Big Ten* in radio). The club owners would pay me $25 in addition to the jock's personal appearance fee, which, at the time, was $150-$200. My mom had sewn this cute little striped black & white satin mini-dress for me to wear on stage, with white cuffs and collar. On a black satin tie, I later cut out silver metallic fabric and glued on our call letters—W-C-F-L. And, of course, I wore long, black boots. At the clubs, I'd walk out on stage with the DJ, carrying albums that he'd give away in contests.

It was almost like being an early version of Vanna White. This was more than a job to me. I was immersed in the music, fun, and the prestige of being a part of this impressive and glamorous radio world.

(Oops—Someone's slipping)

TOP ROCK GIRLY JOCK

I was only sorry that my brother, Jerry, wasn't able to share the fun. He was in the Air Force, with tours of duty that took him to Viet Nam—twice! Besides risking his life, he was having all kinds of ordeals in his military service time.

One Sunday, while heading back from leave to Forbes Air Force Base, and under a deadline to be there by Monday morning, Jerry found himself stranded on the flight line of a shut-down airport after dark, completely deserted.

Then there was that extremely dangerous spy/fly mission. Jerry had had a bad feeling about it, but his first sergeant, who had asked for volunteers, but got none, said Jerry had to go. Another sergeant insisted Jerry should have his eyes checked first. (My brother's vision isn't the greatest, or he would've been a jet pilot by now.) When his vision was found to be inadequate for the mission, Jerry had to be dropped from the list. A very good friend of his was assigned in his place. The plane was lost. They all were killed. My brother is in the process of writing about his *Nam* life. It was a horrendous time for him, but our family was thankful to God that he came home safely. So, while so many young men were sadly dying for our country, most of us could only pray for them as we went on with our lives. There was only so much we could do—after all, none of us were Jane Fonda.

WCFL staffers were always invited to exciting events. We went to all sorts of parties—mostly for record promotion purposes. Usually we just mingled around, so excited to be a part of the celebrity crowd. There was the big star! And here we were!

One party was unexpectedly eventful. It was a combination Henry Mancini/Andy Williams party—two big names on the music scene. I hopped into my little hot-pants outfit (all the rage that year) and called my friend Annette, who worked in the station's accounting department, and off we went.

Before we knew it, we were having our pictures taken with the guests of honor.

PARTY TIME!

Left—
Annette,
Henry Mancini
& me

Right—
Annette,
Andy Williams
& me

Suddenly, Andy Williams invited Annette and me upstairs to *another party*. Now we really felt special. (I remember that happening quite often in those days. There always seemed to be *another party* somewhere away from the main party and we were always getting invited!) So Annette and I took the bait.

There we were in Andy's suite, along with some of his entourage. The first thing he did was put on his new album and crank the volume for all to enjoy. Drinks were all around. Before you knew it, Andy was *getting tired*. (I was learning that many celebrities seemed to get tired a lot.) He drifted off to the bedroom. He must have suddenly been hit with insomnia, because the next thing we knew he was calling for us. He probably wanted us to turn down the volume on his record that was blasting away—that would surely keep anyone awake.

After Annette took one peek, she pushed me back.

"He's in his jockey shorts!—sprawled out on the bed!"

She was stunned. I reminded her he said he was tired. Then we giggled.

I said, "Oooh, let me have a peek!"

("Moon River—wider than a mile—")

We still laugh about that one. Believe me, Andy got the rest he so badly needed and so well deserved. As far as we were concerned, the party was over!

Then Paul Revere and the Raiders came to town! Things were looking up! We managed to get backstage to watch them perform and before you knew it, dates were being set up all around. Paul Revere and Mark Lindsay were the big catches. But we happily settled for the other guys in the band. They were adorable and so much fun. The next day, Annette and I were being treated to a top-of-the-line lunch in the penthouse restaurant of an expensive hotel on Michigan Avenue.

We were "Hungry for those good things—"

"Order anything you want!" they said.

"I'll have soup," I answered (ala Neil Diamond).

"Just kidding," I quickly corrected.

Cherry, Cherry

The guys were treating, and proud of it! OK—here goes!

"Should we start with escargot?" one of them said.

"Exactly what is that," I questioned, before I agreed to let anything enter my body.

"Snails," someone expertly piped up.

That's all I needed to hear. No, thank you, I thought; I'll just check this menu for some normal food—any kielbasa or pierogi here? Everyone ordered freely, anything and everything that sounded yummy. We had a great time, laughing and eating. But then they started *getting tired*. Uh-oh, I thought. We went back to their hotel and tried to be as nice as we could without standing in the way of them getting the rest they seemed to need. Another short night—another party over much too quickly.

Annette and I also sometimes planned vacations together. It was still winter, so we decided on Florida. As we checked in for our flight, the ticket agent whispered to us that Joe Namath, the big football hero, was on our flight. Whoa! The very single and very rich Joe Namath! This reeked of opportunity! Annette and I didn't have to get in a huddle to decide on a pass.

We were in coach, while he was in first class. After getting airborne, we quietly sneaked up to his seat, with our cameras of course! I mean, we had to have proof that we actually met him! He was asleep—adorable. I wanted to start singing, "Rock-a-bye, Baby" but instead reached for my camera.

I snapped my shot quickly and quietly. **TOUCHDOWN!**

"Broadway Joe"

Then it was Annette's turn. ***CLICK-POP-FLASH!***

Annette had forgotten about the ***FLASH!***

He jolted awake! He was livid! He scowled and yelled at us, "How'd you like to have your picture taken while you were sleeping!"

(Fine with me—as long as it didn't end up in a book someday.)

We quickly scrambled back to our seats. At luggage pick-up, we saw him again. He didn't look any happier, but he did pose for a picture with me. (It's not in here, because it didn't come out good. No flash.) That first night in Fort Lauderdale, we went out to a club for some fun—and just as we walked in the door—yes—you guessed it. There he was again! He gave us such a look. By now we were starting to feel like bad pennies.

Annette and I had many fun celebrity moments together, but in the years to come, she would tell me about her best ever! The night she met Elvis in Vegas!

She knew Elvis' Army friend, Joe Esposito, from the old neighborhood in Chicago, and before you knew it, Elvis had sent Joe over to her booth to invite her up to a party at his penthouse suite at the International Hilton. We were seasoned *partyers* by now—but this was ELVIS! She told me how he mingled a bit with everyone, and then told them to help themselves to the food and drinks and to enjoy themselves. He was tired. (Oh, yeah, we know.) But Elvis really *did* go to his room and go to sleep. He was the perfect gentleman.

But before he left, he spent some time talking with Annette. He told her how hard it was, sometimes, to be "Elvis Presley." He said he often tried to escape from it all and that's why he sometimes wore sunglasses—just to shut out everything for a while.

I've always felt that Elvis wasn't a superstar for himself, but for so many others. In a gift shop in Memphis, they sell what they claim to be Elvis' favorite book. It's called *The Impersonal Life*, and it's all about being there for others. I truly think this is how Elvis felt. It may have started with wanting to help his folks with his fortune, but ended by wanting to help as many as he could. He could've walked away anytime, but didn't.

Cherry, Cherry

I envied Annette's moment with Elvis. I had no idea then, that the day would come when I would meet him myself.

Radio station parties and meeting celebrities weren't the only fun times we had! On Friday nights, my girlfriends and I would often bar-hop on Rush Street. One night we were at The Store. I had had two beers. That was one beer over my limit. I was suddenly very, very, very, happy. The band was playing. I was singing along with my beer, when my friend, Sharon, went up to the stage and told the band that I could really sing and play well. ("That's what friends are for.") Suddenly, the band thought they had a secret-celebrity rocker in the crowd. By now, after my second beer, you could've fooled me too.

So I happily went on-stage and the lead singer guitarist handed me his electric weapon. The rest of the guys in the band asked me what song I was going to do—they'd back me up. Since I only knew two songs (but didn't tell them that—or did I?—some of this is a blur). But I do remember singing and strumming that electric guitar, to the Animals' "House of the Rising Sun." When I finished, the place went wild! I couldn't believe my ears! They clapped and hooted & hollered for more! Of course, I'm sure they'd had their two beers by then as well.

So it was encore time! I still knew one more song! I mellowed out with the Beatles' tune, "And I Love Her." And again they hollered for more. But two songs were all I knew. So I bowed and bowed and smiled my way offstage. (Always leave 'em wanting more—Hah!)

My shyness was starting to take a backseat every once in a while. Work at the radio station was fun—everything was "Fun, Fun, Fun." I had finally found that excitement I had been looking for in the working world.

One day a girl called the talent office to ask about one of her favorite DJs. That phone call changed the rest of my life.

TOP ROCK GIRLY JOCK

"Tip-toe through the tulips"
Tiny Tim visited WCFL—
I tried to emulate him, but I think
his hand was on his heart—
while mine was on my stomach—
(They say a picture's worth
a thousand words)

Right—Barbara Sternig, who later became Senior Reporter for
The National Enquirer (& wrote *Secrets of a Tabloid Reporter*)
and the rest of us WCFL Girls—(I'm the one in the hat)

From *Chicago's American*—
Hamming it up for charity at the WCFL studios—
Left— Lynn from WCFL and Dr. Portes of the Cancer Prevention Center
Right—Joel Sebastian and me

WCFL Float—St. Patrick's Day Parade—1969
Jim Stagg, *top left*—Joel Sebastian, *far right* and
Ron Britain next to me—I'm the one in the hat

WCFL studios at
Marina City
Left—
Jerry G. Bishop
Right—
Joel Sebastian

FIVE

Dawn—Go Away, You're No Good for Me

Her name was Penny Lane. I took her call, answered her questions on club events, and told her where her favorite DJ would be appearing. But instead of hanging up, she said,

"You know, you sound like you'd make a good DJ!"

I'll never forget those words but I thought, you're talking to a girl who cracks an egg like she's afraid she'll break it—talk about timidity.

I quickly told her, "Hah! Yeah, right, forget it. I'm so shy, I'm lucky I'm talking on the telephone."

But she persisted. "No, seriously, you sound like you would be a great DJ! And you know all about how radio works—the logs, promos—all that stuff."

(Not really, I thought. I'm just *fakin' it*.)

"Why don't you come down and audition for WSDM-FM?" she coaxed.

"What's that?" I said, "Never heard of it."

"It's an all-girl station. We play blues and jazz. Our slogan is *Smack-Dab-In-The-Middle* because we're in the middle of the FM dial, and that spells out our call letters—WSDM," she explained. You really should come and audition. You'd be great!"

She kept at it, so I said, "Yeah, OK, maybe sometime."

I said anything to make her hang up and go away. A week or two later, she called again.

"When are you coming to audition?" she wanted to know.

I thought, *who is* this girl? And why does she keep calling?

I'm never gonna get rid of her unless I do this. But I know I'll be so bad, that might be the end of it, so, just to get her off my back, I said,

"OK. When, where? I'll be there."

"I'll set it up with Burt Burdeen, the program director," she said, "and I'll get back to you."

Sure enough, she did. Never even met the girl—Penny Lane (her Den Pal name that stays with her 'til today). So I auditioned. I read a few spots—it was over! A few weeks went by. She called me at WCFL again. "Did Burt call you?"

"No," I said, "I told you I'd be bad. I'm too shy for this sort of thing."

"What d'you mean! You'd be perfect! I'll have to ask him!" she said. "He's so busy; he probably just didn't get around to calling you yet."

A few days later I got a call from Burt, asking if I'd like to do the Saturday morning shift, 8 AM 'til Noon. The studio was on 35th and Kedzie on the south side of Chicago. (I lived on the northwest side, about forty-five minutes away.) I would get paid $2 an hour, which was below the minimum wage, so, technically, it wasn't really a *wage*. It was a *gift*, or something like that—can't remember all the details now and not so sure I want to.

Wow! I'm hired! And I'm going to earn $8 total for getting up at 6 AM on a Saturday morning and driving to 35th and Kedzie—and, hopefully, I won't get lost. Wonder what all the other young single girls are doing on a Friday night while I'm getting to sleep early for

Dawn—Go Away, You're No Good for Me

this wonderful gig I never wanted to do in the first place! But I was hired! I'm a dee-jay!

I had to pick an *air* name. I decided, since I was waking up at the crack of dawn, that "Dawn" would be a perfect choice. And so I became "Den Pal Dawn" at WSDM-FM, *"The Station with the Girls—and All That Jazz!"*

WSDM-FM was owned by the Chess family. Phil and Leonard Chess were brothers and owned the Chess record label in Chicago. (Check out the movie, *Cadillac Records*.) Terry was station manager. Many family members played a part in the music scene. Marshall toured regularly with the Rolling Stones as road manager, or so I had heard. At the time I joined them, they also owned WVON-FM in Chicago, and WNOV-FM in Milwaukee, Wisconsin.

My first day finally arrived. Wanda Wells trained me in. (She later became Public Affairs Director at Fox 32 here in Chicago.) Sure, I was shy. But Penny Lane had said I could keep a mirror in my studio and look at it while I was talking on the air, and this would give me confidence. Penny Lane was such a sweetheart. She was always so thoughtful and helpful and now here I sat, *Smack Dab in the Middle* of broadcasting, and I hadn't even met her yet.

So I tried her mirror trick. I wasn't sure it would work. I mean, how would looking at myself, with barely any sleep, and no make-up, make me confident? I looked in that mirror and this scared *plain Jane* looked back.

And what about my grade school classmate, who said I didn't pronounce the word *"the"* correctly? What would she think? What would everybody else think? But there was no time to think about that. I was here. I had a job to do. As a director once told Marilyn Monroe, who also battled insecurity,

"Don't think about it—just *DO IT!*"

I sometimes relate to her dilemmas. Unfortunately, that was the only thing we had in common.

So I started to broadcast. What did I have to lose? If I screwed up, who'd know? I didn't tell any of my friends. And I wasn't even using my real name.

One day, in the middle of a show, Herb Kent, a hot DJ with our sister station, WVON-FM, wandered into the studio, looked at me intently, and said,

"*You* are going *far* in this business."

Whaaaaaaat? Who was this guy and why was he talkin' like this. (I later learned he was the very popular Herb Kent, *The Cool Gent*—another great book you should pick up.)

I wondered what it was that I might be doing right. He made me feel good, but inwardly I thought, how ridiculous. I don't even know what I'm doing or why I'm even here. Oh, yes, I forgot—it must be for the $8 I'm gonna take home. Couldn't be for the music. I was way more into rock and roll.

And the news we had to read was horrific. The *City News* wire was full of reports of Friday night shootings and murders—gangs and family members doing each other in (Chicago living up to its image). We only did two minutes of news. It would've been impossible to report all the killings from the night before.

The studios were as bleak as the news on Saturday morning. Once, while in the middle of broadcasting that *rip-n-read* news, I looked down from the microphone and there was a huge one-inch spider slowly crawling across the control board right in front of me! He was just inches away! Was he poisonous or not, I don't know—how do those look? I almost screamed out loud in the middle of my newscast (which probably would've fit in nicely with the gory killings I was reporting) but instead, I took a deep breath and continued on with the news as the spider continued on with its crawl. I kept my eyes on it 'til it crawled off into the equipment somewhere.

Another time, I was running late, trying desperately to get to the station for my morning show before the overnight automation tape ran out. I finally pulled up, parked the car, and ran frantically down the frozen mud rut that led to the back door. I fell. (Den Pal *DOWN*.)

I twisted my ankle, but "Den Pal Dawn" went on to do the shift in pain. Was this what they meant when they said, "The show must go on?" I limped along—just couldn't move very quickly—not like the mice that lived in the nooks and crannies of the studio. Out of the corner of my eye, I could see them whiz by, trying to catch my attention. Who did they think I was—Cinderella? I don't play with mice.

The other girls had their woes too. I heard that one of them (a week-day morning girl named Copper—for her long red hair) actually fell asleep during her shift. Well, she looked like a hottie—probably had too much party the night before. And who could blame her for trying to catch a few *ZZZZZ's*. There wasn't much to do between stop-sets. When the stop-set came each 15 minutes, we'd press the red button to stop the tapes, do our commercials, or whatever, and then press the green button to start it up again. (*"Green for Go, Red for Stop—"* my childhood plastic records would again play in my head.)

Eventually, I found ways to entertain myself during my shows. I never really liked jazz. I've always explained jazz as a musician hitting a bunch of keys at random, and when he found one he liked, he'd bang on it in triumph for the next five minutes or so. Even I could do that.

Perhaps management realized I wasn't their best choice for the Saturday morning slot, after I got lost driving to the station one morning. My radio was set to the station at 98.7 FM as I headed in. I must have been way too sleepy and missed a turn somewhere. If you know the south side of Chicago, you know that not all the streets go through as they do on the northwest side. Somehow I ran into a dead end. Then it was U-turn time, and another dead end. I had no clue where I was or how to find the street I needed, and everything was closed at this early hour, so there was nowhere I could stop to ask for directions. It was a real quiet Saturday morning and getting even more quiet now with this deafening silence on the radio, as the last reel of automated music ended. It was my turn! But the only turns I was taking was in my little white convertible Spitfire, frantically trying *every* street. I couldn't believe this was happening! As they say, a living nightmare! (But it may have been my inspiration for the *Road Rally* I would later do at another station.)

Did this mean I was going to lose this wonderful $2 an hour gig I had? On the other hand, if my slot was 8 AM 'til noon, maybe I'd get there before my four hours—and management—were up. Now, that's looking on the bright side! I can't recall the exact hour, but when I finally got to the station, no one else was there, so if I didn't tell, who would know! I sneaked in just as quietly as the mice that lived there.

Eventually I worked my way up. I got promoted from Saturday mornings. (Where they ever found an early bird for that slot, I don't know.) But I was given a raise to $5 an hour (bring on the furs and jewels!) and switched to Sunday afternoons! At least I had a better start time of noon.

I started reading the Sunday funnies to entertain myself during the jazz sets and eventually ended up reading some of them on the air. Someone had to liven up this program, I thought. And if I didn't, who would! Later I heard that this had been done before—by Mayor LaGuardia, on his radio show in New York (maybe if I kept this up, I, too, would have an airport named after me some day—Hah!)

But I was starting to learn that nothing was new in radio. Not yet, anyway! But I'd work on it! I did the *Lovey-Dovey Report*, with news of celebrity marriages, divorces and plain ol' hanky-panky—the *Judo Lesson of the Week* for females who needed to defend themselves against aggressive males (or other females)—and *The Bachelor Boy Household Hint of the Day* with cooking tips, cleaning hints and other advice, to encourage a man to think twice before deciding to live without a woman.

Dawn—Go Away, You're No Good for Me

This was starting to become more and more fun. I was Den Pal Dawn, and billed myself as "The World's Most Sensuous Disc Jockey." I chose a signature *sign-on* song, and would start my shows singing,

"Let me entertain you—"

If I was gonna do this, I was gonna do my best to entertain.

Besides the on-air stuff, the Den Pals hosted many station events. The public treated us like celebrities. Such fun!

Den Pals—Hamming It Up!

THESE GIRLS ARE AVAILABLE DAY OR NIGHT –
ALL YOU HAVE TO DO IS TURN THEM ON

WSDM -FM 97.9

I'm on the far left—behind me is Penny Lane—
far right is Danae—Yvonne Daniels is sitting in the middle

We took those shots for our next newsletter—the photo above was one of the rejects. Maybe we overdid it. This is what the station chose to print—

TOP ROCK GIRLY JOCK

A Typical Newsletter—with all the Den Pals!

I'm on the far right, top row—in my "Mary Quant" mini-dress
that my mom sewed for this occasion—
White, with red strawberries

Dawn—Go Away, You're No Good for Me

The Fun Fair—at the Chicago stockyards—where my grandfather once worked—and where I'd be back one day—making my movie debut! Who knew!

What? No Centerfold?

WSDM Nite at the Fun Fair

Troop 97.9 after participating in free chest X-rays at the Fun Fair. Sorry — no requests for copies of the prints. Left to right are Penny Lane, Caress, Dawn, Stephanie, Speakeasy, Wanda, Maybe, Basha and Yvonne.

Den Pal Penny Lane at the mike and Yvonne, Stephanie and Maybe getting ready to announce more winners in the album give-away.

Record albums were given at the Chicago Fun Fair on Den Pal Night. . . Here's Caress with one of those winners.

Den Pal Dawn speaking to the people attending the Chicago Fun Fair.

Big winners at the Fun Fair . . . Den Pals Basha, Stephanie, Maybe, Speakeasy, Caress, Wanda, Penny Lane, Yvonne and Dawn.

TOP ROCK GIRLY JOCK

We handed out our logo bumper stickers—a close-up shot of a girl's waist (her *middle*—because we were *Smack Dab in the Middle*) with a little flower power on her navel.

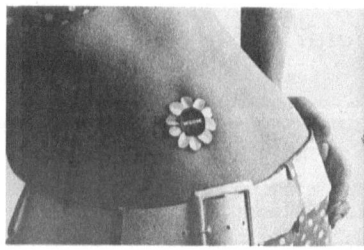

I started getting quite a bit of fan mail at WSDM—which was always a kick to read. Some listeners called me the *female* Larry Lujack. (I only hope they didn't call him the *male* Connie Szerszen—mostly because he was a real DJ and I was a secretary-turned-DJ-and-still-secretary-too.)

But only one fan letter totally stands out in my mind. When I opened it, something fell out—black and fuzzy—and tied with a baby blue string of yarn. I picked it up and started reading the letter:

"This came from my *you-know-what*—now send me some from your *you-know-what*."

ICCCCCCHHHHH! YUCK! ICCCCCCCHHHHHH!

I was holding some guy's pubic hair! As Gildna Radner would later say on *Saturday Night Live*—"I thought I was gonna die!"

Another listener that stands out in my mind was the flight instructor. Would I like to learn to fly a Cessna 150, he wondered. Actually, no, but this might have been my only chance to try it, so I said yes.

I agreed to meet him at Midway Airport. He checked out the plane. I got in the pilot's side and he sat on the passenger side. It was a dual control flight instruction plane. I felt fairly safe knowing that if I screwed up, he could take over the controls. Before you knew it, we were climbing! *I-I-I-I-I-I* was climbing! Oh my! Who'd

Dawn—Go Away, You're No Good for Me

think this thing would just pick up and fly! He did all the hard stuff with the air traffic control tower, while I steered. I learned to press the ailerons when making a turn. He explained that by doing this, a flap would prevent us from slip-sliding sideways and downwards. Sounded like a good idea to me. This flying thing was incredible! There I was, circling the John Hancock building! Such fun! No lanes to watch for; no other traffic around. I flew and flew, pressing those ailerons and cruising around. I really loved it!

Since I was doing so well, he decided I was ready to try and land it myself. He leaned back and watched as he told me to start the descent. Was he nuts? Now we started to hit air pockets. I was, and still am, deathly afraid of air pockets and turbulence. Even more so, with me at the controls! The plane was bouncing around! I felt there was nothing I could do to stop it! He just sat there calmly while I thought, *this is it*. We were gonna crash and this guy wasn't going to help prevent it! I got angry. If he wasn't going to do anything about it, then neither was I. I let go of the wheel, the stupid ailerons, and leaned back just like him.

"Hey, "Sky Pilot," if you don't take over, we're gonna crash," I alerted him.

"No, you can do it—just keep at it!" he insisted.

"No!" I screamed! "We're gonna crash! I'm through trying to land this thing through all this turbulence!"

It took a few moments of the plane in its downward pitch to frighten him enough to believe me. Hurray! Finally! He took over and landed us safely. I later learned that "Sky Pilot" was also often "*Higher than the Sky*—Pilot"—*Hmmm*, maybe that's why he was so brave in turbulence. Eventually he disappeared in the airwaves' vacuum of listeners, and I never heard from him again. I only hoped he was pressing his ailerons.

The odd thing about this experience is that it was so thrilling that I considered going to ground school so that I could really learn to fly. There was something so wonderful about it all—an indefinable freedom! But since I'm not such a technological whiz, I decided that, in the long run, the *mechanics* of it all might bring me down one day. Every so often, though, I have this recurring dream. I take off in a little plane and am flying solo without a glitch. And it's all so beautiful and I land safely. I'm sure this dream's coming from a memory remnant of that day with "Sky Pilot."

Years later I would learn that many air personalities became enthralled with, not only being *on* the air, but *in* the air, as well. The legendary radio DJ, Clark Weber, is an accomplished pilot. Doug Dahlgren (of *Dick & Doug* fame) flew. Bob Collins, the successful morning man at WGN for many years, loved to fly and we sadly lost him to that love.

I remember driving home that day, listening to the plea on WGN radio for Bob to call in if he could hear the station. They knew his plane had crashed after being struck by another plane. What they didn't know at the time was whether or not he, or one of his friends, was actually flying his plane. My date and I once doubled out with Bob Collins and his girlfriend. He was so gifted; so naturally funny and entertaining. When he was around, everyone laughed. It was a huge loss for Chicago radio.

So, I had many new experiences at WSDM, and although I didn't earn much money, it didn't matter since it was only a part-time gig. Everyone there was really nice and I was having fun. Besides, I still had the full-time job at WCFL. And every so often, Penny Lane would land some mobile DJ gigs and share them with me.

One night she asked if I'd sub for her at "The Flower Pot"—a jazz club on Rush Street. Sure! I loved to pick up extra dollars. I got all decked out in my long, yellow dress with ruffles and big red flowers on it (appropriate, I thought, for the *Flower Pot*). I kind of looked like Carmen Miranda lost in the wrong decade. Because I always searched for cheap parking, I finally found a spot near Oak Street, between Dearborn and Clark. There's a square block park there and lots of meters, and you could usually find something. Then I started the trek from Clark to Rush Street.

As I got closer to State Street, a guy walking towards me suddenly grabbed my arm and yanked me into the bushes! I couldn't believe this was happening! I thought I was gonna die right there! But I didn't think for long; instead, I got really angry! I wasn't ready to die now! And not so foolishly!

"Oh, no you don't!" I said, in my meanest voice, while at the same time making quick jerking actions with my elbows, trying to jab at him. Since I'm fairly tall—5'7"—but with platform shoes, even taller, he was just about my height. I couldn't believe he backed off so suddenly, and ran off down the block. (Later I thought my quick movements might've frightened him into thinking I had a Black Belt or something.) I was amazed that it worked! Must have been inspiration from my bit on the radio—the *Judo Lesson of the Week*.

I stepped out from the bushes and tried to walk the rest of the block to State Street where it was lighter and where there were more people. But I could hardly stand. My legs felt like Jello. I was shaking through and through. There was no one around to console me. I slowly crept along and when I finally got to the club, the first words out of my mouth were,

"Somebody, please get me a drink!"

I started to tell some of the patrons about my close brush with death with that sex fiend. Some were so sympathetic and started to hover around, offering to protect me—Oh?—I then thought I'd better shut up. These guys may not have been any less dangerous. Maybe I was paranoid, but I didn't want an instant replay on the walk back.

SIX

All Shook Up

Things went fine for a couple years. I was the talent coordinator/secretary at WCFL, and week-end jock at WSDM.

I was starting to think about college again—something I had skipped as I went from job to job. I wasn't planning on getting a degree; there were just things I wanted to know. Because of my work schedule, I thought I'd better look at night classes and so I checked out the courses at Northwestern University. Studying broadcasting never even crossed my mind; at that time, I didn't even know people did that. All I cared about were subjects that interested me.

Journalism was on my list. In order to get into that class, I had to take the prerequisite, Reading and Writing. How remedial, I thought. But I enrolled. I needed to finish two semesters there before I could advance to the journalism class.

In Reading and Writing, we read many great novels. It was in this class that I discovered F. Scott Fitzgerald and Zelda. It would be several decades later that I'd find myself sitting on the back steps of one of their summer homes in Montgomery, Alabama, which was open to visitors.

"This is where F. Scott Fitzgerald wrote 'Sunday Afternoon'—right here on these back porch steps," the curator pointed out.

They had lived through that crazy Hollywood era—with F. Scott womanizing—and Zelda jumping into fountains, only later to be committed.

Besides reading great fiction, we also had to write. By the end of the first semester, the first paper the teacher raved about was mine. He was thrilled with my report.

"Now, *this* is good writing! And it shows the author really knows her subject!"

I cringed in the back seat. Please don't make me read it, I thought. The paper was on "Love in America." Yeah, like I really know my subject. Haven't been able to make any of my loves last longer than a year, was never married, and at this point in my life, never even engaged. If I had had any insight on love at all, maybe it was because I was inspired. The teacher was getting cuter and cuter with each class. I don't remember how it came about—did he ask me, or did I ask him—but I did have a date with him. We went to the Drake Hotel's posh bar where he told me all about his true love who no longer cared for him. I liked him—he liked her—she liked someone else. (Who was I?—"Dear Abby?") Too bad for me—he was a great kisser.

But he had been so thrilled with my writing that he said I could skip the next semester; so I advanced to the journalism class. By the end of *that* semester, that teacher was also reading my paper to the class as an example of good writing. I was starting to think I might not need too many more of these classes. Besides, there were other things I wanted to learn about. I signed up for Conversational French (D'accord?), Real Estate, Philosophy and Drama. (Connie's own Liberal Arts course.)

It was in drama class that I met Jim Feeley. Another foreshadowing. Later, he would be the PR guy that booked me to emcee celebrity shows in town. I remember one particular class, when we had sensitivity training. Jim was my partner and we had to face each other and hold hands, with our toes touching each other's toes. Then we had to lean as far back as we could and learn to trust one another to keep from falling. Supposedly, this would come in handy in later acting sessions. Jim and I laughed through it all, but when he told me he had dated Ann-Margret (who had also studied acting at Northwestern), I almost let go of him!

Really! Here I was, hanging onto a guy who had dated Ann-Margret! The same Ann-Margret who won first prize in 1957 in the *Morris B. Sachs Amateur Hour*—she won a portable phonograph! I used to dream about singing on the *Amateur Hour*, but knew I was too shy to ever pull it off. I would watch as the winners sang their way to first prize, which often was a gold wristwatch. This very same Ann-Margret would later make movies with Elvis! And she had also dated this cute, blond hunk in my hands right now! When the session ended, I never saw Jim again—until one day, when he walked into WCFL on business. He and his wife, Sunny, have been dear friends ever since.

One evening, as I hurried down the hall to catch a class at NWU, a guy stopped me and asked if he could interview me as "Co-Ed of the Week" for the school paper.

Who? Mousy me? I thought.

"Sure!" I said.

Looking back now, I find that I said *"Sure!"* to almost everyone who asked—well, *almost* everyone. So he took my picture, and I was in the next issue of the *Northwestern News*. The article recapped my jobs, courses, and future goals and ended with—

"Who knows—Northwestern may be cultivating the next Betty Furness."

(Didn't she sell refrigerators in TV commercials?)

The "next Betty Furness?" I didn't know about that. But I did think there was some money to be made in commercial work.

TOP ROCK GIRLY JOCK

Photo by Franz Queen
Connie Szerszen

Before coming to Northwestern, where she is enrolled in an acting class on Thursday evenings, Connie attended the American Academy of Art, and includes oil painting as one of her many hobbies. During the day, she is employed as a talent coordinator for station WCFL, Chicago. She also has a part-time job as a disk jockey with WSDM, the station that features music and all-girl disk jockeys. While on the air, Connie is known as "Dawn," and can be heard from 8 a.m. to noon on Saturdays. In any spare time that she manages to find, Miss Szerszen states she would love to travel. She has been to Europe twice, and would like to spend more time abroad. Connie ultimately would like to do commercials for TV. Who knows —Northwestern may be cultivating the next Betty Furness.

So I made a demo tape and sent them out to advertising agencies, hoping to land some national stuff! Being in the right place at the right time sure helps.

WCFL's Ron Britain was cast to do a TV commercial for Jay's Potato Chips. He told me they were also looking for a female voice for that spot. I jumped at it! Ron suggested I call the agency and drop them a demo tape, which I did. They sort of liked it, but wanted me to audition for their creative department. They wanted to see my range of voices before they made a decision.

So one day, I found myself at the head of a long conference table in front of a couple dozen creative geniuses, singing my heart out—

"On the Good Ship Lollipop—"

They all looked at me rather stone-faced. I felt so stupid, but I knew I was good. (Little Shirley Temple would've been proud.)

I got cast. I had to do two different voices—one as the wife, and one as the girlfriend. Things went fine! I made more money on that spot than I did the entire last month in my full-time job at WCFL. My next commercial was for Walgreens. I was getting hired a lot because I was associated with a big-time radio station, and because I sent out lots of promotional flyers begging for work.

The jocks were always thinking of me. Barney Pip, WCFL's popular evening DJ, played his trumpet and shouted, *"Turn into*

All Shook Up

butter!"—peanut a big hit with the kids. He also sometimes guest-hosted a TV show—the Mulqueens' *Kiddie-A-Go-Go,* on WFLD-TV, FOX 32 Chicago. One day he had a schedule conflict.

Would I like to take his place, he asked. Heyyyyy, would I! He said all I had to do was play games with the children on the show, and talk to the puppets. The next thing I knew they were sending me downtown to Stevens on State Street to pick out a wardrobe to wear on the show. I wasn't going to get paid for filling in for him, but I'd get to keep the clothes! Ah—*clothes*—they said the magic word! My folks watched it at home. The puppets talked on and on and I just ad-libbed with them. It was fun. There was no script, which was just as well. After all, how hard should you have to work for some skirts and sweaters?

I started to feel like *family* with some of the jocks. One day one of the DJs was on the phone with a fan who said he wanted to go out with me, and begged the jock to introduce him. So he handed me the phone, and the guy asked me out. I tried to be kind as I explained I couldn't go out with him, because I was dating someone else at the time (a TV reporter from Channel 32, whom I met one cold winter night when my car wouldn't start, and he gave me a jump. He went on to become a prominent news anchor in Las Vegas).

This radio fan sounded so defeated; I felt sorry for him (one of my weaknesses).

"But you know" I offered, "my cousin, Chris, isn't dating anyone right now. Would you like to go out with her? I could fix you up! Kinda like a blind date."

"Sure," he laughed, "that's right up my alley!"

I gave him Chris's number. He called. They talked for over an hour and laughed a lot together. They got on just great, she said.

When the doorbell rang, she opened it to find him standing there with dark glasses and a white cane. There was a cab waiting at the curb. Her blind date was really blind! She was stunned. But he had been so sweet on the phone; she didn't want to hurt his feelings and so, didn't make a big deal of it. It had just caught her by surprise. They went out to a club—had some drinks—listened to the band, and had a nice time, she said.

But later she told me that she felt so guilty about their first phone conversation. He had *tried* to tell her he was blind—he even told her that old blind joke—you know—the one with *wood eye*. They had laughed and laughed about it together. But Chris had thought he was only joking; she said she had no idea he was really blind. I told her I didn't know either and I'm sure neither did the jock who started this matchmaking. (Or did he?) (Or—was he even really blind?)

Chris was a very dear cousin of mine. One day, for fun, we read some book on fortune-telling and palm reading. There was an illustration in it that showed how to find your *life-line* on your palm. Supposedly, this would predict how long one would live. She seemed to have trouble finding it. So, I showed her my palm and where the line continued on towards the wrist. She said,

"I don't have that."

Trying to help her find it, I grabbed her hand to point it out, and, sure enough, hers stopped right in the middle of her palm.

"Does that mean I won't live long?" she worried.

"No, silly, that means you're not as wrinkled as I am—not yet, anyway."

And I laughed. But I wondered. Everyone I'd seen had this line, and hers stopped short. And, sadly, it was true. She died so unexpectedly—young and in the prime of her life. She was a sweetheart and we all still miss her.

Working at WCFL was extremely helpful to me as a fledgling air personality. I never studied broadcasting since I had never really wanted to do this in the first place. Now, after my shows at WSDM, I would take home the air-checks, and slap them onto my reel-to-reel tape recorder which I kept on the floor in my bedroom closet. I'd shut the door to my room and lie there on my hot pink shag rug, next to the recorder, listening and listening to see what sounded good and what

All Shook Up

didn't. But I really didn't know what to listen for. So I took tapes of my shows on WSDM to the jocks at WCFL, and asked them to help me sound *professional*. They were like personal coaches and gave me all kinds of great tips. Clark Weber encouraged me—he wrote a note for me to take to my shows. "When you sit in that chair at 'SDM tonite, entertain ME!" Ron Britain, Joel Sebastian, and Jim Stagg all gave me many great ideas on how to *relate* to the audience.

Ohhhh? I thought. *Hmmmm*—I think I get it. On a sunny day, you talk about going to the beach. It started to sink in. So that was *relating*. Not hard—but also, not enough—I thought. Shouldn't it be more entertaining than just that? But that would be a good start.

I realize now how lucky I was to have such great talents right there to advise me, to answer questions—to learn from. I think I entered a chameleon stage. Because I was surrounded by all of these creative minds every day, I started to think like them. (Good thing I wasn't still working at the medical center, or I'd probably be cutting cadavers.)

Working at both stations was just one happy rockin' time. I was the talent coordinator at a highly successful AM station, WCFL, at its peak in the late '60s—and having creative fun at my part-time gig at WSDM-FM.

But, like a Teflon pan, it didn't last forever. The shake-ups were starting. Things were getting quirky with the new general manager. He told me he was hiring an assistant for me. He said I should teach her everything I knew—show her the files, etc. I told him I didn't need an assistant, but he insisted.

My vacation was coming up, so I tried to get her briefed on everything before I left. A friend and I were going to London. *Now* I *knew* Jim Stagg—who had toured with the Beatles when they came to America. He knew everyone who was anyone. Jim made arrangements for us to meet Derek Taylor at the Apple Studios in London. We hoped we'd get lucky and the Beatles would be there then too. Maybe I'd finally get to meet Paul! Maybe, maybe, maybe.

But that didn't happen. The day we met Derek, he was all upset because Paul had just started hanging around with a new girl. He said they were driving all over London in her white convertible Corvette—Paul and Linda Eastman. Derek was afraid this would really end Paul's rocky relationship with long-time girlfriend, actress Jane Asher. All I wanted was to see and touch Paul. I knew he couldn't be mine, so I really didn't care who else got him; but I acted concerned. After a short visit, Derek gave us a book with all the Beatles' autographs on the inside page. Later, I licked my index finger and slid it across one signature just to be sure they were truly signed, and not printed. So, yes, now I have a *smudged* Beatles autograph.

Sometime during that vacation, I had a dream. I dreamed that I lost my job as talent coordinator at WCFL. I was devastated! Besides my on-air gig at WSDM, I really loved this job too! I'd never had this much excitement in my personal life as I had at work.

My dream ruined the rest of the trip for me. Even though I knew it was just a dream, I couldn't shake off this bad feeling because I knew I sometimes had pretty accurate dreams or intuitions. Did that kick in when I almost died with the high fever of the measles—or when, as a teenager, my tooth became abscessed, and my head swelled to double its size—the second time I nearly died. Some psychics claim that that's when their abilities appeared—after high fevers or major illnesses. Or did I just inherit this from my folks who were both very psychic.

When I got back from vacation, I told Jim Stagg about my dream. His mouth dropped open. He looked stunned.

"Who told you? Who've you been talking to?" he asked.

"What do you mean, Jim?" I said, "This was a dream. I haven't been talking to anyone!"

Jim looked at me suspiciously, but I had no idea what he was driving at. I was confused with his reaction to my dream. And then he told me. There had been a staff meeting while I was on vacation and the general manager told all the jocks that now that I had trained an

All Shook Up

assistant, he was going to let me go and give her my job—for less money than they were paying me. (Later someone else told me he met her in a bar one night and made all kinds of wonderful promises that he now owed her.)

Since my salary was partly paid by the jocks, and since Jim was then program director, he interceded and asked to put it to a vote. The jocks didn't find it in their hearts to fire me (especially while I was on vacation).

So, my dream had been a real premonition after all. It had really been happening across the Atlantic while I was boppin' around on Carnaby Street in London. Thanks to Jim Stagg and the other jocks, I was allowed to keep my job at WCFL—for the moment, anyway.

One day, one of the girls in the WCFL news department and *also* a Den Pal at WSDM-FM, tipped me off—that the manager of WCFL wanted to get rid of me so that his girlfriend could have my job. (Yeah, I already gathered that.) He was going to *proclaim* that anyone who had a job with another radio station would have to leave WCFL—even though he had previously given us permission to work for WSDM since it was an FM station with a jazz format and not a competitor of ours. She warned that I'd have to make a choice. I was ready. I knew it was coming sooner or later.

For some reason, he didn't want me around any longer. I think he thought I might know something I shouldn't know (*Hmmmmm?*) and just wanted me gone. One day he walked in the talent office, grabbed the steel wastebasket, turned it upside down, and plopped it right over my head. (Good thing it was empty.) There I stood with the wastebasket completely covering my head, half resting on my shoulders. None of the jocks dared say anything as he laughed and ridiculed me as a nitwit. I didn't say anything either—because his behavior scared me. Besides, he wouldn't even have heard me with that big wastebasket over my head. He must've been very angry at not being able to give my job to his girl. I guess I was lucky, though, that he didn't "Bang a Gong" on it too.

TOP ROCK GIRLY JOCK

Although standing there with a wastebasket on my head was humiliating, it wasn't nearly as dangerous as the time the news director threw one of those old manual typewriters—yes, the *whole typewriter*—right at the head of one of our female reporters. Everyone at the station talked about it! The typewriter missed hitting her, and years later I saw her doing the news on national TV! She looked great! She was a brilliant reporter and had eventually become a famous national news broadcaster.

As for her former news director, he went on to enjoy oblivion. And I heard—yes, "I Heard it Through the Grapevine"—that our general manager landed in prison—for some offense or other. I think management should think twice before they mess with their employees' heads. You know—that karma thing.

"Instant karma"—"Gonna knock *YOU* right on the head."

The call letters, "WCFL," stood for the "Chicago Federation of Labor"—if this was labor, it was getting a little too laborious. So when the manager forced me to choose between my full-time position as talent coordinator at WCFL and my part-time DJ job at WSDM (where I now earned $5/hour for a 5 hour shift), I chose my one-day a week job as DJ. The other Den Pal who worked at WCFL, and who had tipped me off that this was coming, chose her full-time gig at WCFL and left the 98 Music Den behind.

This is where I learned one of life's lessons—that sometimes "bad things happen for good." When man closes a door, God opens a microphone. It wasn't long before WSDM asked me to be their new morning personality! However, since I had worked my way up to $5 an hour, the station asked if I'd take a slight cut in pay to $4 an hour. "Sure!" I said. Anything *to work my way up* to a prestigious offer like this! I was honored they wanted me. Anyway, living at home with Mom and Dad was a big help through this period of down-sizing of salary. I earned $80 a week and became the new morning DJ!

Somehow I knew deep down that Yvonne Daniels (daughter of jazz great, Billy Daniels) had to be making way more money than that.

All Shook Up

But then, she was born of talent—and played all her own musical selections, while the rest of us Den Pals just talked during the automated music breaks. (With as little as I knew about radio, I was lucky to be there at all. I probably should've paid WSDM for all that *training*.)

Yvonne had a great reputation because of her dad. Music was in their family history. Many of the Den Pals secretly called her "the Queen Bee." I liked Yvonne. She was always very nice to me and I respected her and admired her expertise—the way she could pick up a music track *just so!* And she always dressed so stylish—even though it was only a radio show where no one ever sees you. I remember one outfit in particular—white blazer, short white skirt, and long white boots. She always looked stunning and classy.

After WSDM, Yvonne worked with Sid McCoy at WCFL, an AM station. But those were still the days when mainstream AM rock and roll radio allowed a woman to be a *sidekick* to a male host, but would not give her a show of her own. News directors were much more open to hiring women than program directors were. Music shows were out of bounds for women. Someone had said that women didn't have enough *authority* in their voices—to play music. But it appeared they had the authority to report the news—just not "Be Bop a Lula"—go figure.

It wasn't until much later that Yvonne would work at the rocker WLS—but only on the late night shift. She eventually left to do mornings, playing jazz at WNUA, which must've felt like being back at WSDM. The radio world also lost her much too soon. She was posthumously inducted into The Museum of Broadcast Communication's "Radio Hall of Fame." Many of the original Den Pals were there to honor her—Penny Lane, Danae (who later worked at WNUA) and Merri Dee of WGN-TV (Channel 9).

I think many of the guys at the ceremony were hoping to catch a peek at former Den Pal, Cindy Morgan, who once had a spicy role as "Lacy Underall" in *Caddyshack*. Well, if they'd seen the movie, I'd say they'd already seen plenty of her. She was very pretty, but most men say they don't remember her face. But then, most men don't remember the other Den Pal faces either. Sometimes there's just too much to remember. Right, guys?

Back, left to right – Yvonne, me, Danae, Jan
Front, left to right—Cheryl, Penny Lane, Janice

After WSDM, many of the girls went on to work in media related jobs—some in radio and television, some worked at the old Gaslight Club, some toured with Second City, and many did free-lance commercial work. You may also remember Linda Ellerbee; she was a major part of WSDM in its early years and later did national TV.

All Shook Up

I loved doing my morning show at WSDM—although it wasn't easy for a night owl like me to get up at 4:15 AM each day. In the morning, there was only enough time to throw on a shirt and jeans and grab some cereal for breakfast. Coffee would have to wait until I got to the station.

I still hadn't grown to appreciate jazz, but I found ways to enjoy doing the show. I brought along my transistor radio and listened to rock & roll on other stations during our taped jazz segments. I really wanted to be a rock jock. I listened to the hot morning guy at the time—Larry Lujack. His show was so entertaining and hysterically funny. And he had always been nice to me. I totally admired him, as did many other DJs. He was so gifted and had the Gemini sun sign just like many other great entertainers. And from what I'd heard, he worked hard at his show. He was finally inducted into the "Radio Hall of Fame," where he should have been years ago—not only because of longevity—but because of talent and popularity.

When I struggled with a formula for comedy, he explained it to me so simply—in one sentence—and then said,

"Or is it the other way around?"

I laughed! Of course, I caught it and it's been some of the best advice I'd ever gotten. No one can ever be Larry Lujack—but Larry! And no one should want to be. One of the greatest things he's pointed out to the radio world is that we are all truly best at being ourselves. We may be influenced by those that came before, but we will never perform the same. Two people may have the same formula for comedy, but each will have different punch lines. Like snowflakes, God didn't make two of us alike.

So there I was, having to do this laid-back jazz thing—soooo boring. But since I really didn't know that much about radio, I guess that was the best place for me to be.

By now, WSDM had moved from their south side, 35th and Kedzie location, to Michigan Avenue. This was exciting. We were in that downtown area where most radio and television studios were located. It wasn't anything exceptionally fancy—but it had location, location, location.

Our studio entry was off of Rush Street. Monday mornings would find me carefully side-stepping some of the homeless—and leftover party-goers—grubby guys with paper-bagged wine bottles sitting on the curbs of Rush and Grand. Mostly, they looked too groggy to be much of a threat; or if they were, I was usually sleep deprived and too groggy to notice.

WSDM—528 N. Michigan Avenue, Chicago

I usually arrived at the station by 5:00 AM, and before my air shift, had a ritual of button-pushing that took about fifteen or twenty minutes. There were tapes to change, as the overnight shows

All Shook Up

were automated, and just a few simple, but highly important, switches and buttons to activate. I didn't exactly remember which switches did what, but knew what I had to do. Or so I thought. Until that awful morning when whatever was supposed to happen—*didn't!* In fact, *nothing* happened. *Nothing* was working! I panicked. Who wouldn't? I quickly phoned our engineer, Bob, who lived *far out* in the suburbs. *HEEEEEEELLLLLPPPPP!*

Even though I had yanked him out of sleep, he calmly went over everything with me. (It's always amazed me how engineers can be so calm and think so meticulously through panic moments.) But nothing helped. He told me to hang tight until he could re-set things at the transmitter. (That was at the John Hancock in downtown Chicago and he was miles and miles from there!) But my air shift started in a half hour! He'd never be able to reach the Hancock from his home in that amount of time. What else could I do? I waited. (By now those winos on the curb with the paper-bagged bottles were starting to look pretty good to me.) The 6:00 hour came and went—then 7:00—and 8:00. It was sometime during the 9:00 hour that everything was finally fixed. Bob called and said I was good to go and could start broadcasting my show (as short as it would be that day). I cringed, worried what my program director would say when I told him.

But he was also very calm about it all—until the next few days, anyway. That's when the irate calls and letters started pouring in—like salt on a hangnail. *Owwwwww!* Tons of listeners who had our station set on their clock radios were livid! (*Hmmm,* guess we had a pretty good-size audience after all.)

"Do you realize I was three hours late for work that day!?!" The angry words jumped off the letters to slap us in the face. I felt so bad.

But, with the "no use crying over spilled milk" proverb in mind, I quickly apologized to my morning listeners, reminding them that they had had some good extra sleep that morning without it even being their fault. How could their bosses blame *them!* Even a big-time

Chicago radio station can sometimes pop off the air for *hours*! Surely, their bosses would believe them, and I'd even back their story.

I pulled several SNAFU's there at WSDM. Like the time I read the news and the word *"communiqué"* came up. Well, I was usually pretty good at pronouncing big words. So, as I read the news, I said, *"kom-u-neek."* Later that day the program director told me the word was pronounced *"kom-u-ni-kay."*

"Oh, please, Burt, don't worry," I reassured him. "I studied French for two years—I'm sure I said it correctly."

He just rolled his eyes. He was a saint, when you come to think of it. Imagine what he had to put up with, with all the girls—and all that jazz.

Then, there was the time I talked on the air about the pet name some military guys had for the girls they dated in Viet Nam. I had no idea the word was a slur. I thought it was a *term of endearment*. Well, I got a letter from an irate listener who said he was married to one. I wrote him back congratulating him on snatching a sweetie. Well, really, who knows about *guy talk* but guys?

I like to think I doubled the ratings in that morning time slot. We had had a "1" but by the next rating book, I brought it to a "2." (Yeah, I know—but they *were* doubled.)

By now I knew this radio thing was my fulfillment. It was what I was meant to do—to be! This was what I could offer to the world with my life—to entertain—to make people chuckle—to uplift them. It was my calling. I again felt like the heroine in those movies that I'd seen growing up! Thank God I had no mortgage payments as I continued to live with Mom and Dad. Is she ever going to get married and move out—I'm sure they wondered. Hah!

"Can't you find some sucker?" my Dad would tease.

Not yet—but I did manage to introduce a Den Pal to a prominent Chicago voice-over talent. They eventually got married. Guess I was better at playing matchmaker than finding my own match. I was just too busy with my career for that.

All Shook Up

WSDM—Smack Dab in the Middle—in downtown Chicago!

5 AM in Engineering—I could do this blindfolded!
(Except for once)

TOP ROCK GIRLY JOCK

Let's see—
I *stop* the tape—the red light comes on—I open the mic and do my thing—I *start* the tape—the green bulb lights up—
"Green for Go, Red for Stop—"

(Or was it the other way around?)

SEVEN

Over the Rainbow

"**W**hy, then, oh, why, can't I?" It was time to seriously put the *broad* in *broad*casting. About now, I became more and more aware that most male DJs were making five times as much money as I was. I decided that I should try and get a job at stations that paid more money and get myself on one of those big payrolls. I started sending my tapes to a couple stations—especially to WIND—because they had hired one of WCFL's star DJs, Ron Britain. They were familiar with the WCFL personalities, and so perhaps, familiar with me, since I'd worked for some of them. My mom worried that I'd be spinning my wheels instead of records,

"Forget it, Connie. You're a girl," she cautioned me. "They're never gonna hire you. They only hire men."

I thought—so far, anyway. But my mom didn't want me to get my hopes up—to dream dreams that might never come true. But I still remembered the feeling of being that heroine in those movies I saw as a young girl. Of course, it could happen. Dreams *can* come true.

So I sent a tape to WIND, which was owned by Westinghouse Broadcasting. They were playing *"'50s, '60s and Now!"* It was the first oldies format in town—and it was a big hit in Chicago. Everyone was jumping on it! By now, some of the DJs who had worked in rock & roll radio were moving on up to the oldies format.

Ron Britain was WIND's new morning jock, and he had been a great catch for them! He had a huge fan base and his skits on WCFL had been hysterical—like *Subterranean Circus*—*Believe It Or Don't Believe It*—and his anonymous *Merry Christmas* calls to random listeners. He was *Saturday Night Live* before its time!

So I continued to bring demo tapes to the program director, Bob Moomey, who was so kind, not wanting to discourage me.

He'd say, "That was good—but you're not ready yet—keep working at it and get back to me with another tape."

I was so naive. I really thought I stood a chance. Had I seen the huge piles of tapes a program director gets from all over the country—experienced jocks, desperately wanting to get into a major market—I might have quit trying. But I didn't know that. I didn't know about major markets. I only knew Chicago because this was where I was born. I didn't know much at all about the *business* of the radio business.

"OK, Bob—be back in a few months!" I promised.

He *never* said, "Don't call us, we'll call you!"

On my second attempt, he again encouraged me to keep working at it, and again I believed.

The third time around, and much later that same year, it was the same response. But, this time he added that they needed a secretary in the sales department, and would I consider working there until they found a replacement? I asked him to give me *that* job, (thinking I could work my way up someday later). But he already saw through that ploy and told me that he knew that was not what I really wanted to do—so would I help them out in the meantime?

"Sure," I said.

Over the Rainbow

After a couple weeks, they found a sales secretary. Now they wondered if I would help out in their continuity department. Could I come by after my morning radio shift at WSDM and work a few hours for them? The stations were now just one block apart. I could walk over. Again, I heard myself saying, "Sure."

Around this time I started telling my woes to Ron Britain, their morning jock.

"They're not ever gonna hire me. They're just humoring me. These jobs only go to men," I hopelessly confided.

Ron said, "Just keep on trying!"

He was so kind and encouraging. It was only later that I learned he had given me a good reference, telling management, when they asked him about me, that I was a serious and hard worker. But I gave up. It was, after all, almost an entire year of trying.

Suddenly, after I hadn't been in touch for several months, the program director called,

"Would you like to come down and audition for the fill-in slot?"

WOULD I!

The audition was simply reading a couple of commercials and a weather forecast. There were two men that they also auditioned. But the station was learning a hard lesson. Every male jock wanted a full-time gig and would only take the part-time position until they were hired full-time elsewhere.

In many cases, jocks were like gypsies, moving from town to town, wherever the best work was. I, on the other hand, was a Chicago girl who wanted to stay in her hometown and I'm guessing that may have swayed things in my favor.

Anyway—I was *hired*! I became the new fill-in jock! The station was an AFTRA Union station and I would be paid the union rate— $100 per shift. This was more than I made all week doing the morning show at WSDM.

When I asked why, after all this time, they suddenly offered me this position, the program director said,

TOP ROCK GIRLY JOCK

"We all laughed at your last audition tape!"

I wondered what could have been so funny, since at WSDM, all I did was back announce songs, give the time and temperature, and a couple minutes of rip-n-read news.

"That line," Bob Moomey said, "the kicker at the end of your news story—about the snake found in someone's house. After you read, 'Everyone wondered where the snake came from,' you tagged it with, 'Well, even *I* know that! The snake came from its mommy and daddy snake,'—we couldn't stop laughing," he said.

I felt so complimented. I guess it was all in the timing. The month they called me to audition was October of 1971—the same month that the Equal Rights Amendment was adopted.

My very first show was on Christmas Day, 1971. For me, this would be *The Beginning of the End* of holidays that people with normal jobs usually enjoy. But this was one of my best Christmas presents ever! Thank you dear God!

Doing a radio show here, though, was so very different from WSDM where almost everything was automated. Here we had to talk every two minutes or so, at the beginning of each song. And most of the songs were short because they were oldies—not like the five-minute songs of today. There was an engineer whom we could see through a window, in the room at the end of the studio. We would raise our hand to ask him to open our microphone, then point to him to start the next song (kinda felt like doing the "Macarena"). At the exact moment we did that, we'd punch a timer button that activated a clock—like a huge stopwatch—that would start ticking off the seconds of the intro time to the song. We would watch the seconds count down in front of us, and rattle off our information over the intro music before the singing started. Things we tried to avoid were, talking over the vocal portion—or having a song end, and having *dead air* before the next song started (hence, the old DJ expression—*you could drive a truck through it*). Sometimes, there'd be a song with a *cold open*, meaning there is no music before the singing—the singing just starts immediately! In those cases you had to talk at the end of the previous song and try and finish your sentence right on the last note before the next one started. Everything had to be tight and moving! Eventually you learned to feel the music and never really looked much at the clock; you just knew when the singing would start.

But that first day was a challenge! I was doing the best I could, projecting the basics as I thought programming would want, and keeping a tight ship. But, my engineer, Chester, on the other side of the glass, kept complaining.

"I can't hear you!"—"Louder!"—"Speak up!"

Bad enough I had all this new format stuff to deal with—now the engineer can't *hear me?* My head was wild with thoughts that perhaps a woman's voice couldn't carry through the microphone on this set-up. Frantically, I spoke louder and *LOUDER!* I was almost shouting. If I shouted any louder, Chicago wouldn't even need a radio to hear me. We could just open the windows. Still the engineer wouldn't let up.

"Get closer to the microphone! Speak right into it!" he ordered.

What could be wrong here, I thought. We never had this problem at WSDM. Maybe because this was the AM band and different than FM? Perhaps I just didn't have the *bazoom* to my voice that the guy jocks had? Some of them could really bellow it out. Maybe the microphones at WSDM had had special adjustments made for female voices, but not here? And since I was their first female, they probably never had this problem before.

Finally, the engineer couldn't stand it any longer. He complained that his pots were way up and my voice was just not getting through! He charged into the studio to inspect my microphone. There was a foam cover on it, like a wind buffer, to prevent P-popping and extraneous noise. He looked and looked and fiddled with the mic, and finally yanked off the foam cover. Surprise! The microphone had been completely turned around 180 degrees and the opening was now on the other side. I was talking into the *back* of the microphone. Well,

TOP ROCK GIRLY JOCK

yeaaaahh, that'll do it! And it's not something anyone would easily notice, since the foam cover was on. It seemed to me this wasn't a usual occurrence or it wouldn't have taken the engineer this long to discover it. He said,

"Oh, the cleaning woman must've accidentally turned it around."

Oh yeah? I thought. Cleaning woman? On Christmas Day?

And I'm sure a cleaning woman would've had instructions to never touch the broadcast equipment. I think Chester was just trying to reassure me that there'd be no more sabotage. He did his best to console me—he was so concerned and sweet.

But deep down I think we both knew there was a prankster on the loose. It doesn't take a rocket scientist to figure out why the microphone didn't work for me, but worked fine for the disc jockey ahead of me. And I do remember who that was. But I'll leave out his name—wouldn't want to tarnish his radio image. Anyway, if *he* hadn't turned it around, would *his* deep voice possibly have come through the back end of that mic? And the guy before him—and the one before him? How many do you think were broadcasting into the back end of the microphone?

After that first six-hour shift, I was exhausted! The assistant program director came in near the end of the show, and I said to him,

"Jeszcze Polska Nie Zginęła!"

This is really the first line of the Polish National Anthem. Literally translated, it means, "Poland is not yet lost." To me, it meant "Polish girl is not yet lost"—since I am of 100% Polish descent; I've always felt people should be proud of their heritage.

So, when the assistant program director heard me say that, he asked what it meant (probably to be sure they weren't curse words) and suggested I say it on the air. I thought that was out of range for the program, but he thought it was fine. The station was very into an ethnic appeal. They had a strong Italian name, Bob *Del Giorno*, who had just been on the air before me—*(Oops!)*—Well, now they had a strong Polish name as well—*Szerszen!*

Over the Rainbow

And so, for the very first time, on Christmas Day, 1971, at the end of my show, I said—

"JESCZE POLSKA NIE ZGINĘŁA!"

It became my signature sign-off and I've been saying it at the end of my radio shows ever since.

The WIND studios were at 625 North Michigan Avenue and WSDM was now at 528 N. Michigan, exactly one block apart. WIND called me whenever they needed a "fill-in"—whenever a jock called in sick at the last minute or took a day off. It was a perfect set-up for WIND and for me. They would call me during my morning show at WSDM in the 9 o-clock hour and ask if I could be at WIND to do the 10 to 2 PM shift.

"Sure," I said.

And I would scramble, asking Penny Lane, whose show followed mine at WSDM, if she would please start fifteen minutes earlier, so I could run down the block to WIND. I had to hustle myself over there! I ran, dodging traffic as I crossed Michigan Avenue; if I tripped and fell, my career could be over. By the time I'd get back on my feet, I might miss the 10 AM show start at WIND. So I ran quickly, but carefully. Please cars, don't hit me! I'm *on my way to a star*.

Once there, I had to settle into their format, and try to focus on who and where I was. The format called for announcing the call letters, WIND, and your name and/or time of day every time you opened your mouth. So I pitched it,

"This is WIND (I had the call letters written on an index card so I wouldn't get confused as to where I was), and it's 10:15 and my name is—my name is—"

Oh, my gosh! I forgot my name. All the listeners now think I don't even know my own name! And what is it anyway? Why didn't I write *that* down! I was sooooooo tired (started to sound like all those celebrities I'd met in the past). I had just been *Den Pal Dawn* for the past four hours. Now, I was supposed to be me, myself, *Connie Szerszen!* And as I struggled to spit out the words, I couldn't believe I had forgotten, not my radio name, but my *real* name! The vocal on the song started, so there was no time for me to say anymore.

Ah, leave them guessing—Hah! And me too. (I know I have a tricky name but I almost always remember it.) I survived.

One morning, the night after a big radio convention in Chicago, Phil Nolan, General Manager of WIND, called me during my broadcast at WSDM. He asked if I could attend a very special luncheon. The Editor of the *Chicago Daily News* would be there; and the Admiral whose brother had captured the U-505 submarine on exhibit at The Museum of Science and Industry, the Brigadier General of the Marines, someone from the Sears Tower planning commission, and other dignitaries. Phil was a great guy and I wouldn't think of letting him down—especially after hiring me as their first female jock.

I said, "Sure, I'll be there—where and when?"

"This morning at 11:30," he said.

Because I was in blue jeans, I decided to drive home which was about twenty-five minutes away, and change into my "Navy" dress—much more appropriate for this special luncheon with so many military guests.

It was at the Press Club, just around the corner from the station. I had slept only one hour due to partying at the radio convention the night before. I arrived at the luncheon, feeling sleepy but fine—until the Bacardi.

Everyone ordered a cocktail, so I did too. Two sips, and the whole room started spinning. With both hands, I grabbed onto the table and smiled. I politely answered all their questions about being a woman in this man's world in radio, and tried to be charming, but thought I might pass out at any moment. Phil Nolan was proudly introducing their "first female" to this prestigious group. It would not look too good for him to have WIND's new acquisition fall off her chair. But how much can one fragile female do on one hour of sleep!

Over the Rainbow

Within a matter of months, WIND's revolving door started spinning again. The week-end guys were leaving for full-time gigs elsewhere. Week-ends were a blur as the male part-timers flew out the door. I might have been their only answer—and so, they promoted me from "fill-in" to regular week-end jock!

Mom and Dad were so proud. And I thanked Mom for spurring me on with the challenge of trying to get hired in all-male territory! I was booked for Saturday, 6-midnight, and Sunday, noon-6 PM. I did week-ends, and filled in on vacation shifts as needed. The promotions department ordered my first pubicity photo.

CONNIE SZERSZEN   WIND RADIO - WEEKENDS

Soon everybody wanted my story. Norman Mark of *The Chicago Daily News* was first with this article on April 12, 1972—

'Sensuous disk jockey' bucks male chauvinism

It's hard to understand why more women are not working as AM radio disk jockeys.

The job does not require one to lift heavy objects. A record, even an LP, weighs a couple of ounces at most and the DJs are usually assisted by burly engineers, who actually place the record on the turntable or push the button that starts the tape recorder.

But when Connie decided to try for bigger and better things, she encountered pure male chauvinism. AM program directors conceded that she had a good voice, but they often added that women are unsuitable for AM air work because of their unstable employment record. (They sometimes get pregnant.) Connie never pointed out that many male DJs last less than nine months. Sometimes they are employed only a matter of weeks.

Another prospective employer told Connie that a woman's voice doesn't have the authority needed for AM radio. It is obvious he never argued with a woman over a checkbook imbalance.

The program directors even became creative in their excuses. They said that lady announcers might be acceptable in New York or Los Angeles, but Chicago wasn't ready for a woman broadcaster. (They forgot Yvonne Daniels, who was heard with Sid McCoy on WCFL in 1965 and who has the sexiest voice in local radio.)

They said that women couldn't learn the complex mechanical requirements of modern radio.

I've seen DJs at work, and their job consists mainly of pointing to an engineer to signal the start of a record. A woman with two hands (and at least one finger on each) should be able to signal as well as a similarly equipped man. FINALLY WIND AGREED to hire her, and Connie began on Christmas Day. She is witty, her voice is pleasant and quite a change from the endless male voices we hear.

She ends each show she does with the words "Jeszcze Polska nie zginęła," meaning "Poland is not yet lost." If Polish men have half the determination of Connie Szerszen, Poland is far from lost.

\#

WIND took his article and created a promo piece for the sales department

'Sensuous disk jockey' bucks male chauvinism

It's hard to understand why more women are not working as AM radio disk jockeys.

The job does not require one to lift heavy objects. A record, even an LP, weighs a couple of ounces at most and the DJs are usually assisted by burly engineers, who actually place the record on the turntable or push the button that starts the tape recorder.

Yet Connie Szerszen, a substitute disk jockey for WIND who is heard on the station mainly on weekends, assures me that she encountered endless problems while trying to get a job on AM radio.

Miss Szerszen (pronounced Szerszen) is heard weekdays on WSDM (97.6 FM) from 6-10 a.m., where she is known as Dawn, the world's most sensuous disk jockey.

It is a title she gave herself, "because it sounds so dumb," she says.

A self-described "100 per cent pedigreed Polish girl" from Chicago's Northwest Side, Miss Szerszen began in radio as a secretary at WCFL, where she arranged record hops for disk jockeys.

ONE DAY she happened to talk to a WSDM hostess. An audition led to a part-time job and then to full-time employment.

But when Connie—a pretty girl who is thin enough so that her parents probably tell her to eat lots of food and put some meat on her bones—decided to try for bigger and better things, she encountered pure male chauvinism.

AM program directors conceded that she had a good voice, but they often added that women are unsuitable for AM air work because of their unstable employment record. (They sometimes get pregnant.)

Connie never pointed out that many male DJs last less than nine months. Sometimes they are employed only a matter of weeks.

Another prospective employer told Connie that a woman's voice doesn't have the authority needed for AM radio. It is obvious he never argued with a woman over a checkbook imbalance.

The program directors even became creative in their excuses. They said that lady announcers might be acceptable in New York or Los Angeles, but Chicago wasn't ready for a woman broadcaster. (They forgot Yvonne Daniels, who was heard with Sid McCoy on WCFL in 1965 and who has the sexiest voice in local radio.)

They said that women couldn't learn the complex mechanical requirements of modern radio.

I've seen DJs at work, and their job consists mainly of pointing to an engineer to signal the start of a record. A woman with two hands (and at least one finger on each) should be able to signal as well as a similarly equipped man.

FINALLY, WIND AGREED to hire her, and Connie began on Christmas Day. She is heard irregularly on WIND (and gets paid almost $100 for every shift she works). She is witty, her voice is pleasant and quite a change from the endless male voices we hear.

She ends each show she does with the words "Jeszcze Polska nie zgineta," meaning "Poland is not yet lost." If Polish men have half the determination of Connie Szerszin, Poland is far from lost.

CHICAGO DAILY NEWS, Wednesday, April 12, 1972

Norman Mark

560 WIND GROUP W

TOP ROCK GIRLY JOCK

I dabbled in so many things (some call it *Renaissance*, some call it *dilettante*, and some say *Jack of all trades, master of none*), and at that time I was also on the career board of *Mademoiselle* magazine. The magazine was planning a series of make-overs. We had to complain about one of our features and they would do a correction. Since I'm great at complaining, I was accepted as one of their projects.

All the chosen girls were flown to New York, all expenses paid. We had a *before* group picture taken. I was the only one in the photograph with her slip showing. It was unintentional, but I would later tell my listeners that showing your slip meant you were looking for a man (Victorian days legend). Tho, there was that one day when I stepped out of the car and my entire half-slip just fell to the ground—not sure what that meant—hopefully not a sign of a loose woman.

Then the magazine's beauty department started to analyze us. I was accused of looking like a Barbie doll (which I personally think looks kinda cute, but then I like dolls). The make-up experts came next. My skin was too pink they said (yeah, they're called *pimples*) as they slathered some green stuff all over my face (helllloooo—I'm an Earthling, not a Martian). They continued on.

"Make her face shiny," one said.

"No, a matte finish is the way to go!" another said, as she tapped on the powder. (Why not just put a mask on me?)

Then someone added, "Her hair is too brassy! Send her to the salon!"

When I got there, the master hairdresser, Leslie Blanchard, asked me what blond products I was using because my hair looked so nice and natural. (I thought the beauty department said it was brassy. Did anyone really know what they were doing? I started to feel like a guinea pig—but, hey, it was, after all, a free trip to the Big Apple!)

The end result was a new formula for coloring my hair, which was now cut in a Buster Brown style, tons of make-up with a lot of green underneath it all, and the best part, a new wardrobe! We were given all sorts of clothes to try on and they helped us choose what looked best for the photo shoot. I ended up with a russet colored coat and aqua blue sweater, which I was allowed to keep.

All the girls were then taken to the rooftop of a New York building where some props had been set up. This is where our *after* photos were taken. It was a dreary day, but we were all out there smiling because now we were beautiful! I remember being asked to sit here, stand there, climb the stepladder a few steps. The photographer was trying to catch our best pose.

When the shoot was finished, everyone celebrated. We were all hustled into a Rolls Royce (the one and only time in my life—ever!) and treated to a spectacular dinner at a posh restaurant.

My folks came along on the trip and, when I visited their hotel after the festivities, they just stared at me. For a split second, they didn't recognize me. When I looked in the mirror, neither did I. In person, I didn't look like myself at all—I actually almost looked like a professional model. It was amazing.

During that week in New York, I tried to squeeze in as much fun as I could. One morning I got up early and went to watch Don Imus broadcasting in his cowboy hat. He was the hot ticket in New York radio. I had to see what all the fuss was about. He didn't appear to be too happy. I thought that that might be *relating* to the New York audience. From what I observed, no one in New York ever smiled or laughed much. When we went to a restaurant and paid the cashier, it was usually a grunt of some sort and the change would be slammed into your hand. If we were living the *American dream*, why was everyone so grumpy? Maybe we just went to the wrong restaurants. But Don Imus seemed to relate well to this grumpiness. I watched him for about a half hour and then left (kind of like when you're at the zoo and you realize not much more is gonna happen at that cage, so you go on to the next).

And the next was fun alright. There's nothing like shopping thrills for us girls! Mom and I just had to stop in at Tiffany's. (Ah,

"Breakfast at Tiffany's"—Audrey Hepburn—here comes that movie-star-feeling again!) An adorable bracelet caught my eye. Purple colored gemstones entwined with green (emeralds?) in a grapevine pattern. It was about one inch in width. The sales guy asked if I'd like to try it on.

"Oh, no, I'm sure I couldn't afford it!" I timidly answered as I backed off a little.

"Oh, come on, you can try it on," he coaxed.

And then suddenly, there it was on my wrist! And there I was, feeling like the poor little, poor girl.

"How much?" I asked out of curiosity.

"$85,000," he said, matter of factly.

I turned to my mom, "So, what d'you think, Mom? Should we sell the house and snap this right up? He did say it looks good on me!"

We laughed and laughed about it later. We were never ever together in a Tiffany's again. I've made a few trips to the Chicago store, but that New York minute was just a special time for my mom and me. We had such fun together!

Finally, the *Mademoiselle* make-over issue came out. The photos were great! In the magazine, the heavy make-up looked completely natural. Little histories on each girl's problem, and what town she was from, accompanied the photos.

I was hoping they would print WIND's call letters to help promote my radio show—but not! I did tell my listeners about it, though, because it was such a kick for me and I thought perhaps a curiosity for them!

And 'til this day, I still use the blond formula that Leslie Blanchard concocted for me (whenever I'm in a blond mood; of course, you know how we girls can be—I mean, sometimes we redheads and brunettes have just as much fun).

Check out the *before* photo—I'm first on the left—the one with her slip showing.

Over the Rainbow

Mademoiselle
big fall beauty issue

October 60¢

HOW TO LOOK LIKE NOBODY ELSE BUT YOU

12 SUPER MAKEOVERS

Twelve "befores," count 'em (well, since these members of MLLE's Career Board were picked from all over the country, only eight made it to New York City for this picture; the other four—Gayle Durkin, Marti Hendrick, Teresa Roth and Brooke Canty—were made over in Cleveland or Los Angeles). Here, from l to r: Connie Szerszen, Marilyn Goodman, Kathleen Allen, Karen Hauge, Barbara Ward, Sheilah Lizman, Janet Joyce and Marie Tylka. A mix of geography, a common plea: each wanted a new look, her own, individual, *best* look. All knew something was wrong but either didn't know what or, knowing, didn't know what to do about it. Mlle's objective, collective eye saw to it that a team of hair and makeup experts got together and got to work, even set up exercise classes as part of the total picture. (Speaking of, it's a good idea to have a friend take a picture of you, you're simply too used to your mirror image to see all of your possibilities.) The problems we ran into were basically two: too little or too much. Some thought the natural look meant wearing little or no makeup, others thought they had to pour it all on—the false lashes, the bleach, the cakey makeup, the whole ageing bit. Underdone, overdone, they hadn't done what they could to live up to their full beauty potential. What we did you'll see—nothing cookie-cutter but separate, speedy regimes they liked, plan to keep up. Each girl came out looking herself—at her best. And that's super

142

TOP ROCK GIRLY JOCK

Bottom—I'm in the middle—the one they said looks like a Barbie doll (after some kid threw her in the toy box)

Over the Rainbow

Right—
My one and only time in *Mademoiselle* magazine—
Still no centerfold—Hah!

TOP ROCK GIRLY JOCK

Also about this time, I was getting more and more interested in writing music. Since I had already learned to play a little guitar at the local high school's adult education classes, my brother and I started jamming together and writing our own songs. We'd play them for each other and it was kind of fun to see what we came up with. (Move over, Karen and Richard Carpenter!) But the Beatles were really the hottest act around, and I thought their early style was sweet, fun, and so melodic. I wanted to write like that!

There was a popular folk singer in town, by the name of Bonnie Koloc. I contacted her producer and asked if he'd like to hear some of my songs. I was astonished when he agreed to meet me and even seemed to really like my songs! He took my music to an arranger, got a band together, bought studio time, and we recorded two of my songs.

When I listened to them in the control room, I could not believe that that was me! What they can do with your voice is unbelievable! I never thought I could sound that good! Finally, the producer explained to me that we would record an entire album of my original songs. I would then be booked at different events like college parties, etc., where I'd perform my songs, and we'd sell the albums! What?

"I can't go on the road!" I said; "I have to DJ at the radio station on the week-ends."

"Well, you'll have to choose between that and this," he said bluntly.

So I chose radio. I never finished the album. I never got copies of the songs I recorded at Streeterville. Somewhere I still have the music tracks from those sessions, but my singing was not on there.

Meanwhile, my radio show was going strong. It was a year down the line now, and the media still found the *woman in radio* story intriguing.

It was March 24, 1973, when Ron Powers of the *Chicago Sun-Times* wrote—

Over the Rainbow

A Female DJ for MCP'S

Attention, male-chauvinist pigs. Your dream girl lives. She is tall, fair-skinned, red-haired and beautiful. Although she has made it in the male-dominated world of radio broadcasting, she would not give you a karate chop in the breadbasket if you jiggled the loose change in your zoot suit, spun your key chain around and muttered rakishly, 'Hubba-hubba, Good-Lookin', what's cookin'?' In fact, she would probably dimple becomingly and invite you up on the front porch for ice tea and apple turnovers.

She is happy to be where she is in life. No cold-eyed femlib spokesperson, she. She is polite, sensible, dresses in soft pink things, likes Elvis's ballads and wants to get married sometime...

She thinks the main thing in broadcasting is 'just being yourself and being a well-rounded person.' She takes night-school courses at Northwestern University...and reads love poems. ("Like, I really like alliteration a lot.")

Her parents are proud of her, and little children send nice letters to her. Her name is Connie Szerszen, and she doesn't have a date this Saturday night because she is working the 6 p.m.-to-midnight shift on radio station WIND.

IF ALL THE ABOVE SOUNDS like a superslick parody of Miss American Pie, it's not really meant to be. The main thing about Connie Szerszen is that she is - here we go again - a pleasant, bright, decent, together, out-front girl who is having the time of her life in a profession (disk jockeying) that is crowded with throbbing egos, neurotic overachievers, dunderheads of all descriptions and strange flower-shirted creatures who believe themselves to be in touch with the Ultimate Intelligence. A plain old everyday garden variety MALE, f'gawdsake, would have trouble keeping his sanity in that zoo. But a woman, in the flood tide of The Movement, has to fight a rear-guard action in the broadcasting milieu as well; against the strident ones who expect her to behave not only as a female but as a Symbol besides.

"I never really wanted to do this," said Connie at the station the other day, between fits of honest-to-June Allyson giggling over the fact that anyone would care to interview her. "But when I really got into it, it became a challenge to do well. At times, along the line, I guess I really did fear I would fail. I mean, a lot of station managers kept telling me that Chicago's not ready for a female disk jockey. Women's voices lack authority, one guy said. I thought that was dumb.

"As for pressure from women like from activist groups --I really hate to talk about it, because I'm kind of like in the middle. I think they have some good points. If women are accepted in broadcasting today, it's partly because of something they started. But I'm not one to get out on the lines and yell for action."

Connie's struggle to get where she is now in radio announcing - weekend and fill-in shifts at WIND - is right out of a Germaine Greer nightmare.

....On Christmas Day, 1971, Connie came to WIND, which considers the world safe for women disk jockeys on weekends, at least...

"I think of it as being on the telephone," she said.

"How I sound on the air depends on how my moods are. I may have personal feelings about a song, based on memories I associate with it. My voice probably shows that. If I'm in a bad mood, I just won't talk as much. I was born under the sign of Cancer; when the moon is full I'm really in a good mood."

Full moons to you, Connie Szerszen. You're a nice lady - uh, person.

#

When I read this, I was amazed at how this guy whom I'd never met, could know so much about me so quickly. He captured my giggles, my favorites and my feelings. He explained a lot of *me* to me. But then, that's what great writers do. Ron Powers went on to win the Pulitzer Prize. I feel so lucky to have been interviewed by such a gifted writer! His creative and kind article sure took me *"Over the Rainbow"* (which, by the way, is my *favorite song ever*) because its message is full of colorful hope.

TOP ROCK GIRLY JOCK

The *Men* Instrumental in Bringing a *Woman* to Chicago Radio!
A first for America!

Right—
WIND Program Director,
Bob Moomey

Above—
WIND General Manager
Phil Nolan

Right—
WIND morning DJ—
Ron Britain

RON BRITAIN   WIND 560 6 – 10 am

Over the Rainbow

Left—Burt Reynolds! Finally! **A Centerfold!** Loved that *Cosmo!*

Below—
As DJ at WIND
Week-ends and fill-in

Right—After our *Mademoiselle* makeover in New York Yessssss—
I'm the one in the hat

TOP ROCK GIRLY JOCK

WCIU·26

141 WEST JACKSON BOULEVARD   CHICAGO, ILLINOIS 60604

PRESS RELEASE

WHAT: "FOR YOUR INFORMATION" ... is a special program produced by the Television Department of Columbia College in association with WCIU-TV. In this series of programs, "FOR YOUR INFORMATION will explore FM and AM radio in Chicago.

WHEN: Saturday, October 6, 1973, at 5:30 PM, "FOR YOUR INFORMATION" explores FM radio in Chicago with guests: Bob Johnson, WBBM-FM; Ed Walters, WYEN-FM; author/critic Bill Brashler and student host, Gil Peters in a super-charged discussion of FM radio.

Saturday, October 13, 1973, at 5:30 PM "FOR YOUR INFORMATION" will answer the question "Is AM radio a listener's answer to a garage sale?" Find out with the top "tonsils" in Chicago -- that's Larry Lujack, WCFL; Connie Szerszen, WIND; Herb Kent, WVON, author/critic Bill Brashler and student host, Gil Peters.

Saturday, October 20, 1973, at 5:30 PM "FOR YOUR INFORMATION" gives you a chance to look back to the days when you knew every tune on the TOP 40. Ron Britain hosts: The New Colony Six, The Buckinghams, and The Shadows of Night.

CHICAGO'S FIRST UHF TELEVISION

Saturday, October 13, 1973, at 5:30 PM "FOR YOUR INFORMATION" will answer the question "Is AM radio a listener's answer to a garage sale?" Find out with the top "tonsils" in Chicago -- that's Larry Lujack, WCFL; Connie Szerszen, WIND; Herb Kent, WVON, author/critic Bill Brashler and student host, Gil Peters.

EIGHT

Rock and Roll All Night

After two years of being the week-end *American woman* at WIND, a new program director was brought in by Westinghouse. Al Mitchell started making changes. I was promoted—and became the full-time, 6-10 PM jock!

This was a *first*. WIND (Westinghouse Broadcasting) now sent out a press release, announcing they had the—

"First female on AM radio to have her own show in prime time in a major market!"

This all happened when AM was the powerhouse on the radio dial; FM was still trying to catch up. The Women's Lib Movement probably had some influence on this. But I myself, had had nothing to do with women's lib. I just wanted to dee-jay.

One day, during a show, Al told me to be sure and be back in the studio before the newscast ended. The news came on at the top of the hour, and that's usually when the jocks ran to the bathroom, or for coffee. I kind of wondered why he was getting his shorts in a bunch, but thought he just wanted to take some precautions for a smooth transition from news to music. Inwardly, I questioned whether or not I had been getting sloppy.

So I quickly ran back into the studio and waited for my turn. And as I sat there, I heard the end of the newscast.

"Today, on her birthday, Connie Szerszen was read into the United States Congressional Record by Congressman John Kluczynski," the newsman announced—then he read the statement—

> "Mr. Speaker, there is nothing nicer in the whole world or nothing better in the whole world than music, unless, perhaps, it is the glory of a lovely woman. We are blessed with the perfect combination in the person of Connie Szerszen, who has blended all the loveliness in one magnificent package for the radio audience of greater Chicago on station WIND. Her charm, her voice, her manner, and the knowledge of her subject have rendered her the darling of the airwaves for many thousands of her devoted fans, of whom I happen to be one of the outstanding examples. It is a great pleasure for me to wish her a very happy birthday this July 3. Perhaps we can account for her success because at long last we have a disc jockey whose voice is as pleasurable to listen to as the records she plays."

#

I was *stunned!* What? Who? Me? I was grateful for our music format with short intros, because after that announcement, I didn't know what to say. I was speechless.

Someone later told me that I was a topic of conversation between our general manager, Phil Nolan, and Congressman Kluczynski, and that's how it came about. It made me feel so good to be working for management that appreciated my efforts. Again, the station prepared copies for advertising purposes.

What a fantastic birthday present from God. Now, not only was I "Over the Rainbow"—I was—**OVER THE MOON!**

Congressional Record

PROCEEDINGS AND DEBATES OF THE 93^d CONGRESS, SECOND SESSION

Vol. 120 — WASHINGTON, WEDNESDAY, JULY 3, 1974 — No. 99

Senate
House of Representatives

WEDNESDAY, JULY 3, 1974

CONNIE SZERSZEN

HON. JOHN C. KLUCZYNSKI
OF ILLINOIS
IN THE HOUSE OF REPRESENTATIVES
Wednesday, July 3, 1974

Mr. KLUCZYNSKI. Mr. Speaker, there is nothing nicer in the whole world or nothing better in the whole world than music, unless, perhaps, it is the glory of a lovely woman. We are blessed with the perfect combination in the person of Connie Szerszen, who has blended all the loveliness in one magnificent package for the radio audience of greater Chicago on station WIND. Her charm, her voice, her manner, and the knowledge of her subject have rendered her the darling of the airwaves for many thousands of her devoted fans, of whom I happen to be one of the outstanding examples. It is a great pleasure for me to wish her a very happy birthday this July 3. Perhaps we can account for her success because at long last we have a disc jockey whose voice is as pleasurable to listen to as the records she plays.

560 WIND GROUP

RADIO ADVERTISING REPRESENTATIVES, INC.

TOP ROCK GIRLY JOCK

PRESS INFORMATION
625 NORTH MICHIGAN AVENUE CHICAGO ILLINOIS 60611 TELEPHONE 527-2170

WESTINGHOUSE BROADCASTING COMPANY INC

CONNIE SZERSZEN

Connie Szerszen, WIND's first female personality, is a native Chicagoan. The daughter of Mary and Stanley Szerszen, Connie lives with her family in a nearby northwest suburb.

Connie attended St. Bartholomew elementary school and Alvernia High School. Interested in art, she also took courses at the American Academy of Art and the Art Institute of Chicago.

Before joining WIND, Connie was heard mornings, Monday through Friday, at WSDM-FM. Her first show on WIND was Christmas Day, 1971. Connie's debut in major market AM radio launched a career that has only just begun to skyrocket. Until March, 1974, Connie was heard weekends (Saturday, 6 P.M. - Midnight and Sunday, Noon - 6 P.M.) and filled in for vacation relief. On March 25, 1974, Connie became the first female personality on AM radio to have her own prime time radio show. Connie can be heard on WIND every evening, Monday through Friday, from 6 P.M. to 10 P.M. and also Sunday, from 5 P.M. to 10 P.M.

Billing herself as WIND Radio's "top rock girlie jock", Connie has become a legend to her legion of fans.

Off the air, Connie enjoys writing music and playing the guitar. She also has an active interest in sports and although she admits she's not too good at any one particular feat, she enjoys just getting out for a good time.

Rock and Roll All Night

I was evolving. I was the now the "Top Rock Girly Jock!" I was the "Polish Princess!" And once in a while, I was the "Chic in Chicago!"

Every so often, I'd spell out my last name on the air at the program director's request. People who didn't have us tuned in perfectly, heard *Thurston* instead of *Szerszen* (which is pronounced *"Ser-zen"*) So, I spelled out my name for the listeners—

S as in *stupid*, *Z* as in *zit*, *E* as in *Elvis*, *R* as in *rock*, *S* as in *sleazy*, *Z* as in *XEROX* (yeah, I know), *E* as in *EEEEEEK!* and *N* as in *nuts*.

I thought this *clarification* just added to the confusion, but you usually didn't argue much with the program director. The trickiest part was trying to find a long enough song intro to say all this stuff.

And, just as at WCFL, the fun extended beyond the work. We again met tons of celebrities. Many would guest on Chicago Eddie Schwartz's overnight talk show like—

The Legendary Steve Allen! *Hi-Ho Steverino!*

TOP ROCK GIRLY JOCK

Karen & Richard Carpenter, WIND's Doug Dahlgren, and me

Rock and Roll All Night

When I had the chance to meeet Karen and Richard Carpenter, I remember someone at the station admiring how wonderfully thin Karen was—poor thing. They were both so sweet.

I always noticed that the more famous the celebrities were, the nicer they were. It was always the one-hit wonders that seemed to be all puffed up about themselves. Well, maybe they had to flaunt it while they could because they knew their fame would be short-lived.

The WIND air personalities were invited to all sorts of events! There were press parties at the Chicago Playboy Mansion. Those were always very special. All the jocks loved them. Everybody who was anybody, and those who wanted to meet somebody who already *was somebody*, was there! (Huh?)

There was a swimming pool in the basement where they handed out paper bathing suits for those who wanted a dip, but not necessarily a skinny dip. You could either carefully step down the narrow winding stairway, or—you could slide down the fireman's pole to get downstairs in a flash! A lot of the guys chose the pole. I was so tempted to follow them for the thrill of it all, but afraid the view from my mini-dress might give the guys too much of a flash.

Besides all the gaiety, the hors d'oeuvres were incredible. I remember oranges half-stuffed with ice cream—*mmmmm*. And, it was here that I tasted my very first oyster. This kinda caught me by surprise. I had no idea you couldn't chew through an oyster. So when the slimy thing totally filled my mouth and I was starting to feel real stupid and unglamorous, I tried to gulp it all down. But it just wouldn't budge. It was in a kind of limbo in my throat somewhere. I thought I might choke to death. I thought of spitting it all out right there on the table! (I mentally pictured guests looking at the mess, "Oh, my, what delectable is this?") 'Til this day, I really don't know how to eat raw oysters because I'll *never* try that again.

But that was where I got to meet Elton John in his white-framed sunglasses; his lyricist, Bernie Taupin, was there too.

TOP ROCK GIRLY JOCK

"Hey, Elton—let's have a hug!"

Bernie Taupin and Elton getting an award from Hef

Rock and Roll All Night

Hef—Hoping Elton would play?

Hef's Playmate, Barbie Benton—(Don't think Elton played)

TOP ROCK GIRLY JOCK

WIND Program Director, Al Mitchell, in back—
and me—draping myself all over Elton in his cute plaid suit—
(I didn't know) (He looks like he enjoyed it, tho)

Rock and Roll All Night

But "Rocket Man" Made a Quick Getaway!

Foosball, anyone?
Left—Elton, DJ John Landecker, me—*Right*—Barbie and Hef

TOP ROCK GIRLY JOCK

Years later, Sharon Fox, a local reporter, sent me that tear-sheet from *Faces* magazine—also the name of the hot club on Rush Street. As celebrity guests took turns playing foosball with Elton—there I was in the background. Can't seem to remember that moment. I must have had a great time!

There were many press parties at the Chicago Playboy Mansion and besides meeting Elton, I also met a hot new group at the time—Fleetwood Mac. A picture of Stevie Nicks and me hangs in the family room, both of us *cocktailing* it. Stevie's a real talent and has done some great music on her own; although I don't know her personally, I hear she's a kind lady and loyal friend.

Decades later, I'd still be playing Elton John and Fleetwood Mac—at WJMK—and remembering the fun of hanging out with rock stars who brought such memorable music to the world.

Right—Stevie Nicks of Fleetwood Mac & me,
at the Chicago Playboy Mansion

Rock and Roll All Night

Another fun time was when the WIND jocks did a photo-shoot for a radio station album of the top oldies. It was a charity album for the Variety Club's Children's Charities and La Rabida. After the kids were through with school for the day, we went to their schoolyard and took pictures dressed in 1950's garb. The station rented costumes for us. I wore an ankle length circle skirt, bobby sox and saddle shoes. It was hilarious. (The only picture *I've* ever had taken blowing bubble gum.)

Back left to right—Chuck Benson, Ron Britain, Dave Baum
Front left to right—Larry "the legend" Johnson, Dick Williamson. "bubble-gum me," and Bob Del Giorno
(Looks like his bubble was bigger than mine)

It's a wonder we didn't get arrested, running around dressed like that–nowhere near Halloween. Can't you just picture the mothers who ran late picking up their kids from school and finding us in the schoolyard.

Another shot showed me and "Chat Champ" Dave Baum, when he flashed open his raincoat. Actually, it was all in fun. There was nothing there. I mean, I don't know if there was anything there or not. I assume there was something there. What I mean is, I didn't see anything. He was completely covered. Later, at the station, we all laughed at it. But this photo never made it on the album cover.

"Chat Champ" Dave Baum—showing off his belt buckle

Rock and Roll All Night

Public appearances for the radio station were also fun! I gave talks to high school students who wanted to know how to get into radio—and especially to encourage girls not to give up in a man's territory.

I appeared at shopping centers for special events. The most fun ones were with Captain Marvel, and another with Spiderman (the '70s version). They were fun because it was all impromptu and neither of us knew what the other was going to say.

Sometimes I wondered why they even wanted me there at all. I never thought I said anything particularly entertaining—and I can't remember them doing that either. But the kids were thrilled. I guess their costumes said it all. (In fact, maybe a little too much—so snug.) Ah, well, something for the kids and something for mommy.

"C'mon, little Johnny, let's get a closer look at Captain *Maaaaaarrrrrvel-lous!*" (Make that *Marvel-lust*.)

TOP ROCK GIRLY JOCK

Rock and Roll All Night

By now I was also starting to appear on stage with some real big time celebrities.

I co-emceed a Bobby Vinton show with Chicago Eddie Schwartz, at the Chicago Amphitheater. My mom sewed a beautiful baby blue satin halter top gown for this appearance, and I added a baby blue feather boa. (I wore a lot of blue in those days, even though my favorite color is pink.)

I remember walking out on stage to join Eddie. The place was packed. He introduced me as the "Polish Princess" from WIND. I have to credit Eddie for giving me that sweet title. The audience applauded and cheered, and I thought this was great—getting all this adulation—and I didn't even *do* anything! No singing, no dancing, nothing! Then together we brought out Bobby—the "Polish Prince!" Bobby's big hit then was "Melody of Love" which had some lyrics in Polish! "Moja droga, ja cię kocham—"

Left—"Chicago Eddie" Schwartz, Bobby Vinton, and me
Backstage at the Chicago Amphitheatre

TOP ROCK GIRLY JOCK

One show with Bobby Vinton was at the Arie Crown Theater at McCormick Place in Chicago. This one was a station sponsored Halloween show co-hosted by all the WIND dee-jays. The jocks had to whip up a costume for this event. "Chicago Eddie" Schwartz, a big, macho guy, came dressed as a pumpkin. (Good thinking, Eddie!) Since Bobby Vinton, the "Polish Prince," was the main attraction, and since I was the "Polish Princess," I decided to dress like him. (Kind of in drag—) (Wasn't that a Buckinghams song?)

My mom sewed a blue satin suit for me. I cut out Bobby's picture from an album cover and made a mask from it. I carried a red rose, which was what Bobby often did when he sang back then. But the best part of the costume, I thought, was the hair on my chest. *(Excuse me? Puleeeeeeze—not for real!)* I cut little snippets of brown fake fur and glued them to my neck area and any exposed skin that peeked from beneath my collar. Bobby loved it! I never did get to see if he actually had any hair on his chest, since his outfit that day was a red and white *princely* uniform that buttoned up to his chin.

Rock and Roll All Night

Above—With Bobby Vinton at Arie Crown Theater

Below—With "Chicago Eddie" Schwartz, on Halloween

Right—Me in my Bobby Vinton costume—mask from his album, Polish eagle in back, and red rose!

Mom, Bobby Vinton, and Dad—*Polish Power!*

Before I emceed a show, I'd get to meet the stars backstage. Tom Jones was a real nice guy. I introduced him to my mom, who usually came with me (not to chaperone, but because she was just as thrilled as I was to meet these celebrities). "Superjock," Larry Lujack, used to call Tom Jones—"Tommy Tightpants"—but with my mom standing right there, I tried not to look down to see just how tight. I gave him a *Radio-gram*—a bit I dreamed up on my show, where listeners left voice messages for Tom—and then I'd give him the tape to cherish forever—and my picture, so he'd never forget me. Hah! Of course, I never met him again.

With Tom Jones—Condessa Del Mar, Alsip, IL

TOP ROCK GIRLY JOCK

I was also mistress of ceremonies for the Wayne Newton show—again at the Condessa Del Mar in Alsip, Illinois—a suburb just south of Chicago. Huge crowds always came to the concerts there because huge acts were packing them in.

With Wayne Newton—Condessa Del Mar, Alsip, IL

And again I got to meet a superstar backstage. Wayne Newton was so sweet. To honor his Native American heritage, he handed out little embroidered black and white feathers that had a tacky back, so you could stick them anywhere! He gave my mom a feather. He liked my mom so much, he even gave her one before me. It was all so exciting! So big-time! My scrapbooks are filled with pictures of my family and me posing with superstars.

Check out the embroidered feathers on Wayne and Mom!

The station promoted many local festivities. Each Spring WIND held its annual Kite Fly in Grant Park on Chicago's lakefront. The jocks each had to make their own kites and compete in a DJ kite contest. I designed a "Top Rock Girly Jock" kite. It had two pink balloons filled with helium for boobs (which I thought would make it fly better). (*Hmmmm*—helium might be just the boost we girls could use—forget the plain ol' air bras or water bras. Now, don't go inventing a helium bra or I'll want a royalty—you read it here first!)

TOP ROCK GIRLY JOCK

Left—
My First Place
Trophy Winning
"Top Rock Girly Jock"
Kite

Below—
My Bobby Vinton
"Polish Prince"
Kite

The next year, I rehabbed it. (I wasn't gonna go through building a kite all over again. This radio job was getting out of hand.) So I removed the balloons from the "Top Rock Girly Jock" kite, put a "Polish Power" tee-shirt on it, took off the skirt, painted the pink legs blue, added the cut-out from the record album of Bobby Vinton's face (left over from the last station event) and called it the "Polish Prince" kite. ("Waste not, want not.")

Since I had won a trophy in the kite-fly last year, chances were pretty good I wasn't going to get it again. This kite was a quicky; but without the two balloons, and a T-shirt on it, it really didn't fly all that well.

Left to right—Bill (my fan club president), Pete, Mom,
me with the Bobby Vinton kite, and Dad
Grant Park—1975

TOP ROCK GIRLY JOCK

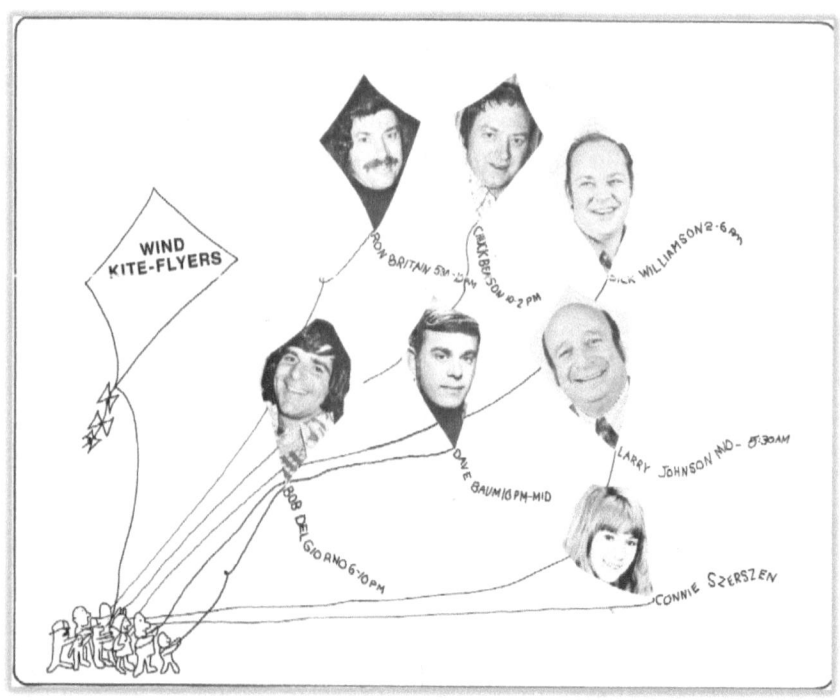

The WIND kite-fly in Grant Park had been an annual event almost from the beginning; but one year, before the 8th Annual Kite-Fly, we were told that kite flying in Chicago was against the law. We could be fined up to $50 for flying a kite. We were criminals. What could we do—but *protest!* And Chicagoans know how to protest.

48th Ward Alderman, Christopher Cohen, discovered the old law and helped set about changing it. (Especially because he had just bought 1,000 kites with his name on them for political reasons—when his constituents give him a hard time, he says he can "hand them a kite and tell them they know what they can do with it.")

We ordered jailbird outfits (just in case) and set out to protest where everyone could help in the demonstration—at that time, it was the Civic Center Plaza. It made all the papers.

KITE-FLYING ILLEGAL! SAY IT ISN'T SO

46th Ward Alderman Christopher Cohen blew the dust off an old city ordinance and discovered it was against the law to fly a kite in Chicago.

But the law could be changed! So the alderman and kite enthusiasts from WIND Radio's audience gathered at the Civic Center Plaza on April 16 to protest the ordinance. Station personalities were intent that the 8th annual WIND Kite Fly would take off as scheduled.

The rally received much press coverage. The protestors were assured they could fly and not be arrested. Back to the drawing boards and string untanglings. The kites would fly!

TOP ROCK GIRLY JOCK

Chicago Daily News

Grounded fliers seek air rights

By Dave Canfield

Chicago Tribune
Monday, April 29, 1974

Ben Franklin's smiling

Crowds here 'go fly a kite'

By Anne Keegan

THEY LOOKED LIKE fishermen with lines up to the sky.

All across the meadow in Grant Park yesterday afternoon these anglers came, reeling in and letting out, pulling and tugging to keep their catch at bay.

There were schools of them in the blue overhead, darting like brilliant tropical fish, tails swishing as they changed their courses at whim.

The afternoon fishermen were kite enthusiasts and their catches were their kites. Baloon kites, box kites, Chinese kites, kites with shimmering aluminum tails. Kites with messages like "Jesus Saves." Kites with futuristic shapes.

STING RAY kites that hovered low over the crowd on a silent breeze. Little store-bought kites that darted and plunged at the end of their lines, tripping on the wind and crashing their delicate frames into the ground.

There were thousands there for the event. It was the 8th annual Kite Fly sponsored by radio station WIND in cooperation with the Chicago Park District. And just about everybody there came to fly—and watch—and swap kite stories.

There were children with their parents, teen-agers with their homemade inventions, and grownups who'd never given up the sport. Their crafts peppered the lakefront sky, riding 20-mile-an-hour wind gusts that lifted them high over Meigs Field. As the afternoon lengthened, the steering lines crossed and recrossed, turning the baseball diamonds into a giant labyrinth of string.

THE SMALLEST kite that flew was less than a half-inch long. The largest was 80 feet— a 60 pound dragon-like chain of triangular sections that snaked into the air long enough to be considered airborne and win first place in the largest kite category.

Other designs were less lucky. A 250-pound replica of a 1902 Wright Brothers glider crashed five times during trial flies and eliminated itself from the running. One of its University of Illinois Circle Campus student designers, commented, "Guess it's back to the drawing board for a while."

But the whimsy of nature chose to interrupt the day. Clouds grayed, the sky opened up, and within 15 minutes the meadow was empty. All that remained was the broken skeletons of homemade kites and miles of water soaked string.

Chicago today, Monday, April 29, 1974

Worse than the Spaghetti Bowl

If you think expressway traffic is tough, you should have seen the kite traffic in Grant Park. A kite-flying event sponsored by the Park District and radio station WIND yesterday attracted thousands. The majority, it seemed, were tangled in other people's string.

Rock and Roll All Night

Left—Me, Bob Del Giorno, and Stu Collins—Civic Center Plaza

TOP ROCK GIRLY JOCK

WIND also held a Lambs Farm fund-raiser each year ou in Libertyville, Illinois. Sometimes I'd have to do a report from one of the activities that were planned for family fun. Ponies were available for little kids to ride. The ponies were tied to a center post so they could only walk in a circle—nice and safe for the kids. I thought, how bad could this be. So I hopped a pony and started doing my on-air report. The little bugger just wiggled and wiggled—how could this be so scary! I felt like I'd flip over its side and maybe even crack my head open—how embarrassing would that be in front of all these little kids! It reminded me of the time I was little myself and my dad had led a pony while I was riding it. The pony stomped right onto his new shoe and Dad got so mad. That was the first time he'd worn those shoes and now one was ruined. Yeah, well, but his foot was OK.

One year at the Lambs Farm, the DJs had to come up with a box lunch that was based on a Chicago landmark. Mine was the "O'Hare Box Lunch." I went to the airport's airline kitchens and picked up airline food for my box lunch. It was easy because I didn't have to prepare it, and actually, in those days, airline food wasn't all that bad. My folks were also there for the day, as they came to most of the events. While I was on stage, auctioning off my box lunch for charity, my dad was proudly watching in the crowd. He turned to the guy next to him and said,

"That's my Connie—that's *my* daughter!"

The guy looked him up and down and said, "Yeah, mine too."

Mom and my brother and I just laughed when he told us no one believed him. We would have liked to have seen the look on his face.

My family always enjoyed going to the Lambs Farm. Besides it being for such a worthy cause—it was a nice day out together—although I can remember how the corners of my mouth hurt at the end of the day because I tried to smile and have fun with—*everyone*. It was real exhausting—but it was also really fun.

Above—Box Lunch Auction for Lambs Farm

Below—"Chat Champ" Dave Baum and me

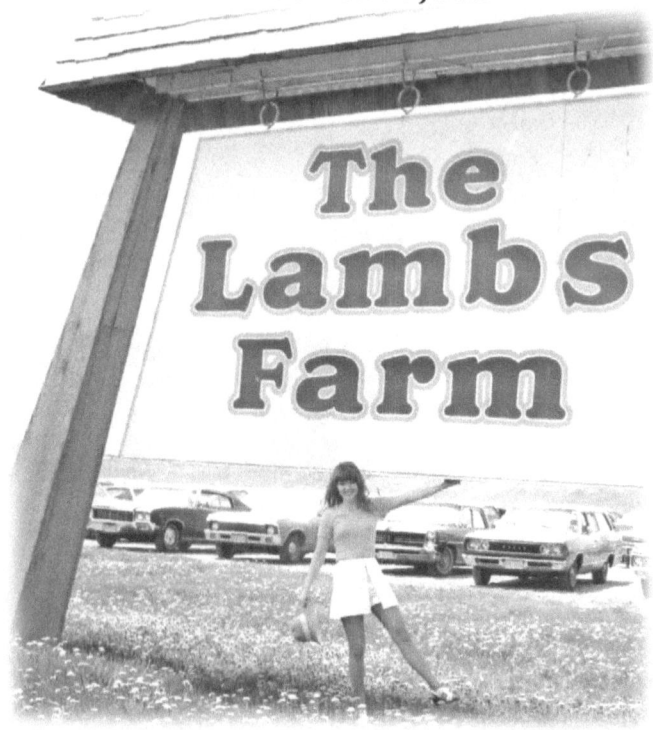

My Very First Lambs Farm Fun—1972
(When both me and my "lucky hat" were in better shape)

Rock and Roll All Night

Each year the WIND Zoo Day would also come around. We'd invite all our listeners to join us at the Lincoln Park Zoo. Each DJ would have an appearance scheduled to interact with the animals.

WELCOME TO WIND RADIO'S DAY AT LINCOLN PARK ZOO

SCHEDULE OF EVENTS		LOCATION ON MAP
Noon	CONNIE SZERSZEN MILKS THE COWS (FARM IN THE ZOO)	1
1:15	ED "CHICAGO" SCHWARTZ FEEDS THE SEA LIONS	2
1:45	STU COLLINS HOSTS A TEA PARTY FOR THE MONKEYS IN THE CHILDREN'S ZOO	3
2:00	CHUCK BENSON FEEDS THE BEARS, WOLVES AND FOXES	4
3:00	BOB DEL GIORNO FEEDS THE MONKEYS AND APES	5
4:00	DAVE BAUM FEEDS THE LIONS	6

WIND RADIO 560

My first zoo duty came in 1974—to milk the cows. They said it would be easy because a machine was attached to the cow to help somehow. (Don't ask me how—I only saw my Aunt Stephi in Poland do this once—without a machine—and the milk smelled awful—warm and stinky.) Still, this procedure was extremely embarrassing for me. There I was pulling on the cow's teats—don't ask why my face was all red, but I could feel it. A crowd watched my every move. And nothing was coming out. So I pulled harder, faster, slower, sideways—nothing! When I finally got a little dribble, everyone cheered. By now my face was purple. I was hot all over. Get me outta here, I screamed inside, as I smiled on the outside. (This was way worse than feeding the porpoises back at Marineland in the '50s!)

(Not the prettiest view—of either one of us)
(Wonder if this hurts her—or him—no, it must be a *her*—
a *him* wouldn't have all those dangling participles—
Okay, *stop it*—I know what you're thinking)

(Where's the *"Green for GO"* button?)

(I don't think I like milk anymore—and sure could use a beer)

The worst Zoo Day of all, though, was my event in Lincoln Park's Kiddie Zoo with the baby chimpanzee. Look now, isn't he cute! Just like a little baby—only more hairy and stinkier. (Notice how there's lots of *stinky* at the zoo?) So there I was, surrounded by radio fans who'd come out to greet me as I lovingly carried the chimp in my arms—showing him to the kids and chatting happily with the people—when, in a flash, it happened!

Once again, the hairy hand is quicker than the eye. That sneaky little chimp grabbed the front of my low-cut blouse and yanked it down in his wild savage way. (I'd had boyfriends like that, but never expected this to happen at the Kiddie Zoo.) Of course, I was wearing a bra (I hadn't burnt them all in the 60's), but I didn't want to show it to the whole crowd! I almost dropped the hairy creature and it would've served him right. "King Kong" would never behave like that. Holding him in one arm, I grabbed my blouse with my free hand and yanked it back up as fast as I could. Of course, I laughed and smiled at the crowd. Again, I could feel my face hot and red. Everyone was in hysterics—even the little kids—but especially their daddies. It was a *Janet Jackson* moment before its time. The zoo attendant hurried to take the chimp from me—yeah—he probably does this to all the girls—and you have to wonder where he learned it.

The right hat for the right occasion, I always say—

Just look at those folks laughing in the background!
(Like they've never seen a bra before)

Rock and Roll All Night

I never found out who did the assigning of these events, but they must have thought I was now ready for the big game. The following year, I was chosen to feed the lions. All I had to do was stand clear outside the cage and toss huge chunks of raw meat at the hungry lions inside. That didn't sound too bad to me, so I agreed.

We were in the Gorilla House, getting instructions from the zoo attendant and discussing our scheduled events, when I wandered off to see the gorillas. Suddenly, and unexpectedly, one of the gorillas was extremely happy to see me (if you know what I mean) just as one of the DJs came looking for me. There I stood—and there was the gorilla in all its excited glory. The jocks wouldn't let me live that one down. They laughed at how easily I could *turn on* a gorilla. (Guess I brought out the *animal* in him.)

I couldn't wait for that Zoo Day to see if any of the lions would reach out between the bars to try and eat me alive as I was trying to feed them. When the day came, I stood as far back as possible and just threw that meat as hard and far as I could. *Grrrrrrrrr!*

WIND Zoo Day—Lincoln Park Zoo—1976

TOP ROCK GIRLY JOCK

The station was hot and we were a part of everything that was new and exciting in Chicagoland. On May 29, 1976, WIND hosted *Opening Day* at Great America in Gurnee, Illinois.

Rock and Roll All Night

One of my old boyfriends showed up to say hello. He had been a medical student back in the days when I was a secretary at the medical center. We only dated a short time; someone told me that he dropped me for a nurse, whom he later married. He sort of mentioned she was there too, but I never got a real close look at who beat me out of a boyfriend. Hey, but she was a nurse and now he was a doctor. Good match.

I really couldn't reminisce with him too much because I had station reports to do every few minutes and had to concentrate on my job. Amusement rides needed reporting! Hah! I boldly went on Willard's Whizzer, so I could give a roller coaster report. Since I'm deathly afraid of roller coasters, it was a challenge. But Chuck Benson tested it out and assured me this one was pretty tame. I actually liked it, although I think Great America has since removed it. Too bad. Kinda reminded me of the Caterpillar at Riverview—only wilder—just wild enough for me.

Again, my family came along to enjoy the big day. Since my brother Jerry was now finished with his Air Force stint in Viet Nam and Brazil, he was able to get in on some of the fun too. Although Jerry had plenty of fun at work. He was a project engineer for the Japanese games at Bally/Midway. Midway decided to license some games from NAMCO. They were really interested in *Rally-X*, but NAMCO insisted they also take *Puc Man*. (The name was later changed to *Pac Man*, for obvious reasons.) So, Jerry was sent to Japan to consult. Once back home, he had to re-engineer it for U.S. production. Midway asked Jerry to work on *Rally-X* first. Jerry had that ready by five o'clock, and then started on *Pac Man*. He ended up staying at work until ten o'clock that night because it was such fun.

Jerry tried to tell them that *Pac Man* was going to be the hot game, but the head of marketing didn't agree. He told Jerry he had his "finger on the pulse of the public," as he tapped his wrist with his index finger. He then asked his secretary to come up with American names for the characters, because the original names were all in

Japanese. She asked Jerry to help. He said, "Let's name the blue one *"Inky"*—and another one to rhyme—*"Blinky."* And she named the pink one, *"Pinky."* (What, no *"Kinky?"*)

Later, for *Ms. Pac Man*, one was named *"Sue"* (after the wife of the head of marketing). And so that was how the characters got their names.

And sure enough, *Pac Man* was all the rage. Midway saw Jerry had been right, when the orders for *Pac Man* came flooding in, while *Rally-X* flopped. I was so proud of my brother who became such an important part of pop culture—and even naming *"Inky"* and *"Blinky"* I told him he had *his* "finger on the pulse of the public."

Today, many in the game industry try and take credit for *Pac Man*—some are even in Wikipedia. I tried to enter some of these true facts, but somebody kicked them out. So goes Wikipedia.

So, while I played on the radio, my brother played video games. (Don't the Szerszen kids ever have real jobs?)

Station events were fun—but sometimes also scary. The DJs were invited to take part in many outside events for charity. There was the celebrity stock car race at Santa Fe Speedway, where I was lifted bodily and shoved through the window of a stock car—because—the door was welded shut! Someone slapped a helmet on my head and said,

"Now, if there's a fire, you push this lever."

Fire?!?! These radio events were really getting dangerous! I overheard another media person say he would never do this again—and he was a big burly guy! I was the only girl. It was a *demolition derby*. I was petrified. I remember letting all the other cars get way ahead of me, so I'd be sure not to get bumped. I was so slow that they all did a full lap and ended up behind me—at which point I raised my hand out the window with thumbs up. For just a split second there, I looked like a winner! Hah! I smiled through the whole thing while secretly promising myself, "never again!"

(Yup—I'm the one in the—*helmet*)

And—The only girl!

And I kept my promise. When the Arlington Race Track event came up and WIND asked for volunteers to ride the race horses, I said, "No, thank you." I wasn't gonna get killed for station promotions.

The Celebrity Tennis Tournament appeared to be safer, so I agreed to that even though I knew nothing about playing tennis; but again, it was for charity. So when I turned and bent over to pick up a stray ball, another came flying hard at my tush! Gosh that hurt! Almost knocked me over, as I struggled to regain my balance. My mom was in the spectator area and was disappointed to hear some woman say,

"What is *she* doing there! She doesn't belong out there!"

My mom turned to her and proudly said, "She's doing it for charity."

That didn't stop my tennis. I did another charity tennis tournament later and Shelly Long was also one of the invited celebrities. This was—*Long* before her TV fame—(pun intended).

Rock and Roll All Night

She was quiet and didn't talk to me much—but very pretty. I heard she had once done some modeling.

The next time I heard about Shelly was when I auditioned for a local TV show. I was invited to read for the co-host position. They called me; I didn't call them. I guess they also called Shelly. At the time I was the "Top Rock Girly Jock" at WIND, she was doing TV commercials for Homemakers furniture (someone told me that her ex-husband produced them). Shelly beat me out of the job as co-host with Bob Smith on *Sorting It Out* on NBC 5.

Eventually, we all ended up at another charity event—this time for the American Cancer Society Bike-a-thon in Grant Park in 1975.

Left to right—Bob Smith, Shelly Long—(*Sorting It Out,* NBC 5)
Johnny and Jeannie Morris—Sports, CBS 2
Right to left—Tom Tully, Chicago political dignitary,
and me—in the hat—the only one in a hat

TOP ROCK GIRLY JOCK

Many charities called on the WIND DJs—We loved to help out.

Right—Mayor Ray Willas, Harwood Hts.—Lions Club Candy Day
(At least I'm not the only one in a hat this time!)

Left—Marty Robinson, WTTW 11, Jerry G. Bishop, and me

Crowning the '75 Easter Seal—NBC 5 Chicago
Right—Jerry G. Bishop, *Chicago's Camera*, me & Easter Seal rep

TOP ROCK GIRLY JOCK

Left—Steve Edwards, *AM Chicago*, ABC 7, me, Irv Kupcinet, *Chicago Sun-Times*—United Cerebral Palsy Telethon

Right—Penny Lane, WSDM, Bob Greene, *Chicago Sun-Times*, and me, drinking for charity (can't remember which one)

Rock and Roll All Night

Above, Left— Sandi Freeman, *AM Chicago*, ABC 7, Doug Dahlgren, WIND, and me

*Left—*WIND's Stu Collins, me, Chuck Benson
Kicking off 50-hour marathon football game
At Weber High School for the Forgotten Children's Fund

TOP ROCK GIRLY JOCK

I was in pretty good company in those days. Radio was such fun! The WIND format was *personality* radio; so I could *PLAY!*

During the summer, on Sunday afternoons, every twenty minutes or so, I would give *Sun-tan Alerts,* reminding listeners at the beach to turn over and fry the other side.

I started doing a *Road Rally* on some of my Friday night shows. With each song, I'd tell listeners in cars, to make a right turn, go through three stoplights, go left, etc. I would just make up wild things and, if they played along, it would be a surprise to see where they'd end up by the end of the show. Some called to say they were at a dead end, while others ended up in a cemetery. (As do most of us, eventually. My listeners always *were* ahead of their time.)

When a hot, sex-symbol celebrity was in town for a show, I'd often do the *Radio-gram*. In those days, disc jockeys had engineers, so it was easy to invite listeners to call in and record a message to their star. The engineer would roll the tape, and record all their sweet words. I never heard them myself, but I'm sure my engineer got an earful as they called in hour after hour. By the end of the show, I had several large reels of tape and I would then hand deliver them to the celebrity—the fun part for me.

I had done that for Tom Jones and now I had a chance to do it for Elvis. Since I wasn't going to be an emcee for Elvis' show, this gave me a good excuse to meet him.

He was in town and staying at the Arlington Hilton in Arlington Heights. How did I know? My cousin's wife, Linda, was working there at the time and kept me posted on the buzz about Elvis. She said she knew exactly which route Elvis took when he came back from his concert, to his suite at the hotel. Really? That's all I needed to hear.

"Linda, you've got to find a way for me to meet Elvis!" I pleaded with her. She agreed, as long as I'd get her some Neil Diamond concert tickets someday. She *loved* Neil—(ahem—I almost did too). She went to work on it with the security guys. Everything was arranged. I was to meet her after my show and I'd bring along the tapes of the *Radio-gram* to Elvis, and personally hand them to him, so he could see how much Chicago loved him. You'd think since I was a Chicago radio DJ, that I'd have an easier time meeting Elvis; but those were the days when his entourage was keeping him away from the media, who had treated him so badly lately.

So there we waited—at the Arlington Hilton—Linda, me, and my boyfriend at the time.

Left—Me holding the *Radio-gram,* and Linda—*Back Right*

We knew we had to surprise Elvis and his bodyguards, or this plan would never work. We quietly slipped down to the lower level of the hotel near the freight elevator, which Elvis used to get to his suite. There were huge rolling steel racks filled with dirty linen. We hid behind them, so if any of Elvis' security were scouting ahead, they would not be able to spot us. And again we waited. And waited.

Finally, the freight elevator started to rumble. We cautiously peeked out from behind our hiding place. The doors opened slowly, and out stepped a big group of guys. Lots of guys, but I didn't see Elvis. I hesitated. Linda gave me a shove in the back, yelling,

"Go, Connie! Now!"

I lunged forward from behind the dirty linen racks.

Suddenly the whole group that had just stepped off the elevator froze.

"Stop!" they shouted.

I still didn't see Elvis. I tried to explain.

"I'm from a Chicago radio station. I have a gift for Elvis from his fans!"

Suddenly they parted (like the Red Sea) and there stood Elvis in the middle. By his side was a woman in a red dress with a white fur coat. "Ginger," I thought. Darn!

Elvis was wearing a dark blue jacket and sunglasses. I walked up to him and handed him the tapes (more than any others ever had). I explained that these were love messages from all his Chicago fans.

And as I stood there before him, I just trembled. How could anyone be so handsome and have such charisma. He was quiet. I thought he almost looked sad. Looking at him closely, I got the feeling that he was truly a kind, sincere, and generous person—so generous with the gifts he had been blessed with—with his good fortune and with his time—his whole life. I thought back to when my friend Annette told me how he had said to her, "how hard it was sometimes, to be 'Elvis Presley.'" All I remember him saying, was "Thank you." I still couldn't believe I was standing there with him. Even with all the others around, it felt like such an intimate moment—as if there were just the two of us.

I then asked if I could have my picture taken with him and he agreed, and at this point, because I was so overwhelmed with being there next to Elvis, I didn't realize what was happening. I didn't try to hug him as I had done to so many celebrities before. I was frozen in time.

My boyfriend took my picture with Elvis. He stood directly behind me. I stood directly in front of Elvis. Since I'm fairly tall and because I wore my high platform heels, Elvis and I were about the same height. My cherished photo of this moment shows *my back* and a bunch of bodyguards. I completely blocked the view of Elvis! *How could my stupid boyfriend* do this to me!!!! If it weren't for Linda, I'd have no memory at all of that special night, but she was able to get me a photograph of Elvis posing with the Hawaiian musical group that was performing at the hotel. They had also ambushed him further on down the hall. They gave him a banana. And so, I at least have a picture of Elvis from that night in 1977—holding a banana.

"ELVIS! Marry me!"

TOP ROCK GIRLY JOCK

I often proposed to Elvis on my show—not that I thought he was listening—but just in case.

He would only live less than four more months. I remember leaving for the station and was just walking out the door, when my mom called out for me to come back. I was running late and couldn't imagine what was so important. Then she told me. She had just heard it on the radio—Elvis died. I couldn't believe it—she must not have heard right. But then I heard the news myself. It was like the end of everything. My mom had actually discovered Elvis before I did—she loved his "Heartbreak Hotel" and would always crank the radio when it came on. And now *she* "Was the One" who first discovered he'd died. From "Heartbreak Hotel" to the ultimate heartbreak.

I had to do a live radio show that same night. I didn't know how I could. Everyone at the station knew what an Elvis fan I was. My program director gave me permission to do a special show that night—with Elvis tributes—putting callers on the air who had stories to share about Elvis. I cried—listeners choked up, and cried in their calls. Our *rock and roll king* was gone.

The media had been criticizing Elvis at this stage of his life, but I found him to be beautiful. And I cherish the day I was lucky enough to meet him in person. Until this day I feel a special bond with Elvis. I grew up loving him. He epitomized the *prince* that young girls search for—love's fantasy—and the American dream. He was genuine—and throughout all this, very humble, polite, and generous. Anyone who would have had to live such a public life and deal with all the stress and intrusion that comes with extreme fame, couldn't have done any better. Fame often steals the treasures of real life. Entertainers become a commodity—just like the records they sell, or the movies they make. I will *always* love him tender—and will never let him go—from my heart.

The *Radio-gram* for Elvis was the last one I did. But I found other games to play. Adding another layer of fun to the music that folks already tuned in for, could only give them more entertainment.

Rock and Roll All Night

So I invented *Strip Radio*. With each song, I'd ask the listeners to take off something. Keeping it family radio, I stuck to things like corn plasters, hearing aids, dental bridges—so by the end of the show, nothing too risqué would have been eliminated, just in case they were not alone. A loyal listener, David, loved it and told the papers. On June 12, 1977, the *Chicago Sun-Times* made me the cover girl of their Sunday magazine, "Midwest."

TOP ROCK GIRLY JOCK

The headline read—

THE WOMAN WHO INVENTED 'STRIP RADIO'

I was mortified! It looked like something out of the *National Enquirer*! The two-and-a-half-page spread started with—

"Wow! There I was having a bowl of soup with Neil Diamond! So I asked him, 'Neil, how do you write songs?' 'Cause I like to write songs myself, you know? And he said, 'Well, if I told you how, you'd be able to do it too.' I thought that was kind of sarcastic. I mean, I just wanted to know if he wrote the music first or the words. Then he started to get fresh with me—gee, I don't know if I should be telling you this. I mean, I never even told my mother—It was OK when we were in the restaurant. But as soon as we got in my car—well, I didn't think he should start ripping my clothes off. I mean, he's a married man, isn't he? I was just an innocent little secretary. He probably thought I was a 100 per cent, Grade A groupie. Actually, I'm very straight - although if you listened to me on the radio, you might not think so. I'm a strict Catholic girl—wow! This is probably gonna blow my whole image!"

By quoting me as saying, "I never even told my mother," I now had some explaining to do at home, and tried to convince my family that the papers sometimes exaggerate and misquote—which was what had happened in that report. It *was* a little twisted. The die-hard Neil Diamond fans were livid. And they couldn't believe I walked away from such ecstasy. Who did I think I was?—they wanted to know. Well, who did he think he was? And who do they think *they* are! But I knew how they felt. I would've done the same for Elvis! Other than that, the story was great! I especially appreciated the comments from management.

> "People are always asking me, 'Is she for real or is she just doing a flaky act?'" says Phil Nolan, general manager of WIND. "All I can say is that if it's an act, she's fooled me too. She's the same when you play softball with her—when you have lunch with her—She just says exactly what's on her mind. In a plastic, homogenized radio world, you turn on Connie and she's real. She really enjoys what she does. And there's nothing more fun than listening to someone else having fun—"

"Breezy," is the word Phil Nolan finally comes up with in an attempt to describe Connie's unique style.
"In one way, she's naïve. In another way, she says some really outrageous things. She just isn't your everyday, average announcer."

Once again, I was grateful for having *me* explained to me. I will always treasure Phil Nolan's words, although I never knew what he thought until I read it in the article. Everyone at WIND was great to work with—we just didn't talk about stuff like this. (The last I heard, Phil and his family ran their own radio station in Minnesota—KAUS (AM 1480/FM 100)—and knowing his talent, I'm sure it's a success!)

Anyway, our promotions department loved the story. *ANY* publicity was *GOOD* publicity, they said. Any reaction from listeners only proved they were still listening. They cleaned up the story and made reprints for the sales department.

Soon after, *People* magazine wanted to do a story on me. I was thrilled until I found out the program secretary had told them my real age! What? I was stunned. No DJ tells their real age! I learned that back from the guys at WCFL. It would totally affect how the listeners heard you. Even Hollywood actors didn't give a real age with their headshots. They were told to keep their pictures current, and directors chose them as they saw them. The same held true for radio. But it was too late. *People* magazine refused to do the story unless I agreed to let them print my age. So I declined the story. Oh, vanity of vanities! But I was starting to think *NO* publicity was better than *BAD* publicity.

A nice bit of publicity came from CBS 2 Chicago. They wanted to do a feature story on me for their 5 PM newscast anchored by Bill Kurtis. I got all prepped for this one.

Reporter Edwina Moore came to the radio station with a camera crew. They taped me while I was broadcasting.

I wore my now torn and battered, straw "lucky hat" with holes all over it. Then they taped another segment in a side studio, where I explained how I felt about doing the show. I told how it was like being in a little den, playing music, and sometimes painting my fingernails between songs. When they aired the interview on the newscast, they ended with a shot of me saying,

"I'm a really good disc jockey, because God made me, and God *don't* make *no* junk!" (Not sure where I heard that—and don't two negatives make a positive?—*Hmmmm*—)

Anyway, I was having the time of my life!

Since I am of 100% Polish descent, I was invited to many Polish American festivities. The Polish Constitution Day Parade in Chicago is always very popular; they say there are more Poles in Chicago than Warsaw. I was invited to help introduce the floats—and again, my name was entered into the U. S. Congressional Record. It also made the papers—the *Chicago Tribune,* and the *Dziennik Zwiazkowy*, the premier Polish newspaper in Chicago. I know the print is kinda small so you might not be able to read it—but I'm guessing since it's in Polish, you probably can't read it anyway. I could probably write all sorts of things in Polish here—Daj mi buzi—Ja cię kocham. (How're we doin' so far, my little gołąbki?)

But I can't tell you how many Chicago listeners of Polish descent were glad to hear that finally someone in the media was there to represent them—to show the city that it didn't take three of us to change a lightbulb. Maybe for a while, the Polish jokes would be squelched. Not only was a girl of Polish descent able to change a lightbulb—she was able to deliver an entire radio show. I felt honored to be a spokesperson for our heritage. I was invited to many local Polish TV shows—like the Chet Gulinski show—I was their *Polish Princess.*

(At least now my name was spelled right!)

TOP ROCK GIRLY JOCK

Commemoration Of Poland's May 3, 1791 Constitution

Saturday, May 3, 1975

Program At Reviewing Stand
State and Madison Streets — 12 Noon

WELCOME:
Mrs. Helen M. Szymanowicz,
Vice President, Polish National Alliance
General Chairman, Poland's Constitution Day

NATIONAL ANTHEMS:
Mr. Stefan Wicik,
accompanied by 81st United States Army Band

PARADE NARRATORS:
Connie Szerszen, WIND Radio
Bob Lewandowski, WCIU-TV, WSBC Radio

Program At Civic Center Plaza
1:30 P. M.

WELCOME:
Mr. Thomas Paczynski,
Commissioner District 12, Polish National Alliance

INVOCATION:
Most Reverend Alfred L. Abramowicz, DD
Auxiliary Bishop, Vicar General

MASTER OF CEREMONIES:
Hon. Aloysius A. Mazewski,
President Polish National Alliance;
President Polish American Congress

REMARKS:
Honorable Neil F. Hartigan,
Lieutenant Governor, State of Illinois

REMARKS:
Honorable Richard J. Daley,
Mayor, City of Chicago

PRINCIPAL ADDRESS:
Honorable Birch Bayh,
U.S. Senator, State of Indiana

INTRODUCTION OF GUESTS:
Mrs. Sophie Buczkowski,
Commissioner, District 13, Polish National Alliance

BENEDICTION:
The Rt. Rev. Francis C. Rowinski,
Bishop, Western Diocese,
Polish National Catholic Church

CONCLUSION:

Sunday, May 4, 1975

ASSEMBLY FOR SOLEMN MASS:
10:00 a. m. —
Polish National Alliance, 1520 West Division St.

MARCH TO CHURCH:
10:15 a. m. —
to Holy Trinity Church, 1118 Noble Street,
led by Council 60, PNA, Drum and Bugle Corps

SOLEMN MASS:
10:30 a. m. —
Reverend Casimir J. Czaplicki, C.S.C.
Pastor, Celebrant and Homilist

---

2 Section 3 Chicago Tribune, Friday, May 2, 1975

Tower Ticker
By Aaron Gold

CBS NETWORK EXECS are blowing their collective tops because they found out that Michael Evans refuses to return to The Jeffersons. He asked the producers for more money and was turned down. . . . Arts and Leisure's Carolyn and Jack Solomon hope to reopen London House in early June with jazz acts but the lunch and dinner food operations will be run by someone else.

SEVERAL OUT OF TOWN investors are interested in buying Dick Jansen's Ivanhoe Theater and Restaurant complex [105,000 square feet] that goes on the auction block May 27 with a minimum bid of $1.7 million. [One contractor said it

Buffone   Christie   Brando

LEE STERN'S CHICAGO STING soccer team kicks off its first home game Friday at Soldier Field against the Denver Dynamos. And there'll be a 10-minute half-time game with members of the media, myself included, opposing a team that includes Bobby Douglass, Doug Buffone, Miro Roder of the Chicago Bears. . . . Other Friday Happenings: Jo Mapes at Orphans; Jim Toriakson's new paintings at the Dobrick Gallery; and Carolyn and Cathy Ford at the Northside Auditorium Bar. . . . Pixie Ackerman is the new manager of the Bonwit Teller men's department. . . . Studs Terkel begins a new evening show Monday on WFMT. . . . And Eddie Hubbard will emcee Monday's tribute [and every Monday in May] to the 1930 big band era at Ratso's with the Eddie Barrett Band, Alma Baller, and David Bacarr.

THE VILLAGE OF OAK PARK canceled plans to unveil two large fountains in its new mall because they weren't completed on time. And none of the recent fire damage to the shops in the mall area has been repaired, and won't be, until an arson investigation is completed. . . . WIND's Connie Szerzsen will intro the floats in Saturday's Polish Constitution Day Parade down State Street [noon].

TICKER BITS: Noriko will unveil her fall fashions June 30 at Tango. . . . WLS' Bob Sirott is the newly appointed executive vice president of Chicago's Muscular Dystrophy Association. . . . P.R. woman Barbara Lee Cohen is not, repeat not, the same Barbara Lee Cohen who recently was married at the Four Torches. . . . Mercury Records is talking contracts with the Gill Theater's Denise LeBrun. . . . Cafe Angelo's Friday gourmet feast is a tribute to New Orleans and features some of the recipes from the town's famous Brennans Restaurant. . . . Happy Birthday to Ch. 5 news boss Ed Planner, Bing Crosby and Englebert Humperdinck. . . . And George Deacon knows of a company that advertises it can reduce your bills. "And they can, too," he laughs, "they put them all on microfilm."

Rock and Roll All Night

Polish American
Police Association

Left—
At the
Baby Doll
Polka Club
1976

Left—Illinois State Representative, Ted Lechowicz,
Chicago Mayor Michael Bilandic, and me—1977

TOP ROCK GIRLY JOCK

EXECUTIVE COMMITTEE

Top Row: Paul A. Kolpak, Ronald L. Sieczkowski, Frank Gondela, Joseph Kotlarz, Ted R. Sajewski, Michael Jasinski, Henry P. Wozniol, Leonard F. Krajkiewicz, Roman W. Lobodzinski, Thomas Korzeniowki.

Center Row: Arthur T. Siemion, Richard Owens, Jeanette Sajewski Turly, Pauline G. Dembici, Chester Marcyn, Wanda Kalin, Donald F. Koualic, Sophia Skrzypek, William Reczek, Raymond Kwasniewski, Walter Mieczynski.

Bottom Row: Reneta P. Siemion, Estelle Wawrzynaik, Marilyn Mazewski, Connie Szerszen, Sonja Bell, Karen Mackay, Lori Sobin, Loretta Wardzala, Helen Wozniel, Tillie Kwasniewski, Harriet Reczek.

Cutting the ribbon—

Celebrating the expansion of
Przybyło's—
The White Eagle—
The premier Polish restaurant
in Chicagoland (Niles, IL)

(Their mushroom-barley soup
is to die for!)

NBC 5 Chicago—*Tilmon's Tempo*, "Christmas Show"

All sorts of invitations were always coming in—to speak to various groups, appear here and there, judge this and that. I judged a Groucho Marx look-alike contest, a "Mr. America" preliminary contest (it was way more fun watching guys parade on stage in bikinis instead of girls).

Judging a Miss Indiana pageant was interesting, though. The winner would go on to participate in the Miss America pageant. This round was a fairly important pageant, so I took real care to vote accurately. What amazed me was that the girl I thought should have won, did not. Overall, I thought she was the best choice, but when you started adding up points given to the different girls, you really had no way of knowing who would come out ahead, unless you purposely *threw* the point count to favor your choice. By being fair to all the girls, and giving them each the points they deserved in a certain category, could upset the total points that your favorite would need to win. But I aimed to be a fair judge to all.

Rock and Roll All Night

Once I was invited to the Blossomtime Festival in St. Joseph, Michigan, to help judge the best float in their parade. Guests of honor were Jim Palmer of the Chicago Fire football team and actress Adrienne Barbeau. (I secretly called her Adrienne Bar*boobs*—she had every man's attention.)

There were two other judges besides myself. When I saw the adorable *Snoopy* float, I immediately cast my vote for them! The float was exquisite. Every detail was in place, so beautifully done and not just slapped together. The other two judges agreed with me. But the dignitaries who had invited me to be a judge asked if I would like to reconsider. Did I really want to vote for this one—or for the other float—the one that contributed tons of money to the event each year the one with the bumblebees, etc., etc.

I said, "No, I really like the *Snoopy* float—it's so well done!"

But, they countered, the other company has so many more people in their float—and they win every year! Really! Why's that?

"Are we judging on volume?" I asked. "I thought it was creative appeal. Well, yes, if it's based on volume, then the other float should definitely win—they do have the most people in it. But if it's based on how well a theme is portrayed and executed—then, in my opinion (as judge), the *Snoopy* float wins, hands down!"

Blossomtime Festival—1974

St. Joseph, Michigan

The other two judges agreed with me. The *Snoopy* float got the trophy that year. It was a real upset. I was never invited to judge their Blossomtime Festival again.

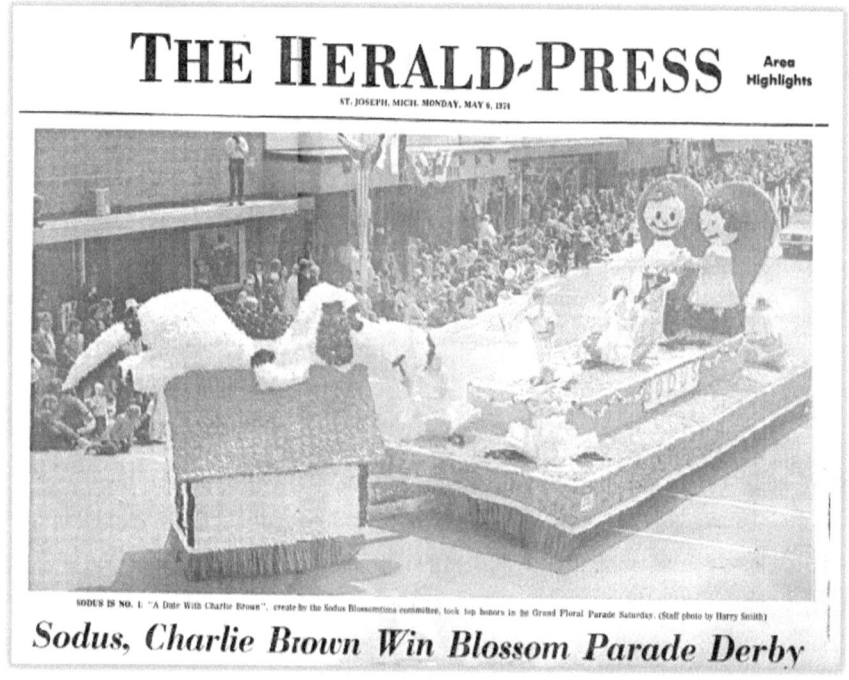

Front Page News—(I still love it—*soooo* cute!)

We got many perks along with our DJ jobs, but sometimes a *perk* ended up being a real *SNAFU*. WIND had just acquired a new client—a prominent hair salon. I was offered a free treatment. Because I was lightening my hair, they thought they could improve on my *blond*. (Didn't I go through this once before in New York with *Mademoiselle* magazine?) The hairstylist explained how they were going to give me *blond on blond*. There would be wonderful highlights in a lighter shade, which would make my hair color so much more naturally blond and attractive. I was all for it. The stylist applied the formula to my hair and said she'd be back after the time needed for processing.

After an hour or longer, I started to wonder if she was ever coming back. I knew this was a free-bee and they probably had paying clients to attend to, so I didn't want to impose. But, finally, my head was feeling warmer and warmer, so, with a mush of chemical junk on my head, I went to look for her. Everyone was stunned. They all had completely forgotten about me!

Quickly, they rushed to shampoo the formula from my hair. But I was already fried. I almost cried as I looked at my hair, which now resembled something like my old doll's mohair wig. And it wasn't even blond anymore! It was ugly, mousy brown hair. And it looked like it was ready to fall out. I ran out of there as fast as I could. They wanted to correct it. I cried, "Don't touch me—leave me alone!" and ran to my car and drove off.

In desperation, I started looking for another beauty salon. Not knowing the neighborhood, I drove around and around until I finally saw one that looked up-scale, and ran inside, almost in tears. "Please, help me," I pleaded!

They wanted to know who did this to me. So there went that other hair salon's *promotion*, as I told these hairstylists my story. I begged them to fix it because I had to be at work in just a couple hours, and I couldn't face anyone with this hair!

They were all shocked. They said the only thing they could do now was to give me heavy-duty vitamin treatments. My mousy hair color would have to stay as it was, because any attempt at changing my color might make it all fall out. When they were finished, I drove straight home and quickly slapped on a wig and headed downtown for my show. That *prominent* hair salon is doing very well today, with branches all over Chicagoland. Not for me, thank you. I now cut and color my hair myself. (Oh? Connie's not a real blonde?)

TOP ROCK GIRLY JOCK

But many sweet fans made any of my struggles worth it. Through the years, the listening audience at WIND continued to build.

There was Francis, who made up bumper stickers for my show which he freely handed out everywhere. He'd go to flea markets and buy me unusual novelties. I remember a couple of ruby rings, and a book on his fave, Marilyn Monroe, and of course, lots of Elvis stuff. He made a wooden calendar, and a wooden carving of Elvis for me. He was a devoted listener, who was also a great family man, and was just happy to hear someone with a Polish name on the radio. He put this sign on his car's back windshield—

A local florist, The Greenhouse, once sent me three dozen and three (?) roses. I got all sorts of wonderful gifts from listeners—perfume, knick-knacks, jewelry, etc. One couple even created a little crown of velvet, and inscribed it with the words *"Polish Princess."*

A girl named Pat, a devoted Donny Osmond fan, wrote regularly, asking for more Donny songs. I later helped her jump-start a career in radio when I heard of an opening, and from there she went on to have her own show and is a talented writer today.

Some of my listeners started a fan club. They wrote newsletters, and, Bill, who had started a fan club for me, also created a comic strip to send to members. He depicted some of the stuff he and others had heard me say on the show—with some added variations—Hah!

Some made up stamps printed with my picture that they had snapped at a station event.

TOP ROCK GIRLY JOCK

The listeners at WIND were always full of surprises. I got tons of mail. I couldn't even answer it all. Some of it was hilarious.

One young guy wrote to *thank me* for my on-air story about Cedar Lake. It was a real hot day and I had gone to the lake before my show. I talked on the air about how I knelt in the water to cool off (because I can't swim) when something socked me hard from behind! I turned to see this huge fish! I think it was aiming for the beauty mark on my back—probably thinking it was food. So my punch line to the story was,

"Now, I know what they mean when they say *the fish are really biting today.*"

Well, this listener was so upset, because he and his girlfriend happened to be driving up to his family's cabin in Cedar Lake for the week-end, when they heard me say this on the radio. His girlfriend was afraid of fish at the beach and he had spent weeks convincing her that there weren't any there. I blew his whole story—and probably his chance at week-end bliss. Ah, it's all in the timing.

But some mail was as weird as it had been at WSDM. I got a letter from a young girl who said she gave up her boyfriend after listening to me. She tried to entice me, telling me how pretty she was and that she had green eyes. I answered her on-air by playing "Green-Eyed Lady," saying, "*Les-Be-On*-ly friends."

One loyal listener would regularly send me rent money he collected from his apartment building. Sometimes it would be hundreds of dollars. There was no return address, so we couldn't send it back; and, besides, he wrote that if his wife found out he was doing this, she'd kill him. So I turned it over to the programming department who donated it to charity.

One day, I received a letter with a colored pencil drawing of a house on it. A note on it pointed to *my bedroom*. The letter said that he knew where I lived, and that soon I would find myself at the bottom of the Chicago River, because I failed to meet him one night after my show. He had been writing, asking me to meet him at 10:30 at night behind the Museum of Science and Industry. Yeah, right.

I showed the letter to my program director, and he immediately called the police. A private detective was assigned to the case, and he came down to the station to take a report. His after-shave about knocked me over. He smelled better than I did—and—said he was real interested in my case. Real interested, huh? Here we go again, I thought. I never did find out all the details. However, this strange fan who had threatened me (using the name, *"Doctor-So-and-So"*) was contacted by the police, and told to leave me alone. He was not considered dangerous, I guess, but had previously been treated for his psychotic behavior.

I also got mail from prisoners. Incarcerated men loved me—perhaps because I was their only available fantasy girl. Talk about a captive audience. I never responded much to their letters; at least not as much as actress Tuesday Weld who, I'd heard, married an incarcerated fan. But some could write very romantic letters.

There were many complimentary letters, as well, from prominent people in town, mayors of suburbs, and even *Chicago Sun-Times* columnist (and now famed movie critic) Roger Ebert (which really impressed me.) The late Gene Siskel also said he loved our station, when I joined him at a benefit at WTTW, a PBS station in Chicago. The whole city was into our music and format. We were *hot*.

One prominent businessman, and leader in the Polish community in Chicago, called and encouraged me to move on to TV, as a reporter. He said he'd talked to the station, NBC 5 Chicago, and they were very interested.

I didn't have to think long. I just explained that at this point in my career I really loved where I was, and what I was doing, and hadn't thought much about TV. (Talk about "looking a gift horse in the mouth.") Years later, when I needed work and auditioned for a staff announcer position at that same station, I was rejected. They said I had too much *personality* in my voice. Go figure.

As the years went by, I got to know some listeners pretty well since they regularly showed up at station events, and sometimes even waited for me outside after my shows. I introduced some fans to each other and they got married. (I was actually pretty good at this matchmaker stuff.) Meanwhile I was still single!

But then, I think I may be a late bloomer. I know for a fact that I'm usually just plain *late*. Once I was asked to be godmother for my cousin's new baby. On the day of the Christening I suddenly realized I didn't have the right hat to match my outfit. (Hats are important, y'know.) So I quickly bopped over to the closest store to pick one up, and headed for the south side of Chicago. (Oh, no, here we go again!) Yes, that's right. I got lost. I got to the church just as everyone was coming out. They had baptized little Maggie by proxy.

Another embarrassing *late* moment was when I was the Maid of Honor at another cousin's wedding. It was a small wedding, and as I was driving along, I suddenly remembered I'd forgotten the bride's white orchid corsage. ("I Forgot to Remember to Forget"—reminds me of an Elvis song—only I forgot to remember to remember—Huh?) If I didn't bring it, she'd have no flowers on her wedding day. So I U-turned back home, grabbed the corsage from the fridge and rushed to the church. When I walked in, the priest said to the congregation,

"Is that her? Can we get started now?"

But the most frantic *late* moment was when I drove in for the show while a huge snowstorm suddenly sprang up, slowing traffic. As I parked the car, I heard the engineer play Sonny & Cher—one of their two-minute songs. I hopped the elevator to the third floor, plopped into the chair and slapped on headphones just as the song ended. Later I chewed him out for not picking another song—"American Pie" would've given me six more minutes!

I made many sacrifices for the show! Having had a bad bout of teenage acne, I was seeing a dermatologist in New York.

Rock and Roll All Night

Mom and I would get up at dawn and fly there for a 10 AM appointment. Later we'd treat ourselves and shop at Bloomingdale's, (where we once bumped into Yoko Ono in the bargain basement—hey, Yoko, *"designer"* is *up*stairs). Then a quick stop for lunch at Yellowfingers across the street, after which we'd catch a cab to the airport. Back home, I'd hop in the car and drive downtown to do my show. Yes, I was *tired*. (Just like so many of those celebrities I met in the past—Hah!)

I did get a lot of free time with the show, though—because when Bulls basketball season started, the games were played during my time slot. So I'd do the station breaks and otherwise occupy myself until it was time for me to go back on the air. Sometimes I went down to the restaurant/bar on the main level of the building. I couldn't really get into it, though, because if the Bulls finished early, I'd have to pick up again with music—if they went into overtime, I might not go back on the air—but I never knew which would happen.

But I felt a part of their team in a way—Hah!—can't remember who sent me this photo—**but check out the left side, first row**. Folks at WIND were always so full of fun.

1974-75 CHICAGO BULLS

SEATED FROM LEFT: Assistant Coach Ed Badger, Rowland Garrett, Jerry Sloan, Bob Wilson, Norm Van Lier, Leon Benbow, Matt Guokas, Coach Dick Motta.
STANDING FROM LEFT: Trainer Dr. Bob Biel, Bob Love, Cliff Pondexter, Micky Johnson, Nate Thurmond, Tom Boerwinkle, John Block, Chet Walker, Business Manager John Kerr.

TOP ROCK GIRLY JOCK

And we had a great team of news and weather folks!

WIND NEWS TEAM

Back from left - Ed Dorsey, Dick Stone, Ian Hunter
Dave Newman, Jim Boutet, Ralph Howard
Front from left – Jim Gannon, Eleanor Richards, Jim Morris
John Kerans, Jack Fleming, Dick Elliott

(Remember "Finckle's Sprinkles?")

Rock and Roll All Night

Come to think of it, I got a lot of free time in this job—at least four weeks of vacation to start. So I made the most of it.

One year my friend Sharon and I went to Aspen. Since neither of us really ski that well, a lot of our time was spent shopping, eating and checking out bars at night. One night we were at the Jerome Hotel, sipping cocktails at the bar, wrapped up in our girl-talk, when someone shouted over from a table behind us. We turned to see five or six guys all drinking and laughing and calling us over. Nothing real unusual about that, except that one of these guys was *John Denver!*

"Sharon," I said, "Do you know who that blond guy is? That's John Denver!"

Sharon wasn't sure. She had never met John in person, but I had. When my reporter friend, Sharon Fox, wrote for the local paper, I'd often tag along. There was a club called The Quiet Knight, that brought in new acts fairly regularly. We saw Carly Simon perform there, and many entertainers that are now famous but were then in the early stages of their careers. And that was where, one night, we saw John Denver perform. During intermission, we were invited to his dressing room with some of his friends. He excused himself from the conversation to make a long distance call to his Annie. I remember how his face lit up when he talked with her, and how gentle he sounded with her on the phone. Any woman could see this guy was in love. I can't remember if they were married then or shortly after. So, *excuuuuuse me*, but I *do know* what John Denver looks like.

I always thought he was adorable! I loved his music, his passion for what he did, and his *normality*. It was sad to hear as the years went by, how he lost Annie, and probably a lot of the hopes and dreams that were entwined in that love-of-his-life-time. And when his plane went down in the Pacific, I heard it on the news driving home late one night. Just too sad. He was too young. I didn't want to believe it. I thought back to that night at the

Jerome Hotel in Aspen. We never did go over to their table. We were too shy. But I sure wanted to.

Now that I think back on it, years ago we hadn't been too shy to get on the band's bus to hunt down Joe Cocker. We knew just where he'd be after the show at the Aragon (we'd seen the bus parked outside). By the time we got to Joe's seat near the back of the bus—he was sitting there alone, opening a little bottle of something or other—a tiny bottle—about an inch or two. Cologne? Anyway, he was kind enough to give us an autograph, and we got outta there before the band showed up. The old Aragon Ballroom had been a real hotspot for early rock & roll—saw the Byrds there—and many other great acts.

Another singer I felt lucky to see perform, was Janis Joplin. It was my one and only time at Ravinia at that point. Sure enough, just as the press reported, Janis sang, slugging her Southern Comfort. She wasn't what the tabloids would call *beautiful*, but there was a beauty in her love of music. Sometimes I think she may have pursued her career to combat the rejection she got in high school from the other kids. I remember reading how disappointed she was that her hometown never really appreciated her, even after all her success. On stage, with her own style of carefree clothes—there were feathers—in purples, lavenders, and pinks—and a see-through whimsy of a blouse, and disheveled hair, tossed wildly as she sang and drank. Janice was gutsy enough to live her passion, whether or not anyone else approved. I admired that. "Freedom's just another word for nothing left to lose—"

In the mid '70s, WIND was at the top of its game. The station ran ads in the Chicago papers promoting the jocks, their events, contests and give-aways.

Look closely at the next picture—check out who's driving the give-away car—none other than legendary Clark Weber! (Clark, by the way, has a great book out, titled, *Clark Weber's Rock and Roll Radio,* with a CD of some of his shows and some *great* photos of fun radio days—like the day he hosted the Bra Burning at WCFL!)

TOP ROCK GIRLY JOCK

Below—
"Clark Weber Bra Burning" back at WCFL—
Yup, that's me on the far right
and my friend Annette holding the sign!

(That chimp at the zoo would've had a field day with these bras!)

Rock and Roll All Night

TOP ROCK GIRLY JOCK

Left—
WIND often ran full-page ads like this in the *Chicago Sun-Times* and later reprinted them for the sales department.

Right—
They posed me in front of an Art Institute lion (an omen?)

Rock and Roll All Night

TOP ROCK GIRLY JOCK

Rock and Roll All Night

TOP ROCK GIRLY JOCK

Rock and Roll All Night

The WIND Studios—625 North Michigan Avenue, Chicago
Broadcasting in my "lucky hat"

NINE

I'm Not in Love

Overall, things at the station were going fine; my show's ratings were up. I was pulling a "10" on week-ends and close to that during the week. We were hot. But my personal life was as screwed up as usual.

At the time all this great career stuff was happening, I was sort of happily dating someone, or so I thought. A friend and I were out bar-hopping one night and met twins. By the end of the evening we had switched twins with each other and ended up dating the one the other had met. Like, they both looked so much alike, it made no difference to us. It's times like these, tho, that you learn that looks aren't as important as character.

He seemed like a nice guy and we were having fun until he started getting nit-picky. Being a non-practicing Lutheran, he didn't care for the fact that I was a Catholic. He introduced me to his sister, hoping she might convert me to the "born again" Christianity that she found so appealing. She tried—and I complimented her on being so sincere and true to her religion—but I tried to explain that I felt the same way about mine. It was soon after that that he started calling me "mackerel snapper." (Catholics are often still derided for their former no-fish-on-

Friday practice.) He warned that if we ever married, the kids would *NOT* be raised Catholic. I suggested we should have two children. I'd raise one Catholic and he could raise the other his way, as a non-practicing Lutheran. He didn't find that too amusing.

One evening we were watching the news on TV, when he started admiring the anchorwoman. He asked if I knew her.

I said, "No, but maybe I can find a way to introduce you to her."

It was becoming clear to me that dating a radio jock had run its course and he was now working his way up to TV news. I wondered where it might end—would Hollywood be next? I got the feeling that he really didn't care for me, but was enamored with the glory of my job.

"It's the Same Old Song." When you met guys in bars, they always asked what you *did*. The real good answers were *nurse*, *flight attendant*, or *nothing* (because Daddy's so rich). When I was a secretary, I always wished I could answer something more glamorous. But when I finally had a glamour job, I told all the guys I met that I was a secretary. If I told them what I did, they'd be all over me like a tie-dyed t-shirt and jeans. If they still liked me as a secretary, then I felt there might be some genuine attraction going on, beyond what I *did*. Of course, we women are just as bad. All my friends were so impressed when I met a medical student who was planning a career as a heart surgeon. My folks were a little disappointed when I ended that one.

But at that time, I wasn't ready for a serious relationship. I had places to go and people to see and get to know! I wanted to travel and to experience the world—like—shopping in Paris!

I had been to Paris for only four days on the way back from a two week vacation in Poland with my mom. I was wiped out from trying to communicate in Polish "Day After Day." In Paris I could finally speak English again, and, instead, get wiped out from trying to communicate in French. Hah!

I'm Not in Love

From right—Me, Mom, and our relatives in Poland

Although Poland was rough traveling, I did learned to drive one of those horse-drawn carts, shouting out orders in Polish for the horse to go left, right, or stop. *Stop* was a funny sound you made with your tongue rattling—kinda like *"DRRRRRRR."*

Now that I'm older and wiser (who said that?) I cherish the days we spent visiting Poland. We went to Kraków—and Wawel, where a castle displayed a golden box, said to hold the heart of a former king—and Mielec, where flower stands filled the plaza—and where everything was so inexpensive, I had trouble spending $10.00.

Some of the finest exports of Poland are amber jewelry, hand-carved wooden décor, goose down for comforters, and Polish mushrooms (which at times could cost $100 an ounce here in America).

But Paris held many magical movie-star images for me! The song, "The Night They Invented Champagne," floated in my head as I thought back to Louis Jordan in *Gigi*. And, after those weeks in

Poland, behind the reins of a horse-drawn buggy, sleeping on hay mattresses with chickens running near our beds on clay floors, and no electricity in some parts of the Polish villages, Paris was pure *glamour*.

Mom and I on tour in Paris—in the center—in *black and white*

Some of my favorite memories of Paris were of a night at the Moulin Rouge (it was exquisite!)—and eating crepe suzettes in Montmarte where the artists hung out. One of my not so favorite memories was being stopped by security as I aimed my flash camera at the "Mona Lisa." Guards stopped me in a flash (pun intended)—ah, flashing Mona was not allowed. But, hey, she was already smiling; I could almost hear her saying—*Cheeeeeeese!* I get in *more trouble* with a flash camera.

And, of course, shopping in Paris was the best! My French wasn't that great, but I had practiced saying "How much?"—"Too much!" which served me pretty well. Until this day, I have a wonderful Daniel Hector designer suit that I bought at Galeries Lafayette—woolen, camel-colored, with real leather trim on the

I'm Not in Love

pockets and shiny silver buttons. Although I can no longer squeeze into it, it's waiting for me when I diet-down. (Such inspiration!)

So, since my wanderlust was still so unfulfilled, I wasn't really looking for any serious relationships. Anyway, someone once told me, "Guys are like buses—if you miss one, there's always another."

My next *amour* was waiting for me when I walked out of the radio station one night. Out in front, at the curb, right by the bus stop sign. (Maybe guys *are* like buses.) He was standing next to a Chicago Police car. He was a cop. As he approached me, I thought he was going to ticket my car (which was usually parked illegally in the alley alongside the building—closer and cheaper). But instead, he asked why I wasn't playing more Frank Sinatra. I explained our format to him and the fact that the songs played by the disc jockeys, in most cases, were not chosen by the disc jockeys. He was full of fun and mischief and it didn't take me long to figure out he was hitting on me. (Ah, that Connie catches on fast.) He did make me smile, but, gosh, gee, he just wasn't my type (whatever that is).

Next thing I knew, it was "Betcha By Golly Wow!" I was his #1, his *main squeeze*, or so he called me—but his old girlfriend was still in the picture. He told me his mom hated her and loved me. (Great, but I didn't plan on dating his mom.) I think he cared for both me *and* his old girlfriend (a terrible male affliction). But he was never getting married, he said. Well, yeah, 'cause then he'd have to choose only *one* of us. So I questioned what I was doing with this guy! But there were romantic nights in Olive Park where we stayed out 'til dawn. I was in love. I bought him little gifts (something I always do when enamored and so typical for my astrological sign, Cancer, or *Moonchild* as we're sometimes called). Some of us even jump up and down on couches—ala Tom Cruise—I see nothing wrong with that. When you're in love, you're in love. (But then, Tom Cruise and I share a July 3 birthday.)

One day I received a beautiful bouquet of flowers at the station. He and I had just had another fight. The attached note wasn't signed, but all the right, meaningful words were there. He was making up with me. I thought this was especially sweet since it really wasn't like him to send flowers. He was in no way romantic, unless he was talking about Frank Sinatra. (Ain't That a Kick in the Head!)

So I drove over to his place to accept his apology—to kiss and make-up. He came to the door in his robe and wouldn't let me in. He said he was busy. I immediately started having second thoughts about the flowers, but it was too late. Here I was, making a big fool of myself. I asked him anyway. Did he send them? He had no idea what I was talking about and abruptly shut the door, leaving me standing there. I started wondering if his old girlfriend might have replaced me as *main squeeze*. (Maybe it was her turn again.)

I thought back to that recent Friday night when he canceled our date at the last minute. He called while I was on the air—sometime between 6 and 10 PM. He said one of the guys didn't show up for work and he'd have to cover the late shift and couldn't keep our date.

Something in my gut (my guardian angel?—but what would my guardian angel be doing in my gut?) told me this wasn't true. A woman just *knows*, you know. I knew his old girlfriend lived where most swingin' singles lived—near Lincoln & Belmont. So that night I decided to take the long way home—through the Lincoln Park neighborhood—even though this meant a longer drive home. I was disappointed, in no hurry to get home anyway, and just wanted to somehow be a part of the action I felt I was missing.

After my show ended, I hopped into my car and headed onto Lake Shore Drive (the same "LSD" Aliotta, Haynes, & Jeremiah sang about)—*very* crowded on a Friday night. Now this is really *SPOOKY*.

I turned onto the exit ramp at Belmont Avenue and, what to my wondering eyes should appear, but *HIS CAR*—unmistakably *HIS*—with his special vanity plate! And there was a woman in the passenger seat! My heart sank. So I followed. *"Green for Go, Red for Stop."* Left turn, right turn, *stop light*. I pulled alongside on the right, and looked over to my left, past her, right at him. He looked at

I'm Not in Love

me. I smiled. She looked at me, then him, then me, then him again. ("Strangers in the night, exchanging glances—") The light turned green and I lost them as he careened out of there like something out of *Knightrider!* But I knew he had to be close by. So I cruised and eventually found his car parked near a hi-rise. (I didn't watch all that *Columbo* for nothing!) I parked and waited, and waited, for him to come back to his car to explain why he had lied to me. Of course, he never came out. So I went home in tears. But it was now becoming very clear to me why his favorite song was "I'm Not in Love."

I realized then, that if he had lied once, he'd probably lie again—and perhaps had been lying all along. It seemed like "Someone left the cake out in the rain"—a "MacArthur's Park" moment for me—it was *OVER*.

That night I cried to my mom. My poor mom. She listened and worried. I'd never been this emotional before. She just couldn't understand why I was so upset over this guy. I tried to explain how I had given this relationship my whole heart—and now—

"My heart's been broken!" I cried.

And she reminded me of the time when I was only four years old and something had really crushed me. I had said the exact same words to her then—"My heart is broken."

But we all live through broken hearts. About a half year later, he called me at the station, and asked if I would give a tour to a cop buddy of his. Graciously, I gave them both a tour and that was all. I didn't need to repeat the heartbreak.

It was only a couple of months after our break-up that another eager amour started asking me out. I thought, please—let's give the last scab some time to heal. I turned him down month after month. He kept asking. I kept saying *NO!* One day, I thought, why not. Why shouldn't I have some fun while my ex-Officer Friendly was having his. So I told this new guy I'd be *drinking buddies* with him, and that's *all*. Little did I know *drinking* was the magic word.

TOP ROCK GIRLY JOCK

We'd meet after my shift ended at 10 PM, and head to the local bar for a couple. Then we'd stop at my house where I'd say *Hi* to Mom and Dad before they went to sleep. Then he and I would head off to a local restaurant/bar for more drinks and dinner, which would now be around 2 AM. (How fresh was this food?) Pretty soon I noticed I had gained five pounds. Well, yeah, two beers and dinner right before you go to sleep will do it every time. I wished I would've known this as a kid; I was so skinny, they nicknamed me *toothpick*.

Anyway, he was great fun! We laughed back and forth through our beers, and the more we drank, the funnier things were! Some dates sure do look better through the end of a shot-glass. And then history started to repeat itself.

One evening we'd planned to meet as usual—he was working late. I was supposed to meet him at his office. When I got there, he was "Already Gone." "Stood up, brokenhearted again." The night guard said he left with a co-worker. I thought I'd find them at the bar we usually hung out at. The bartender said they just left. Since he had once mentioned their friendship, I knew who she was and where she lived, so I went to her hi-rise and rang her bell (that shy little Connie did).

She answered and asked me to *waaaaaaait*—she was just getting ready for bed (the girl moves fast!) and said she'd let me up in a minute. As I went up one elevator, I'm sure he was going down the other. She said she hadn't seen him and offered me tea. I sipped my tea as I told her how the bartender said he saw the two of them leave together, at which point she suddenly remembered she *did* see him (so *young* for such short term memory problems). She said she only saw him for a drink and that was it. Well, yes, in my mind, that *was* it!

I remembered the time he and I snapped some pictures at his place and when he gave me the negatives to make extra prints, I ran across one of a woman posing in his apartment in a low-cut sundress. When I questioned him, he said it was me. (On negatives we all look alike.) I told him I didn't have a low-cut dress like that. But then I knew it was his co-worker!

And there were many more. I knew I cared for him. I just didn't care for his other women. And he was starting to look like a package deal.

One night there was a company party. Most of the employees were gathering at a favorite hang-out in Chicago—a great Mexican restaurant, if the roaches didn't climb off the wall and eat your food before you did. But they had great nachos! By the end of the night, and one-too-many-Coronas-for-him later, I was dragging him to his car. Some of his co-workers helped me load him in while they questioned whether or not I knew how to drive his four-speed. No problem, I said—it would still be safer than letting him drive.

When we got to his place, I dragged him out of the car and spilled him onto the sidewalk just outside his door. The dog in the neighbor's yard started barking. He barked back. The dog barked again. He barked back at the dog. They seemed to be having a two-way conversation. (*Man* is dog's best friend.) He was out of control. And that was not the only thing he lost control of. When I finally dragged him inside his apartment, I was exhausted. I left and drove myself home.

It was always a soap opera with him. We had been dating for about a year. One evening, we were celebrating a *sort of* anniversary. At about 9 PM, he started yawning, and wanted to end our date. He said he was getting sleepy and still had to clean his apartment. Sleepy and clean? So out of character, I thought. So I offered to help him clean. It was then that he suddenly remembered he had promised to show the *lady* (who lived upstairs) some home movies of her daughter's graduation. I said, fine, we'll show her the home movies and then we'll clean your apartment.

When we got to his place, we went upstairs to fetch her. She came to the door in her negligee—wearing gobs of eye make-up—shadow, liner, mascara—the works! She said she was just getting ready for bed. (Out of cold cream?) We invited her and her daughter to his apartment to watch the graduation movies. The reel lasted about twenty minutes, but three hours later she was still there!

She was all curled up on his couch in her flimsy negligee, while her daughter had enough sense to wear a robe. She kept asking her mom to leave. It was getting late. Eventually, the daughter left, but the mom stayed on. I think she was waiting for *me* to leave. I decided it was time to give her the ol' heave-ho. I told her to take herself in her flimsy negligee back upstairs where she belonged, with her daughter, because we wanted some private time. She was shocked at my rudeness. Really? Hey, *lay-dee*—paradise is closed for the night—and don't forget your apple.

She finally slithered back upstairs, and he followed to make sure she got home OK. (Long trip, upstairs.) I peeked out the door after them and heard a squishy kissy sound coming from above.

When he came back, I screamed at him at the top of my Top-Rock-Girly-Jock lungs!

All he could say was, "Ssssshhhh—she'll hear you!"

So I screamed even louder! At which point he lunged for all his favorite things—his expensive and precious electronic toys—and swiped everything in sight off the counter 'til they came crashing down on the floor in pieces. And then he said it was all my fault.

I wasn't too worried when he said his bedroom caught on fire. (Guess he was hotter than I thought.) Not to worry. Though I knew both he and the *lady* upstairs were smokers, I figured that with the waterbed, they'd put themselves out. Meanwhile, inside, I was smoldering more and more.

One evening we came back to his place from a date, and he asked me to wait in the car while he ran in to *straighten up*. (To me, that was a euphemism for *hide something*.) So I nodded innocently, and while he ran in to unlock the front lobby door, I quickly slid out of the car and climbed in through the kitchen window of his garden apartment. I got inside before he did—only to find feminine undies on the floor, and some moldy homemade cookies in his fridge. She was obviously no *Mrs. Fields*—and how long had she been there?

When he finally opened the door and saw me, it was another smashing moment. Grabbing his favorite hollow-body guitar, he cracked it against the wall. Better the guitar than me, I thought. But to his credit, he never laid a hand on me when he lost his temper. Of course, my body wouldn't have made that melodious, crashing sound as the guitar splintered into itsy bitsy pieces. That was the perfect instrument for such a crescendo! ("While My Guitar Gently Weeps?")

The last straw came when we were out for pizza one night and he told me a young girl (how young?) was at his apartment waiting for him. I didn't believe him. He dared me to call his house. So I went to the pay phone and dialed his number. Sure enough, a girl answered.

"He told me he broke up with you," she said.

I told her to pack up her stuff and be gone by the time we got back. But she had planned on spending the week-end, she said. Too bad, I thought—your fun is just beginning. Get used to it.

Since I had spent almost every day of the past year with him, this was going to be a "Hard Habit to Break." I finally suggested that we not see each other for a month. After that, I suggested a second month. My line of thinking was, if he isn't around me, I can't get hurt. It took a while, but we slowly grew apart and I no longer missed this torturous relationship. My friend, Florence, used to say that if someone stopped hitting you on the head with a hammer, you'd miss that too.

I started to wonder how I had let my personal life deteriorate my career life. After all, we are each our own best friend. To let your life backslide because of someone who doesn't really care about you is stupid—"Stupid Cupid." I decided to never let that happen again. Did you ever see that cartoon—an old, old woman sitting on a bench next to several skeletons—the caption says, "Waiting for the perfect man." That might be me.

As for the jewelry and gifts he gave me, I decided that I had earned them with all my heartaches. Besides, he had spent plenty of money on many women before me—flying them off for romantic little getaways. Don't think they gave him airline tickets when it was over.

Later that year, my home was broken into. I was working "live" on the air 'til "After Midnight." When I got home, the sliding glass doors had been smashed with a rock and the wooden door to the basement had been bashed in and kicked into splinters. The dining room drawers were dumped out all over the floor. Stunned and petrified, I carefully tiptoed back to the kitchen and quietly called the police. While I was still on the phone with them (they insisted I stay on the line), I heard a voice call out behind me. There was a guy standing at my back kitchen door! I screamed! The police on the other end of the phone panicked.

"What!"—"Who's there?"

Just then, the guy at my door started flashing a badge, announcing he was a plain-clothes policeman! Yeah, well thanks for almost giving me a heart attack! I thought the burglars were back for the kill!

Later, the police said there had been a string of burglaries in the neighborhood. All my necklaces, gold chains and bracelets were untouched. Only my rings were stolen. My high school ring—a ruby ring from my parents—a silver ring I had bought on vacation and others I had gotten as gifts from friends and fans. But the crooks didn't get my most precious ones because those were safely tucked away in the safety deposit box at the bank. They got away with some small stuff—but for the big heist, they're gonna need Bonnie & Clyde!

(You may wonder why there are no pictures in this chapter of my
old boyfriends—
that's because I burnt them all—
got the last bit of spark out of the old flames!)

TEN

Another One Bites the Dust

Besides my romances crumbling around me, my career was now at a crossroads. Westinghouse Broadcasting brought in new management. I usually never knew what was happening 'til it hit me in the face. But whenever I turned a corner down the hall at the station and ran into the new manager, that's exactly what happened. I'd bump into him and jump with fright. It was eery—I couldn't put my finger on it. Why did I run into him so often when I least expected it, and why did it make me scream out "*Eeeeeek*" like that. Again, I guess my gut knew it before I did. Anyway, I should've guessed after someone broke into my locked drawer in the talent office—and stole my "lucky hat."

After he came on board, I was told not to say or do anything entertaining on the air. I was just supposed to announce the song titles and call letters—the basics. I was not allowed to show any emotion and I was told to talk softer—more bland—to try and sound more like FM did in those days—like they'd been shot with a tranquilizer gun.

Jim Stagg was now program director at WMAQ and occasionally called to say *Hi*. He called me on the air one day during this period. He had tuned in and was worried that I might have been sick—or depressed. He couldn't understand why I didn't sound like me. I explained that those were my orders. Jim was always very nice to me and once even offered me a job at WMAQ radio when they went *country*. I turned him down because I really loved working at WIND, but maybe that wasn't the smartest move.

I remember the day they let me go. They asked me to come in for a meeting early that day, which was unusual because evening jocks were hardly ever asked to come in early. But I didn't make much of it. So there I sat, in the meeting with the program director and the new general manager. The manager said they had decided they wouldn't be needing me any more. I felt the blood drain from my face; I thought I might faint. I couldn't believe this was happening. In my purse, I had a copy of the latest ratings that showed I had made the most gains at the station. And now they were letting me go?????

It made no sense to me until later, when I found out that they had also dropped Chuck Benson right before me. They were changing formats—going *news-talk*. Music was out—they just wanted to talk. (Though I've always claimed music was *more* than mere words, beat and melody—music speaks to your soul.) The other jocks saw this coming. The new station wanted a fresh, new sound. And although I could easily have done *talk*, I was part of the old sound.

Going from working six days a week to none at all was a jolt. Another oldies station was interested in hiring me, but I had to wait six weeks before I could work on the air again in Chicago. Stations were afraid that if you showed up somewhere else on the dial, that your loyal listeners would follow. It was part of my contractual agreement, which I found to be quite unfair, since *they* let *me* go. But this was the first and only contract I'd ever had; so I signed whatever they presented. I started hanging around the house and tried to humor myself with hobbies. I took up doll collecting—anything to distract myself. I was so disenchanted with the business. All this dedication—for nothing. There was no logic to working in radio. You build something up for someone else to tear down. I was confused and didn't know where I should look for work next.

It was during this time that the legendary Wally Phillips at WGN radio called, out of the blue. (He was also a *Moonchild* like me and I was proud to hear we shared that.) I had pre-recorded some drop-ins for him once when I was visiting the studios and checking for openings. He used drop-ins when he read commercials—actually, I heard his engineer popped them in at random so Wally would be caught unawares and that would be fun. I remember thinking up some lines that might catch him off-guard—like, *"I like a guy who knows his tools."* It was fun.

I never really knew Wally or heard his show very often because I was usually sleeping when he was on and probably vice versa. The closest contact I'd had with him had been at the Women in Motion Pictures Industry "Man of the Year" luncheon at the Ambassador Hotel.

I was an invited guest along with Wally, and actor Cesar Romero—whom you might remember as the "Joker" in the ABC-TV series, *Batman*. He also had a running role in TV's *Falcon Crest*; besides starring in many major movies throughout his life.

I actually met Cesar once before—when he was appearing at a menswear store at the Harlem-Irving Plaza in Norridge. My mom and I went to see him, had a picture taken, and got his autograph. It was so weird, now, to be an invited guest, just like him. There were only three "honored guests"—Cesar, Wally, and *me!* It just amazed me.

So when Wally called asking a favor—I was thrilled! He was the hot morning man—and wanted me to do a bit on his show. I had to set my alarm for this one. He asked me to impersonate Bo Derek from the hit movie *10*. I hadn't seen it, so I hesitated. Wally reassured me—he said she only spoke a couple lines in the whole movie. He said I should just be myself—dumb—blonde. Oh, OK, I thought. No problem there; it was always easy for me to dumb down—kinda came naturally.

TOP ROCK GIRLY JOCK

From left—4th, Wally Phillips, *6th*, Cesar Romero—me, *far right*
Women in Motion Pictures Industry—1974

On the air, Wally kept calling me "Bo," but by the end of the bit, he told the listeners I was "Bo—*Schwartz*." We ad-libbed the whole thing—neither of us knew where the other was going. I remember telling him that *less is more* (figuring Bo must've had on *less* than *more* in that movie). It was such a kick!

Eventually I heard from WJJD and WJEZ-FM. They wondered if I'd be interested in doing country radio. I rather liked country music, because when I'd get burnt out hearing oldies, I'd listen to country. So I agreed.

The sister stations were owned by Schering-Plough Broadcasting. WJJD, at 1160 on the AM dial, was a 50,000 watt powerhouse. In the good old days, it was a huge rocker and catapulted many jocks to Chicago radio fame. Their FM station, WJEZ, offered what they called *beautiful* country. (The songs were so mellow and sad, that later, when I heard there was a high suicide rate among people who listened to country music, it didn't surprise me.)

They offered me the midnight-6 AM shift on WJEZ at 104.3 on the FM dial. I turned them down. I didn't want to live like a vampire. (Little did I know that almost twenty years later, I'd be working at that spot on the dial again.) But as for that graveyard shift—they got a girl from New York to take it and she was as happy as twang on a steel guitar. Great for her, I thought. Congratulations!

But I did agree to work part-time for them. One day, they were extremely short-handed—running low on DJs. They asked if I'd do the show on WJJD, then run across the hall and also do their sister-station, WJEZ-FM, during the same time slot. (I started to get a little deja-vu from those years of running down the block between WIND and WSDM.) Would I get double pay, I asked. No, they said—just double duty. *Hmmmm*, now that I think about it, if I could have done that, I might have locked in double-duty for good. I said,

"No, but thanks for the offer."

(My days of saying "Sure" were coming to an end.) The legal ID had to be done "live" in a two-minute window at the top of the hour. How could I be sure the songs at both stations would not end at exactly the same time? And so, how could I announce both station ID's at the correct times, if I could only physically be in one place at one time. (I'm not Padre Pio, you know—he's now a saint that was able to bi-locate in his earthly life in Italy.)

Things there were always, as they say, "half-baked." (You guys might have another term for that, but I'm trying to be a lady.) I came in to do the 6 PM shift one afternoon, and, as the DJ before me was running out the door, he quickly told me I would have to interview John Schneider of the *Dukes of Hazzard* in less than an hour, to talk about his new country song. John was promoting it in town, and was running late. (Yeah, probably trying to find this big-time Chicago radio station next to a forest preserve in Des Plaines, IL.)

TOP ROCK GIRLY JOCK

It was a hot, humid, day and I had just run in from a full day at the mall (we girls know how exhausting that can be); I was a mess! But even worse than that, I had never really watched *Dukes of Hazzard* (I was probably doing radio shows)—and no one even had his "bio" for me. I knew *zip* about this guy, and I had only minutes to think up questions for an interview! I felt this was a low blow.

So, when John showed up, I invited him to sit at the microphone next to mine and told him that after the stop-set (when we ran commercials), I'd do his interview. The more I looked at this guy, the cuter he got! He was tall and blond, and had a charming, sweet way about him. At this point, I wasn't as concerned about how the interview would go. I mean, what could the station expect after not giving me any advance notice for prep time. So I did what any girl in this situation would do.

I was no longer a DJ interviewing John Schneider, I was just a single girl sitting next to a hot lookin' guy. I'd let nature take its course. Suddenly, the commercials were over and now it was time to talk to John on the air. I gathered up my most professional demeanor, but before I could mentally edit my comment, I heard myself say,

"So, John, tell us—how did you get to be so—*CUUUUUUTE!*"

At which point he smiled warmly and looked even cuter than before my question, which now erased any possible traces of journalistic thoughts from my mind. (Little did I know that he shared a birthday with one of my other boyfriends—chemistry at work again?) We both then laughed together, and he took it from there. I could see he was a real pro and he knew better than to expect any good questions from me. I started thinking, this was great! He can talk about all the stuff he wants to plug—his new country songs, his TV show, his career.

I fell into an "uh-huh" stage as I continued to marvel at this guy. I couldn't have asked any questions that would have pleased him more, even if I'd had his bio. What I do remember him saying is something to the effect of having *lucked into* his TV role. Well, yeeeeeaaah, when you look the look, talk the talk, and sing the song—he had everything going for him.

I knew I'd never see him again after this interview and again, I was right! Who'd want to hook up with a hot and sweaty DJ, with straggly, limp hair, and half her make-up faded off! What a contrast I must have been to the Daisy Duke he worked with! I did manage to get a picture with him before he left. It makes me laugh 'til this day—like the prince stuck with one of Cinderella's stepsisters.

WJJD/WJEZ-FM Studios in Des Plaines, IL
" Hey, John—how 'bout I show you around Chicago—
I know a restaurant on Rush Street that has great soup!"

The WJJD format had been country for some time. It was one Saturday morning, when I came in to do my shift, that I saw the memo from the program director. Surprise after surprise! (Kinda like

Christmas when you never know what you're gonna find under the tree—only difference is gifts under the tree usually work just fine.) We were no longer playing country & western music. We were going *Big Band!* Excuse me?

This had all been kept hush-hush so that we could beat the *other* station to the new format. Really! Might it not have been a good idea to inform the DJ who's supposed to be the first one on the air with this stuff? (Again, just like the Schneider interview—no warning.) I usually didn't arrive hours before show time, so I had to quickly assimilate everything. Because it had been decided at the last minute, the engineers didn't have time to place all the songs on cartridges, which is what we played in those days. So the memo instructed me to play many of the scheduled songs from the turntable in the studio.

Right off, I could see the problem. The microphone was about four feet away from the turntable. I would have to introduce the song, then try to quietly wheel my squeaky swivel stool over to the turntable and start the record. (This was even more antiquated than the first station I worked for—I was starting to miss *"Green for Go, Red for Stop."*)

So, I tried talking v-e-ry s-l-o-w-l-y—stretching my words—so that the *dead air* between my last word and the time I was actually able to start the turntable, would be less noticeable. It was the best I could do. Also, since no one had bothered to tell me of this format change, I had no time to get prepped on the music or artists.

At one point, I introduced the Dorsey Brothers, Tommy and Johnny! Oh? It was *Jimmy?* (I found out later.) Another time, "The Flight of the Canary," or whatever that song was, seemed to be over in a flash. I thought it sounded rather *perky* but noticed too late that I had played it at the wrong speed. But hey, we were *first* to hit the Chicago market with "Big Band!"

It was here that another odd management encounter took place. The program director was a big, heavy-set guy who bellowed when he talked and laughed. He came up to me one day and just flat-out said, "You know—I don't like your laugh."

The same giggle-laugh that Pulitzer-Prize-winner, Ron Powers, had admired in a *Chicago Sun-Times* article in the '70s—and the same giggle-laugh that would be complimented in 2008, in Rich Appel's "JOCK 100" List in *Hz So Good*, when I was voted into the Top 100 jocks in the country—as #99—but only 15 spots away from the late, great, Johnny Carson. Of course, I was both shocked and honored!

But there in the 80's, I had to defend my laugh.

"What? My laugh?" I giggled in response.

"Yeah, see—there it is—you just did it again."

"I did?" I tried to re-wind my mind to try and hear what it was I just did that he heard and I didn't.

"When you laugh on the air, I want you to laugh like this—*Harty-Har-Har*," he bellowed.

I looked at his 300 pounds of belly-laughter, and said, "I don't think I can do that. *MY* laugh just comes out different. Besides, if I try and laugh like that, they'll think I'm *YOU*," I giggled.

("Ooops, I Did It Again"—mea culpa, mea culpa.) After that I tried not to laugh at all. Since I couldn't do it his way, and since he didn't like "My Way," perhaps no way was the safest way. Of course, maybe if I could've laughed more on the show, I might have prevented some of the suicides they said came from listening to country music. My giggles could have been sort of a public service announcement.

Our PSA's were scripted and ready on a roll-a-dex and we had to read them as scheduled on the log. They were usually very dry and droll, and it's just times like that that make you wanna laugh—you know—when you shouldn't. My most memorable PSA was for a local fire department. I had to read the words, "fire-fighter" but somehow, "fire-*farter*" came out. When I realized what I just said, I tried again. Again, I said "fire-*farter*." I did this three times. My brain was skipping like a needle on a scratched 33-1/3. It struck me so funny—I started—*giggling!* (How to lose a radio job in one minute.)

TOP ROCK GIRLY JOCK

Left—
OK—John Schneider!
You can come back now
—got my make-up on

Below—
Gary Deeb,
TV/Radio critic,
announced my show in
the *Chicago Sun-Times*

Another One Bites the Dust

**WJJD
1160 AM**
Mark Edwards
Bill Hart
Bob Dayton
Johnny Todd

Below—
**WJEZ
104.3 FM**

Randy Price, Norm Miller, Carol Mason
John Anthony, John Charleston

TOP ROCK GIRLY JOCK

The station also did a lot of promotion for their country format. This ad ran in *Time* magazine.

As Appearing in Time Magazine.

Another One Bites the Dust

And there was always a fun concert to emcee!
Above right—Jeannie C. Riley, "Harper Valley PTA"—Sweet lady!

The *Chicago Tribune's* Maggie Daly plugged Steve King & me
Today Steve & his wife Johnny have a highly rated show at WGN!

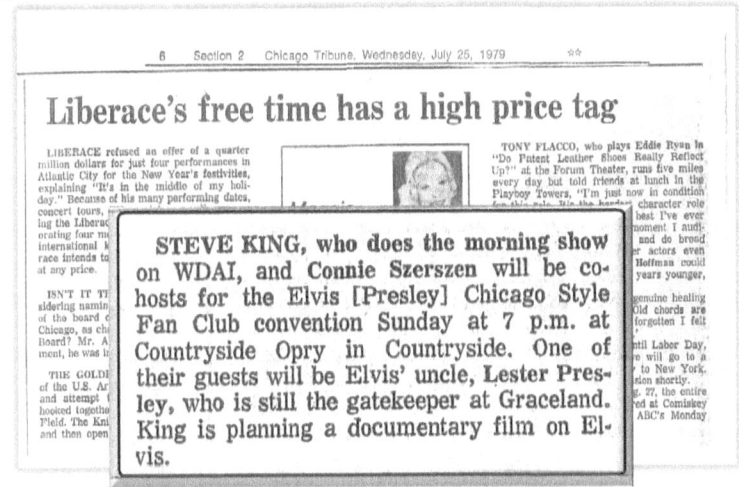

TOP ROCK GIRLY JOCK

Right about this time, my love of music and of the many great people I'd worked with, started to gel into new work situations. A former WIND newsman, and dear friend, Fred Barton, was spinning country & western records at The Barn—a swanky restaurant/bar in suburban Barrington. The *Urban Cowboy* thing was getting to be a real hit-kicker! Next thing I knew, Fred had asked me to co-host some dance nights, and I found myself in a cowgirl hat, playing the "Cotton-Eyed Joe." Perfect! I love hats—and this straw hat had little holes where you could screw on little pins that you collected.

FRED BARTON
WIND Radio 560 ... NEWS

Never did ride the mechanical bull, but there was a *quick-draw* night to see who could be the fastest to draw a pistol out of a holster and shoot. Connie, get your gun. A snap for me! I was quick in those days, and even outdrew the pros who supplied the guns for the show. Move over, Wyatt Earp!

It was great fun! And those country & western nights weren't a drag on my wardrobe budget, since all I needed were jeans, cowboy shirts and boots. You could wear the same stuff over and over—no one really cared. What we cared about was learning the latest dance steps—the Two-step, Three-step, Shottische, Cotton-Eyed Joe, Slappin' Leather. I was out there on the floor, learning right along with the guests—at least until near the end of the song, when I'd have to run back to the DJ booth to start another record—so that the music would never stop.

One day they held an arm-wrestling competition. Since I'm pretty much a weakling, I had no intention of even trying; but someone talked me into competing. They only had one other girl (?) contestant. Well, sure, what fragile female wants to do *THIS!* Then it occurred to me that if there were only two of us competing, I was bound to win something. We got our arms set on the table, wrists in place, hands clasped. Someone yelled *"GO!"* Smash-down! I won second-place! Hah! The trophy looks great on the mantel! (Wards off intruders.) (Should've had this back before the burglary.)

And, speaking of the mantel, most of my budget went towards decorating my new house. I reveled in the fact that I was free to put knick-knacks on the mantel ever since another old boyfriend had warned me—

"The fireplace mantle is *not* for your knick-knacks! It's there to set down a beer can—and ashtray! And I don't want to see any artificial anything around here!" (Had he looked closely enough at me, I wondered?)

"I don't want to see any imitation stuff—like on wallpaper. If you're decorating with flowers, they have to be *real* flowers—or *real* wood," he ordered.

It didn't take me long to think he was *real* crazy! He didn't live here. He never paid any *real* money for this house. I was the one who paid the *real* down payment and had the *real* mortgage. And did he think I would ever *really* marry someone like him so I could be *real* miserable the rest of my life?

After lining drawers and shelves with obscure looking paper (so he couldn't tell what it was an imitation of), I decided he wasn't worth the bother and made sure he was *real gone.*

When I worked at WIND, I had lived at home with Mom and Dad. It was a long time before I moved out. We had a great family life and they just couldn't get rid of me. Besides, Mom did all my cooking, cleaning, washing and ironing. And with working full-time radio, I really had had very little time for domestics. All my energy went into preparing for the show.

And, just as I had done back in high school, I kept that notebook by my bed so if a great idea popped into my head at night, I could jot it down. Years later my brother, Jerry, told me that that's what Seinfeld did. I thought, what's new about that! The bad part is that sometimes it takes forever to finally get to sleep!

I sleep a lot. People have told me, way too much. I need nine to ten hours to wake up naturally without an alarm clock. I used to feel bad about this, until I met a singer at a mobile DJ job who said he slept eleven hours a night. And that, without lots of sleep, he just couldn't perform well. He said it was a known fact that creative people really need much more sleep than others. Recently I learned that singer Mariah Carey sleeps 15 hours a night. And let's not forget President Calvin Coolidge and Mae West—both needed 10 hours. *Sigh!* Another relief! I wasn't as abnormal as everyone thought, after all!

It was in the early 80's when I got a call from the Program Manager at ABC 7, here in Chicago. Jeff McGrath wanted to interview me for a show they were planning.

The show was going to replace *AM Chicago,* which had been hosted by Sandi Freeman and Steve Edwards (same Steve Edwards from *Good Day Live* and who now has a star on the Hollywood Walk of Fame, and who also interviewed me at a telethon in the '70s).

ABC 7 was looking for a new hostess, he explained. He asked to see a tape. I'd done a few TV guest shots in town, and once co-hosted with the NBC 5's famed weatherman, Jim Tilmon. Jim had invited me to talk "Rock and Roll" on his show, *Tilmon's Tempo.* So I brought that tape along. I remember thinking that wasn't my best day as I was having cramps the day of the taping and had to take painkillers—so I wouldn't be rolled over in pain talking about rock and roll. But I made it through the segment and no one ever knew—'til now.

The interview with Jeff McGrath went quite well. He said I looked very comfortable on camera—and I'm sure he knew my history in radio in the city.

But right before I left with my hopes up, he said he was also going to be talking to a woman who was doing a TV talk show out of town. He asked if I'd ever heard of her. Her name was **OPRAH WINFREY.**

Another One Bites the Dust

"Who?" I said.

(And I thought, who has a name like that—I used to think mine sounded strange—but **"Oprah Winfrey"**???)

"Never heard of her," I shrugged.

(Excuse me while I eat those words.)

But I'll say this for Jeff McGrath—he sure knew how to pick 'em! I never followed up on the job, figuring they'd call if they wanted me.

After my part-time stint at WJJD, a DJ friend, Tony Russell (a successful voice-over talent today), who worked for WUSN-FM (US-99), called to say the program director was interested in hiring me for the 6-10 PM slot there. I took it. Things were fine until, one day, I did a bit of *personality*, and imitated a Cabbage Patch doll (which we were giving away in a promotion). The program director went ballistic. Here we go again, I thought.

"How *DARE* you do a Cabbage Patch voice! Don't you know our newsgirl is the only one who does those!" (The newsgirl was his girlfriend.)

"No," I said. "I didn't know."

(But I was now also wondering how he liked my laugh.) There was no memo saying we should *not* do Cabbage Patch voices. I never understood what his problem was; the way he yelled at me frightened me. I finally decided that if all I was supposed to do was push buttons, they could get a monkey to do that. *("—one monkey don't stop no show!")*

I gave my two weeks notice. He asked for a month. I saw no reason to be lenient with him when he hadn't been with me. He said it would take time to find a replacement. I figured maybe the newsgirl could do it since she was already doing Cabbage Patch voices. I stuck to my two weeks, but agreed to work one day a week for the fun of it. But a month later, after getting up at 3 AM, driving for over an hour through winter slush on the expressway, with barely no sleep, for $11 an hour; it didn't seem like fun anymore. I quit that too.

TOP ROCK GIRLY JOCK

I remember that emotional moment—when my mom met me at the radio station one morning. She sometimes drove me in and picked me up so we could have more chat time together and then maybe we'd go shopping a bit and stop for a bite to eat. I knew how proud my parents were of my radio achievements—but I also knew how miserable I was at this place. And so, I asked my mom that very last day at US-99,

"Would you mind very much if I just didn't do this anymore? I really don't want to do this anymore."

My mom looked surprised, but with such understanding, she said,

"Of course not! Don't do it if you don't want to!"

And I knew again, at that moment, that it didn't matter what I did. My folks would always love me for *me*—not for what I did.

It was something that was easy to lose track of when you worked in such a public arena. Friends would sometimes not want to be friends any more and other people whom you hardly knew, suddenly wanted to be your best friend—because of your radio job. It was all jumbled up. But the closeness my family and I shared kept me totally grounded. They always supported me—in good times and in bad.

The year I quit, I made more money working part-time than I had earned full-time at US-99. Even my secretary friends were earning more money than I made as a DJ there. It's so funny because the public often thinks you're raking in all these big bucks as a big celebrity DJ. There *are* six or seven figures for some—usually the morning jocks, or those with good agents—and almost always, men.

At that time US-99 was owned by the Marriott's. Someone said it was specifically the Marriott children's investment. They were later bought out by the media giant, Infinity (CBS), and is now the professional operation it always hoped to be. Today the station is run by highly gifted management and is one of the highest rated country stations in the country! The last I heard, the week-end pay rate had gone up—from $11 to $15 an hour.

Another One Bites the Dust

And from there, some great radio talents went on to do "talk" at WLS—Don Wade and Roma. From the few promotions that we had, I remember how Roma always worked the US-99 booth. She was just as sweet and kind then as she is now on the air. It sure impressed me because such kindness could sometimes be hard to find in radio. (If you're wondering why there are no pictures from US-99—that's because no one bothered to take any of me, or I wasn't there long enough.)

But every bit of show news always made Robert Feder's TV & RADIO column in the *Chicago Sun-Times*.

ELEVEN

Stayin' Alive

After some of the most exciting years of my life, I was now convinced that a radio career would only lead you nowhere. I took some classes, got my real estate license, and started selling. I would now work for myself. My energy would go to establishing some security in my working world. But it didn't take long for me to learn that I didn't like selling. There wasn't any creativity here. And the real estate world with its shrewd sharks was swallowing me up. Besides, I had very little credibility with buyers and sellers. There was too much *fluff* about me. I wasn't all that aggressive, and didn't really want to be. I didn't want to manipulate the public so I could make a living. I wanted to entertain them—to make them feel happy and light-spirited. And I didn't want to live for money alone. I wanted to live my life with my God-given gifts—my stardust. We all have some. But selling wasn't one of mine. My SAT tests in school showed the best fields for me would be in either music or biology. Thinking back to those depressing days at the medical center, there was no doubt in my mind that working with music would always be my first choice. ("I've Got the Music in Me.")

TOP ROCK GIRLY JOCK

When I walked away from radio to sell real estate, I didn't really want to walk away from music in my work life, so I had also started a mobile DJ business. This was a natural progression, sprouting from the gigs I had done with my former WIND newsman, Fred Barton. For a while there, we worked together at various dance clubs and restaurants, but eventually got so many bookings that we each ended up doing events by ourselves, just to fill all the dates. I did weddings, birthday parties, pool parties, company parties, bar mitzvahs—anything that came along.

It was at one bar mitzvah that the mom started complaining to me that the kids were not dancing. I reminded her they were all boys.

"Well, get them to do *something*!" she screamed. "They're all in the bathroom, throwing up. Somebody sneaked in some beer!"

She was frantic, but it seemed to me the boys were already *having* a good time—what with the beer and all. Finally, most of them were corralled in the banquet hall. I tried my darndest to get them to do some sort of line dancing or something, but all they seemed to want to do was climb the pillars. And once again, it was *MY* fault!

Some of those jobs could sure take a toll on the DJ! The corporate parties usually came around Christmas time. Most of the company employees would be there, especially the bosses who planned it in the first place. Nobody wanted to make a fool of themselves by drinking too much, and so, of course, nobody wanted to dance much either. I had to really work the crowd. Sometimes a Snowball Dance with the company president and his wife would get things rolling. (I often thought that a dance with the boss, the wife, and the girlfriend—would've livened things up even quicker—Hah!) I eventually discovered that if I made a fool of myself at these events, they'd loosen up. Next to me, they couldn't possibly look too foolish. (Everything is relative—who said that?) Anyway, it usually worked and I got call-backs regularly.

Stayin' Alive

Of course, there was that one event on a Friday night, that I thought was for *Saturday* night. Those folks were *screaaaaming!* When they called my house and I answered, they asked where I was.

"Where?" was my calm reply, "I'm home—why?"

But, when I realized what had happened, I was devastated. It only has to happen once for it to never ever happen again. I'm just glad it was only a birthday party and not a wedding.

Formal Gigs—
Love wearing anything glitzy!

TOP ROCK GIRLY JOCK

Theme and Tent Parties in the 80's and 90's!

Stayin' Alive

OK—Take a real good look at those ruffles. Many of my DJ outfits were made by—me. Like this one. (A subconscious desire to be in the Ice Capades?) It was an Oscar de la Renta pattern which called for organdy or a similar fabric. But since I like glitz so much, I decided to use a metallic gold. If you know about sewing, this is not an easy fabric to work with. The ruffles were 4" wide; there were 14 ruffles in all. I hand hemmed each ruffle because I didn't have a serger and the fabric kept slipping out from under the needle. So hand stitch was the only way to go. I first wore this to a New Year's Eve gig at St.Thomas Villanova in Palatine, safety-pinned in back. No time to sew on buttons. The blouse took me two months to finish.

Above—2005 Friendship Village, Schaumburg, IL (I sewed that midnight blue sequin dress, too)

Right—2009 The Garlands of Barrington, Barrington, IL

Stayin' Alive

In my free-lance days, I also pursued acting. I had professional headshots taken and stapled a resume on the back. I got loads of "extra" work when Hollywood came to Chicago. I got to meet actor hunks like Tom Hanks, Tim Matheson, Burt Reynolds, David Hasselhoff, and more.

TOP ROCK GIRLY JOCK

It was while doing extra work in *Dr. Detroit,* that I met Dan Aykroyd, and his wife-to-be, Donna Dixon. There I was, standing next to this beautiful, buxom blonde, who was so sweet and friendly. She was from the South, and asked if I was too, because I seemed to have a little bit of a southern accent. I explained,

"No, but I worked for some country & western stations—so maybe a little rubbed off on me."

We laughed. Then Dan came up to her and I could see it already. There were Cupid arrows darting back and forth between them. Oh, I thought, so this is how you have to look to catch Dan Aykroyd's eye. I wouldn't have had a snowball's chance, as they say. Later I heard they got married and still are. But hey, I still have a dark blue satin jacket with *"Dr. Detroit"* on the back.

When a film needed children as extras, I'd scout my relatives. My cousins got great close-ups in the Jackie Gleason/Tom Hanks movie, *Nothing in Common.* If you get a chance to see it, they're the little boy and girl sitting on the stoop while Jackie stops and tries to talk to them. Little Marta broke down in tears; she was so afraid of this big guy.

I also took my mom along. We were put in scenes together. She was a natural! It was such fun—although sometimes our cars got better shots than we did, as we sometimes ended up on that ol' cutting room floor. Our cars also got paid more than us humans. Back then, I think it was something like $50/day for us, and $65/day for the car.

I often brought along several wigs, so that if they used me once as a blonde, they could use me again as a redhead. I remember director, Andy Davis, once suggesting I should be more aggressive if I wanted to work in this business. When I told him I wasn't exactly the Hollywood type—so I probably wouldn't make it in movies anyway, he said I was a pretty girl and shouldn't consider myself less. (I tried to see if he wore contacts.)

He was just being kind and encouraging, I'm sure. But that bit of kindness sure impressed me with what a nice guy he was and it was great to see someone at the top of his game being so sweet to a lowly extra. He didn't know I had any media connections and so I knew he wasn't being kind for any possible publicity.

Years later, when I was on vacation in Nantucket with my friend, Sue, we ran into actor John Shea in the local supermarket check-out line. He was right ahead of us. Sue said,

"I think I know that guy from somewhere."

I never seem to recognize anyone, but as I looked closer, I said,

"Yeah, I think I've seen him somewhere before."

As we were whispering about him, a young boy standing next to him, overheard us and said,

"Yeah, you've seen him on TV—he's my dad—he's been in tons of TV shows, and movies too—like *Missing* with Jack Lemmon."

Now we all started talking. John was so friendly and when I mentioned doing extra work with Andy Davis, he smiled and said what a sincere, great guy Andy was! I felt pretty important there for a few minutes, actually talking shop with John. I asked if we could shoot some video, and he played a part just for us. As he paid the cashier, John smiled at my camera and commented on how fast money would leave your hands in Nantucket! Hah!

Ever since the grade school plays, a bit of the acting bug stayed with me. Since I didn't have any full-time commitments, I thought I'd brush up and take more acting classes. I started studying at Wisdom Bridge Theater and with Kordos & Charbonneau.

One day a talent agent called and asked if I'd like to read for a speaking part in a PBS film titled, *The Killing Floor*. I was thrilled. I brought Mom along, who was my good-luck charm. Besides, Mom could speak great Polish and the part I was reading for was a Polish woman who spoke broken English. I wasn't sure I could pull this off. I mean, I spoke broken Polish—my English was great. But my character was supposed to be on the witness stand and distressed. I guess I did the distressed part pretty well (I knew I could cry on stage way back in second grade). Well, I didn't get the part I read for, but they did cast me in another. My character was a 1917 labor union worker who was supposed to get hysterical as she fought for her union job. (Kinda like back when I worked at WCFL—The Voice of Labor—where they tried to fire me; it was almost like typecasting—Hah!) There were only three lines, but a meaty role, I thought.

So the day of my acting debut came around. By now I had already been through *wardrobe*, and was being prepped in *make-up* in the trailer on the lot. I sat there, looking in the mirror with great expectations—this was my first time *ever* in make-up for a movie—and I watched as they removed all of my own make-up and started penciling in heavy, bushy black eyebrows. This was not gonna be a *Charlie's Angels* moment—I could see that. Then they pulled back my hair into sort of a bun, and put a babushka on my head. It was getting worse by the minute. I was glad when they stopped.

The scene took place in the old Chicago stockyards. It was winter and 30 degrees outside. But for the film, it was supposed to be a hot July day. There were tons of extras all dressed as labor union workers—short-sleeved, cotton, apron-type dresses (just like mine). In one angry mob scene, droves of security police on horseback, bayonets and all, fought back the crowd.

I was shown where to stand and told when to shout out my lines! I was feeling pretty good about myself right about then, knowing I was a principal instead of an extra as before. I shouted my lines as hysterically as I could!

"Oh, my God! Don't take our jobs from us!!! Don't break our Union!"

We did take after take. Somebody always screwed up something. But I was doing just fine. Until, suddenly, I looked at my burning wrist. I was bleeding! And some extra on his horse in front of me was still whipping around his bayonet, or whatever it was. I thought those things were supposed to be plastic! I hailed down an assistant—asking if maybe we should do something about this before I bled to death.

Stayin' Alive

They all were real concerned and very helpful. They wanted me to check in at their first aid station, but I said no. I was afraid I'd miss my big chance and they'd film without me. So they patched me up and we went on with more takes. Finally, we were done. It was, as I learned to say, *a wrap!* They then took me into the alley to record my lines for overdubbing; I had to do them all over again, because I guess the crowd noise drowned out my voice during the earlier filming.

On the day I made my acting debut, my mom was in the hospital recovering from carotid artery surgery. But she had been so happy for me. So, as soon as were finished in the stockyards, I drove straight over to tell her all about it. She was waiting for me in the visitor's lounge. When I stepped off the elevator she turned and looked at me. Then she turned away. Oh, my gosh! My own mother didn't recognize me! I couldn't believe it! Way back she couldn't recognize me when the *Mademoiselle* make-over made me prettier, and now couldn't recognize me when the make-up department made me uglier. We laughed about that for a long time!

My acting debut made the prestigious *Chicago Sun-Times*, "Kup's Column." I was thrilled. It wasn't every day someone could get applauded in this way—on the same page with Zsa-Zsa, yet!

TOP ROCK GIRLY JOCK

KUP'S COLUMN

Irv Kupcinet

Zsa Zsa Gabor is striking back in that Philadelphia fiasco by filing a $5 million lawsuit against the City Line Dinner Theater and its owner **Daniel Tabas**. Zsa Zsa, through her New York attorney, **William Greenawalt**, maintains she was a victim of a frameup and was not responsible for removing the wheelchair patients, who allegedly were disturbing her performance in "Forty Carats." The suit will point out that the alleged incident occurred on May 31, after which she gave two performances (matinee and evening) the next day and another performance the following night before the decision to fire her. The delay, the suit will maintain, indicates her firing was contrived and not instantaneous, as first reported.

MEANWHILE, GABOR, WHILE nursing her damaged reputation, is making plans for another trek down the aisle. This time, she told this reporter, she'll wed German Crown Prince **Frederick von Anhalt**. He was at her side during the Philadelphia engagement. . . . Cook County Treasurer **Edward Rosewell**, indicted on charges of lying to five banks about his debts in obtaining $168,500 in loans, reports he's confident that he'll be acquitted as was TV weatherman **Jim Tilmon** on a similar charge.

THE FUND-RAISER FOR Mayor "Here-e-e's Harold" Washington next Thursday at the Palmer House will raise an estimated $600,000. That will wipe out his $300,000 mayoral campaign deficit and provide an equal amount for his "mayor's fund." **Ed "Bill" Berry** and **Angelo Geocaris**, chairing the event, report some 4,000 tickets at $150 per, have been sold. . . . TV producer **Charles Fries**, filming "The Voyeur" here, is rushing a TV movie on the life of **Jack Dempsey**. He's in a race with other Hollywood producers to be first with the story of the late and legendary champ.

Zsa Zsa Gabor

HOW'S THIS FOR a mind boggler: Newspaper stories report Moses Malone of the champion Philadelphia 76ers will

Veteran actor **Moses Gunn** is brightening Our Town for the filming of Public Broadcasting's "The Killing Floor," the story of the bitter battle to unionize stockyard workers. Also in the cast: local deejay **Connie Szerszen**, known as the "Polish princess" to her radio fans.

Stayin' Alive

It was such a kick to finally get a speaking part in a film, but I continued to do as much extra work as I could get. I was cast as so many different characters—from bar-fly to nun. In the movie, *Above The Law,* in one scene, I played the part of a nun, walking down the hall, consoling some people who were grieving.

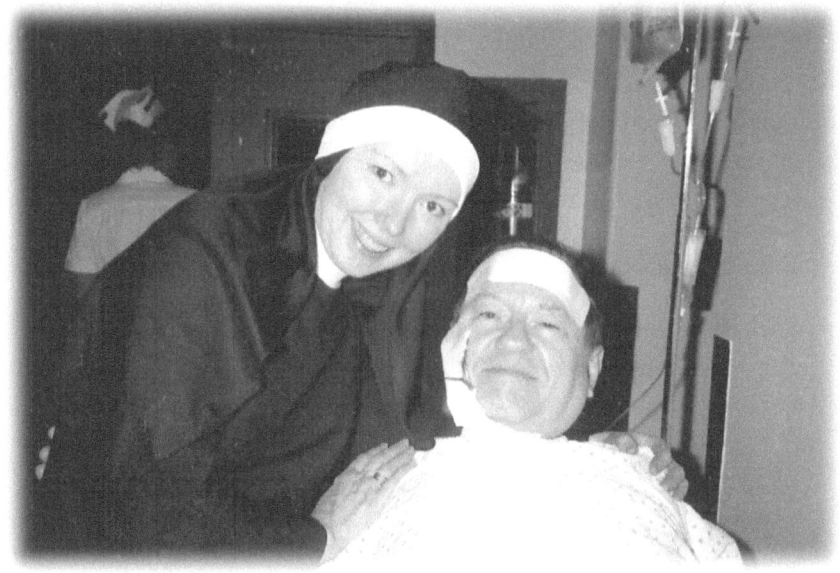

Above—
On the set—
Above the Law

Did they know I had won a prize with my nun's outfit that Mom sewed for me in the '50s—for Halloween?

Typecasting?

TOP ROCK GIRLY JOCK

My happy-go-lucky career change made the neighborhood papers—like *Lerner*. I was flitting from one job to another. I eventually left the other real estate office to work at Realty Stars on Chicago's northwest side, where so many folks spoke Polish. I sold homes without speaking any English—just my broken Polish! Again, I'd get my name in the *Dziennik Związkowy*—this time as a sales agent. The president, Mark Rzepkowski, now also has a highly successful radio show in Chicago and is often called "the Polish Rush Limbaugh!" Catch him Saturday afternoons at WNVR (1030 AM)—but, of course, it's all in Polish, moja droga.

APRIL 4, 1984   Section One—Page Seven

Career change

CONNIE SZERSZEN, WUSN-FM radio personality, has left the evening shift to become a sales associate at Zittel Realtors, 4950 N. Harlem Ave., Harwood Heights. Szerszen, a Norridge resident, will continue to do a Sunday morning radio show on WUSN and will make her acting debut in "The Killing Floor," which will premiere April on Channel 11.

Stayin' Alive

I was so caught up in free-lancing. It was usually great fun, working at different bookings. And it gave me much more flexibilty—not a whole lot of money, but more than I made in radio—and a lot more flexibility.

TWELVE

Catch Us If You Can

So when my friend Mary invited me to Orchestra Hall for an AT&T benefit, I was thrilled! I had free time now to enjoy concerts as I never had when working full-time radio. I used to get all sorts of free press invitations and gave them to my Mom and relatives to enjoy—because I was usually on the air when those events took place.

Mary said Tom Hulce was going to emcee the benefit. I had just seen him in *Amadeus* and thought he was—*MOZART*—come alive! I fell in love with his character, his giddy laugh, (after all, I had one of my own—Hah!) and his prankish ways. She admired him too. This was gonna be a fun evening! My camera was loaded—fresh film, ready to go. We had pretty good seats, not far from the stage.

Suddenly, there he was. I flashed away. Security came up almost immediately, and confiscated my camera. I was crushed. (And, also embarrassed—I felt like some kind of criminal.)

Worst of all, I'd have no memories of this special night. But you know what they say, "When man closes a door, God opens an elevator."

After the concert ended, I retrieved my camera from security and we started heading for the door, when we noticed a group of people standing near an elevator. Nosying around, we learned that this elevator was taking a special group of people up to a private *after-party* with Tom Hulce. Alright! This was where we had to be! Mary and I looked at each other and knew instantly what we had to do.

We quietly cozied up to the crowd, and when the elevator opened, we stepped in with this elite group. At the other end it was a little trickier, though. Because, as people filed out of the elevator to enter the party room, there was a couple at the top of the stairs, greeting everyone. These guests, I was starting to figure out, were probably special subscribers. Everyone seemed to know everyone else. I thought back to times I'd heard of, how people sometimes met other people they didn't know were important, but they didn't want to let on that they didn't know. I thought this had to be one of those times if we were ever going to have a chance at getting in on this private party. So, as we approached the greeting man and woman, I extended my hand to them and said,

"Oh, the concert was just lovely! We *loooooooved* it! The children performed incredibly—they're so gifted!"

I gushed and gushed in my best attempt at a high society voice. They looked at us a bit curiously—there was that split-second of non-recognition from the greeters—but then the smiles kicked in and they agreed—the concert had been wonderful—as we walked right past them into the *PARTY ROOM*!

TOM HULCE! WE'RE HERE!

There was a fantastic long table set with exotic hors d'oeuvres. Champagne was being poured. ("The Night They Invented Champagne"—the magic of music, movies and movie stars filled my spirit!) The balcony doors had been opened to let in the fresh night air. Looking down, you could see the bright lights of Chicago—my little ol' hometown, but now like part of a movie. Everyone was dressed to the nines! (Except us, because we hadn't planned on being there.) The night definitely oozed Hollywood fantasy!

But we still seemed to be getting some questioning glances from the crowd. Then I spotted Marty Robinson from the PBS station, WTTW 11.

"Marty—Hi! How are you!" I said, as loud as I could, so the others would hear and realize I belonged in this group. Luckily, Marty remembered me from the days I had done some charity appearances at the station. He smiled and we talked, and everything was fine from then on. (I never told Marty we'd crashed the party.)

And *NOW*, I had my camera. So, I snapped away!

"Excuse me, Tom—would you mind posing with my friend and me for a few shots."

It was unbelievable! TOM HULCE here—there—he was so accommodating. I had the entire roll almost filled, as I snapped him from every angle. We left the party excited, and giggled about how we had not been discovered!

I couldn't wait to get that film developed. The next day I took snapshots of my garden. The flowers—the trees—the grass—the weeds—ants—I kept snapping and snapping away. (You can see this coming, can't you?) Still the roll wasn't finished. Gosh, I wondered, how many more do I have to take to get to the end?

That's when I noticed the camera was on its 45th shot—on a roll of 36. Something was seriously wrong. I went into a dark bathroom to open the camera and check the film. Yup, you guessed it. (Crime does not pay.) Security at Orchestral Hall must have removed the film when they confiscated my camera. (Don't they owe me $4.00 for that roll?)

We do have a photo from that night, however, thanks to a professional photographer friend that was there on assignment—thanks Terry! (When man closes a camera, God opens another—and He even gets a professional photographer to snap the picture!)

TOP ROCK GIRLY JOCK

Left—My friend Mary Tevis, Tom Hulce (*Amadeus*) & me
Orchestra Hall—1985

(Boy, we sure look like a couple of groupies)

(He had no clue what we went through to get to this point)
(Tee-hee-hee-hee!)

Hey, Tom—I'll trade you my giggle—
for that *Amadeus* laugh!

THIRTEEN

The Wind Beneath My Wings

In the mid-80's, my family's health was in trouble again. My mom needed a triple by-pass. But I trusted she'd be in great hands at Loyola Medical Center. Her cardiologist was Dr. Joseph Hartmann (once lauded in *The Reader's Digest*). Dr. Sullivan was chosen to be her surgeon because of his great reputation.

I remember running into him near the elevator on the morning of mom's operation. He assured me things would go fine, but also informed me that 30% of patients needing this type of bypass do die on the operating table. He explained that her blockages were not the usual kind that most patients had, but that hers were at the junction of where the arteries connect to the heart.

For a second there, my own heart almost stopped when he said that, but then I looked at him and quietly reassured him that my mom would make it through. I just knew it. We were praying for her, and for him, and God would help him. Over six hours later, they phoned the waiting room to say she had survived the operation and was in Cardiac Intensive Care. I could go see her.

Just the day before, a nurse had taken me to the CIC Unit to view other heart by-pass patients. It was to acquaint you with the state of recovery—to see all those tubes, and the heart-lung machine at work on a human being clinging to life through these machines. As we approached a patient, the nurse started to explain things to me, and my knees started to buckle at just the thought of my dear mom having to go through all this. The nurse grabbed me by both elbows to catch me.

"Are you all right?" she asked, as if expecting this to happen.

"I'm fine," I assured her.

And my mom would be fine too. When the going gets tough, the tough get going. We were gonna go through this thing, and we'd all be fine, because God was going to get us through it! But after mom's operation, she just wouldn't wake up. They even nicknamed her *Sleeping Beauty*.

Since the operation had been on Friday, and it was now Sunday, I was really getting worried. I questioned the doctor on duty. He explained, that because they had to raise her blood sugar level for the operation, and since she was diabetic, that that could account for her drowsiness. When he told me what her sugar level was; I was stunned.

"That's way too high!" I warned him.

"No, that's pretty normal for a diabetic," he said.

"But not for *my* mom—she's usually in the 140-150 range!"

He immediately called over a nurse and asked to "cover her again!" (I assumed this was another insulin shot.) He was great—moving so quickly once he had more background on my mom. By that evening, when I was allowed to visit again, Mom was propped up on pillows, awkwardly trying to turn the pages of a magazine. She was groggy, but awake. I almost cried, I was so happy to have my mom back!

We were so close—the best of pals. We could finish each other's sentences. We thought alike. Ours was a magical friendship. My mom almost died when I was only four. A priest had even been called to give her the Last Rites. She told me how she remembered feeling her legs starting to get numb, and she was asking relatives at her bedside to help Dad care for me and my brother.

We were at my uncle's house when she had this attack. My uncle called in *his* doctor—telling him they had an emergency and could he please come as fast as he could. When he got there, he flushed Mom's pills down the toilet, and started treating her immediately. He said the medication she had been given by her doctor, was slowly stopping her heart. Eventually Mom recovered. I have always been so grateful to God for being able to share so much of my life with my mom, and I feel sorry for those who have lost theirs much too soon.

So after Mom came home from the heart by-pass operation, my dad and brother stopped smoking around her—the doctor's idea. We all helped with her exercises and pitched in with the housework. Soon she seemd like herself again, and as we looked at old photographs, we noticed how pale she had been before the operation and how once again, her cheeks were nice and rosy! Things were going to be fine—we were so relieved.

We were living in Norridge, at 4344 N. Nordica Avenue. We had moved there from Six Corners—at 4908 West Byron Street, which had the reputation of being the oldest, and only, farmhouse for miles around, before the area got developed.

I remember how my brother and I helped Mom and Dad as we tried to rehab the thing. Often we were given wallpaper-scraping duty which was kind of fun, because we'd find layers and layers of different papers—some floral—some with cowboys on them. Mom and Dad stripped and re-varnished the woodwork, lowered the ceilings, and divided rooms so we could have three bedrooms instead of two. The funniest part of the whole process was when Dad put up a new garage—and the roof started to slowly sink. (Bob Vila, where are you?) We thought the whole thing might come down one day. But what's even funnier is that, when we moved to Norridge and hired professional carpenters to build the garage, *that* roof did come down— right on top of them. No one got hurt—but it was hysterical. Dad felt vindicated—Mom ran for her camera. She liked taking pictures as much as I do. (Great shot, Mom!) (She also snapped a good shot of our chimney when it got struck by lightning.) Never a dull moment.

But the house in Norridge was our dream home. It was a single-story Chicago raised ranch with a full basement. With Mom working part-time at Motorola to add to Dad's salary, we were finally able to buy this brand new home! We took home movies as it was being built, with shots of the foundation, the framing, the finish, and landscaping (which we mostly did ourselves).

In the early '80s, Mom started sprucing up the decor. Our new furniture was delivered. New wall units and cocktail table! The table was adorable! A distressed-walnut, rattan-bottom shelf and a top shelf of two glass panels separated by a thin strip of walnut.

Dad was celebrating! He stumbled over to admire the new cocktail table, and when I say stumbled, I mean, *stumbled*. The next thing we heard was a loud yelp coming from the living room, along with an indefinable loud crashing noise. We all ran over to find Dad laid out in the cocktail table! He had crashed right through the glass panels—his bottom resting gently on the rattan lower shelf, head, arms and legs dangling out through the broken glass and splintered wood (the Rolling Stones song, "Shattered," comes to mind). Mom, Jerry, and I ran to help, pulling him out as gently as we could. Of course, after we noticed he wasn't hurt, we couldn't stop laughing. The distressed walnut table was now *really distressed.* Since the furniture had just been delivered, we called the store and told them it had been damaged in delivery—well, in a way, it sort of had been—*Sssshhhh!*

The next time Dad stumbled, it was on the pool table in the basement. He cracked some ribs. In *X-Ray*, they discovered the lump. It was golf-ball sized already. The operation followed. In surgical intensive care, he seemed to be in such pain. I asked the nurse to do something! She said they'd already given him the regular dose of morphine, and unless he was a heavy smoker, he wouldn't need any more. I asked her to please give him some more. After she did, the pain must have lessened because he settled down, and seemed to sleep more peacefully. (I think it's very helpful for a family member to give as much information as they can to the nurses and doctors on duty, especially when your loved ones are in intensive care. The staff can't possibly know everything about everyone—but each little bit of information may give them enough direction to make the patient's healing easier.) Eventually Dad recovered.

But nearly five years later, the cancer came back. I went with him, downtown to Wacker and Wabash, for acupuncture treatments which, supposedly, would help him stop smoking. After he died, the staples the doctor put in his ear to help him quit, were still there. It was too late. But I remember what a psychic once told me—that Dad would die—that he'd get sick from one of his former jobs—from working around chemicals or fumes. Mom said he used to clean out coffee vats with chemicals and would come home complaining about the smell, feeling like he'd inhaled all that! He was a sheet metal worker, but sometimes his job called for additional duties. I believe those chemicals were what really killed him.

TOP ROCK GIRLY JOCK

The nightmare began while I was on a ski vacation in Aspen. This was so weird. My friend and I were sitting in a piano bar, relaxing after dinner. As we sipped our wines, I told her of this strange dream I'd had last night. I saw four footprints in the mud. Two of them were deeply set, and the other two were lighter. I had no idea that this could really mean anything, but it bothered me because of the fact that there were four footprints, and four of us in our family. My mom had always believed that dreams of mud were a premonition of sickness.

It bothered me so much that I just had to call home. Since Dad's condition seemed to be under control at that time, and since Mom had the fragile heart, I asked how she was feeling. She said she was fine. But something still bothered me. So then I asked how Dad was feeling.

"Oh, he's doing just great! He's been so sweet all week!"

Almost sounded like a second honeymoon, I thought. (Highly unusual behavior for my folks who seemed long past that stage.) Then I thought of how strangely Dad had acted when he and Mom had driven me to the train station.

We were waiting on the platform, but the train just wasn't coming. My dad was usually the impatient one, but this time he stood with Mom and me, shivering from head to toe. It was a cold February day and he had on his work shoes, with the steel toes! Of course, he was cold—*steel cold*. I finally realized the train must've been on a holiday schedule and we'd better hurry and drive downtown, if I was going to catch the AMTRAK.

When we got there, my dad wanted to carry my luggage to the gate for me. He almost insisted. He wanted so badly to help me. What? I thought this was really unusual—I usually beat him to the punch when it came to asking for things.

"No, Dad, stay with Mom. If I don't come back in fifteen minutes, that means I caught the train. So take care of Mom (she was driving) and help her watch the road."

The Wind Beneath My Wings

(My dad's favorite expression, whenever I drove away from home was, "Watch yourself!" as he usually rushed to wipe my front windshield before I pulled away.)

After I called to check on them that Wednesday, I felt relieved to hear everything was fine. And they did too. Dad had read about an avalanche in Aspen and they were worried about me being out there. But by now, we were in Vail. (Anyhow, most of our time was spent shopping and eating. We were hardly ever in danger—gotta be on the slopes for that—Hah!)

So, on Friday, our last vacation night, we decided to go to a fancy restaurant and splurge! I checked the tourist guide book, and found this really neat Victorian style restaurant that had great reviews. We finally decided to have dinner there, and as we talked with the waiter, he told us the restaurant's history, and how it had once been a funeral parlor. It was eerie hearing that and really bothered me.

When we got back to the hotel, I called home again. This time I heard Dad screaming in the background! Really *screaming!*

"Mom! What's wrong?"

"I don't know! Dad's in such pain!" she cried, nearly hysterical.

"Call the hospital, call the ambulance!" I told her.

"He won't let me! He knows they'll take him to the closest hospital, and he doesn't want to go anywhere but Hines."

(Hines was the Veteran's Administration Hospital where Dad had previously been treated.)

"Mom, you have to call the ambulance! If you can't, I can do it from here! Don't listen to Dad—he needs help!"

"No—I'll do it," my mom whispered as she cried, "but I'm so scared."

My mom—*scared?* My mom was *never* scared. What was happening to my folks while I was so far away!

And I had taken the train because I hate to fly (a fear of those secretly rehabbed third world parts, and sloppy maintenance). I started calling every airline to try and find a return flight so I could get home ASAP. My friend looked at me.

"You're going to cut short our vacation?" she said accusingly.

"My dad might be dying! I've got to get home! We were gonna leave tomorrow anyway, so it's only one day. You can take the train back, or I'll pay for your airline ticket if you want to fly back with me."

Never one to turn down a deal, she accepted the free-bee, and flew back with me. ("That's What Friends Are For?")

From the airport, I hopped a cab and went straight to the hospital. It was now Sunday afternoon. My dad, with an oxygen mask over his face, looked at me desperately to help him. But there was nothing I could do. We squeezed each other's hands, as I reminded him how he had taken the train from the Army Air Force base to see me when I was born. Now I had flown in just to see him. But I didn't know, at that moment, that this would be the day he would die.

Mom and Jerry were there at his side too, but they made us all leave. Dad died while we were in the waiting room, waiting for the next allowed visiting time.

My dad was laid out on February 24, 1987. This was exactly one year later—to the date—that I had been operated on for a ruptured appendix. I always wondered if he had bargained with God to spare my life and take him instead.

My ruptured appendix had been diagnosed as the flu, or a pregnancy, or the need for a colostomy. (Yes, the same hospital that my dad died in, and that my mom would later have a stroke in while hospitalized for observation.) The docs sent me for an ultrasound but couldn't find a baby. Over and over, I kept telling them that I wasn't even dating anyone—and that this had only ever happened once—in the *Bible. There is no baby, I screamed!* But they wouldn't listen. So when they said they wanted to operate, I asked why. For the flu? Or the baby?

"Exploratory," is what the resident said.

The Wind Beneath My Wings

"Uh-huh."

I said I'd think about it. Then after a couple days in the hospital, for observation (yeah, let's observe me suffering here), my heart became very erratic. It was "After Midnight." I rang for the nurse. She said,

"You're probably gonna die because you refused to go for the operation! We were just talking about you at the nurses desk."

"What? OK! I'll go! No one ever told me it was a matter of life or death," I said, "I'll go right now."

"Well, you can't go *now*; the doctor is home sleeping," she answered calmly. (How can he sleep while I might be dying, I wondered.) "We'll tell him in the morning."

(Would they do this on *Trapper John* or *Marcus Welby*?—or even *Dr. Kildare*?)

The next morning they operated. The doc said I was lucky. It seemed my appendix had already burst. (Yeah, I'm sure it had—I tried to tell them about that extreme pain five days ago.) They took a quart and a half of fluid out of me. He said my intestines were also almost ready to burst. But because they had become inflamed and enlarged, they blocked the peritonitis from spreading, which had settled in a pocket on the lower left side of my tummy. My mom was hysterical. She had never forgotten how her baby sister died from a ruptured appendix at the age of ten. It had shattered their whole family. Grandma had died just the year before, and when little Janka was dying, she begged her siblings to understand—that she just wanted to be with their mom in heaven—"what God has revealed to little ones."

The date of my operation was February 24, 1986, and I still find it very strange that my dad was waked *exactly* one year later to the day. The autopsy said he'd had a pulmonary embolism.

On the day of his funeral, Jerry and I went back with Mom to our home in Norridge. Mom came into the family room just as I was taking a thermometer out of my mouth. It read 106 degrees. I felt like I might be catching something, but this reading seemed a little ridiculous. I must have looked shocked because she looked concerned and asked,

"What? Is it high?"

"No, Mom," I assured her, "I don't think it's ready just yet," and stuck it back in my mouth.

When I took it out a few minutes later, it was 110 degrees! Uh-oh, I thought, I must be dead. Mom was still curious about my temperature—so I told her it malfunctioned and I had to start all over again. But this was a brand new digital thermometer. Grabbing the instructions, I looked to see if I'd done anything wrong. The only thing I noticed was the warning to not get it near an electromagnetic field. Like what, I thought—like maybe the TV? But that was way across the room. So what else could have created an electromagnetic field on the day of my dad's funeral? *Now* I'm sure—it was his spirit that was in the room that day. This has never happened since; the thermometer still works just fine.

About a week later, when I stopped to visit, Mom was in the family room and had just awakened from a nap. She seemed a bit disoriented.

"Oh, I thought Jerry came over. I was just taking a little nap and I woke up smelling cigarette smoke, and I thought Dad was home. But then I thought, no, Dad's gone. It must be Jerry."

(He was the only smoker in our family now.)

My brother and I both thought she was just half-dreaming and definitely mourning. We just said, "Really?" We were all mourning. None of us were thinking that clearly.

Even though I had already moved out, I often stayed over at our house in Norridge. One night both Mom and I slept in my old bedroom because it was an extremely cold night and that was the warmest room in the house. While the other rooms were barely comfortable, mine would be boiling.

The Wind Beneath My Wings

It had been about a month since Dad had died, and I was suffering from esophagitis. I woke up around 7 AM (unusual for me) feeling nauseous, and with a pressure in my chest. Mom slept soundly, as I got up and went to the kitchen for some Tagament. I quietly lay back down in bed so as not to wake her, and *Suddenly—there it was! I smelled cigarette smoke!* It was so strong; it was unmistakable! I didn't *think* I smelled it—I *knew* it. But I didn't *see* any smoke—I just *smelled* it—throughout my bedroom.

Well, I couldn't fall back to sleep until I knew where this was coming from. I thought that since Mom had camped out with me in my old room that night, that perhaps she grabbed Dad's pillows by mistake. Maybe Dad's pillows had the cigarette scent on them and maybe, when I lay my head down on the pillow, the scent wafted upward. Maybe that's where it came from. I turned my head face down into the pillows, inhaling as hard as I could, but it wasn't coming from there. Then I thought, since Dad and Jerry had started smoking in the basement ever since Mom's by-pass, that maybe when the furnace kicked on, the cigarette scent was forced up through the heat vents. I started sniffing around the vents. But the heat hadn't gone on and no air was coming out. In fact, the vents were shut because that room always got so hot. So then, I knew. When Jerry came over, I couldn't wait to tell him.

"Jer, do you remember when Mom said she smelled cigarette smoke that week after Dad died—"

He interrupted before I could finish.

"Oh! I gotta tell you! Last week when I came to see Mom, I went downstairs to light up a cigarette. I just sat down on the last step, where Dad and I used to smoke together. The ashtray was clean. I hadn't even lit my cigarette yet, when all of a sudden, *I smelled cigarette smoke!* It was so strong, all around me. But I didn't see it, I just smelled it!"

"Exactly!" I said, and then told him how it had happened to me.

Before you think we're all just a bunch of crazies, I have to tell you that after each of us experienced this, I was on a mission to find others who'd experienced the same things. And I found many. This is God's work. "Those who mourn shall be comforted." It was such a comfort for us to know that Dad had reached out to each one of us on three separate occasions. And we will always be so thankful to God for these special blessings.

Six months later my mom's new, blue Pontiac Phoenix was hit broadside after spinning out on an oil slick. Six days later, she had a severe stroke. They expected her to die, but I knew, that with prayer and faith in God's help, she'd live.

I was sitting on the left side of the hospital bed as the therapist worked on Mom. She said she'd never be able to move her right arm again. When she got through massaging Mom's arm, she laid it back down on the bed. My mom then picked up her arm and crossed it over her chest.

"Did you see that?!" The therapist's mouth was a huge gaping hole.

"I thought you said she couldn't do that," I reminded her.

"She *can't!*"

"But she *did!*" I said.

"Yeah, I know," she almost speechlessly agreed.

The next incident had to do with Mom's leg. Since I had been sleeping on a chair at her bedside, I watched for every little sign of recovery. I noticed that she moved her right leg—the side that the stroke affected. Excitedly, I ran to the nurse's station to tell the resident, who was busily writing reports. He was agitated that I was bothering him.

"She moved her right leg! She can move her leg!" I was so thrilled.

"That's just an involuntary movement," he calmly explained, thinking that, as a lay person, I couldn't tell the difference.

"No, *no!* This is different! Come see her!" I begged.

The Wind Beneath My Wings

Again, he tried to brush me off. I finally convinced him I wasn't going away until he came to see her.

"Oh, so you think if you ask her to raise her leg for me, that she can do it?" he taunted.

"Yes, *yes*! I *know* she can!"

So, just to get me out of his face, he followed me to her room.

"Mom," I calmly said, "lift up your right leg for the doctor!"

She did exactly as I asked. I never saw anyone so astonished (except for the therapist the other day), as the resident ran from the room to call three other doctors, who were all there in minutes, examining her. It was some time later that the head neurologist confided to me that, in fifteen years of practice, he'd never seen anyone survive with such severe brain damage, much less regain use of their limbs. He said she did have a highly developed Circle of Willis— perhaps that explained it medically. My explanation was the grace of God and the Blessed Virgin Mary who must've heard our prayers.

After six weeks of rehab, Mom came home. I took her home to live with me, and actually did not leave the house without her for nearly three years. We went everywhere together. When I needed to do grocery shopping, she'd wait in the car and nap 'til I got back. Jerry would often take over to give me some *away* time—but it was hard to be away because I was always worried about her. I had to learn to give her insulin shots, and she had to take 38 pills a day, all of which had to be perfectly timed and spaced. I had now switched hospitals and doctors, so her new doctor was now Dr. Robert Zimmanck at Lutheran General Hospital in Park Ridge, IL. I was relieved that she would finally be under expert, careful, care. We had speech therapy sessions and physical therapy; and by the end of the day, we both were exhausted.

Sometime during that period, I had a dream in which the Blessed Mother told me Mom would live only one more year. I remember crying in my sleep—please, *longer*. She lived two more years after that dream.

TOP ROCK GIRLY JOCK

When she died, I felt my life was over. She died in July. Her birthday was in November, so of course, I went to her gravesite and prayed for her on her special day. It was raining and cold. I prayed the rosary for her there and shivered through it all, hoping (subconsciously or consciously, I'm not sure which) that I'd catch pneumonia and die and be with her, just as her baby sister had done when their mom died.

I did catch pneumonia. (Don't try this at home.) It was no fun. And living alone made it torture! When I'd finally awake and make breakfast, I was wiped out for the rest of the day and could hardly find the strength to make lunch or dinner.

(This was soon after Jim Henson of *The Muppets* died of pneumonia, so it was a scary thing to have back then.) But Dr. Zimmanck made sure I had the right meds to kick it. And my brother, Jerry, was there to help whenever I needed him. As I started to feel better, I was still too weak to work and could barely even sit up for five hours to do a job. But I had mobile DJ commitments. So Jer went with me, carried and set up the equipment, and ran the show—while I struggled to sit up, introduce the music, and smile through it all. The pneumonia finally left me.

FOURTEEN

Alone Again, Naturally

Again, I was at a crossroads in my life. I wanted to tell my mom, "my heart is broken," as I had always done before—but she was gone. Hanging around the empty house was now just too sad. I'd turn to look for her, but she wasn't there. So, I went out to eat, took long walks in forest preserves, and prayed a lot.

Little by little, God sent me all sorts of wonderful spiritual experiences to help me heal. They were so amazing that I talked with a priest about them and he suggested I write them down so as to never forget. They were gifts of the Holy Spirit, he said. Well, one thing I knew for sure—they were *not* of this world. And that is the other book I am writing. Books can help others gain insight, I believe. And if my experiences can help others who are grieving, why not share them.

But I wondered about what to do with the rest of my life. Surely God wants us to be fruitful and use the gifts He's given us. There's something about that in the *Bible*. But what should I do? Go back to radio? I was too sad to try and make other people happy. What about art? That was another of my gifts.

So I decided to take classes and pray, and let God lead me. I studied doll sculpting. Even in high school, I had found sculpting easy and fun. We once had to sculpt an animal out of clay. Mine was an elephant, and looked pretty good! And since I've always loved dolls, I thought this might be a good diversion for me.

While most students used other doll artists molds to cast in porcelain, I wanted to start from scratch—to take a chunk of clay, sculpt the doll, cast the mold in plaster, pour the porcelain, have it fired, and later think about painting and finishing the doll. It was a healing time for me, and I met many nice ladies as *into it* as I was. My first doll was a little weird looking. But the second was so adorable that the owner of the doll school asked if she could make a doll from my mold. That was such a compliment! I never finished the dolls. I just loved sculpting them. As far as I was concerned, the doll was done when the clay sculpture was finished! Ready to bake. Hah!

Doll Sculpting at Angelic Creations—Naperville, IL

During this same healing time, I started studying art again. At the American Academy of Art, I studied watercolor with David Becker who was a protégé of Irv Shapiro. Great talents! I wanted to learn more about using color and creating fine art. Soon, that led to studies at the Long Grove Art Gallery, where I studied with Romel de la Torre and focused on portraits in pastel and oil. I won an award for a watercolor portrait, made some T-shirts (a failed enterprise, mostly because I never marketed them), and just experimented with different art forms to see what would click—what would make me feel the most fulfilled.

Finally, things started to take some direction. Carol and Joel Warren, who ran the Waterfront Gallery at The Abbey Resort in Lake Geneva, Wisconsin, liked my work and agreed to display my portraits. Carol Warren is a highly sought after photographer in the Lake Geneva area and often photographed the subjects I would later paint. Working from good photos is very important. Most clients don't want the artist's interpretation; they want a particular expression or view, that portrays their loved one as *they* want them remembered. Everyone sees everyone else differently. So before I paint a portrait, I am sure to let the client choose the smile or expression that is most meaningful to them.

Commissions started flowing in. I became a successful portrait artist (with many thanks to Carol and Joel Warren) and until this day continue this passion as time allows.

As part of the American Society of Portrait Artists (ASOPA), some of my works are displayed on *The Stroke of Genius* site, *www.portraitartist.com/szerszen*. I also maintain a local site, *www.portraitartchicago.com*.

Bernie Tafoya of WBBM "Newsradio 78" in Chicago, did a feature story on my portraits, as did Kevin Davis of *Crain's Chicago Business*. Kimbriell Granderson of *The Daily Herald* wrote a full-page for Chicago's northwest suburban section.

TOP ROCK GIRLY JOCK

George San Jose, President and COO, The San Jose Group commissioned an oil portrait of his wife, Jennifer

Alone Again, Naturally

Daily Herald — SUNDAY, OCTOBER 19, 2003

Neighbor

Adoration, inspiration

The works of Connie Szerszen, who painted an image of Pope John Paul II that she treasures, can be seen around the suburbs.

Priceless painting means more than money to local artist

BY KIMBERLI GRANDERSON

Palatine Township artist Connie Szerszen was commissioned to create this portrait of the Rev. Pat Brennan by his parish, Holy Family Church in Inverness.

Szerszen chose watercolor to depict various aspects of Barrington, including images of the Catlow Theater and the Octagon House on Main Street.

This portrait of a mother and daughter was painted in oil.

Palatine Township artist Connie Szerszen captures the image of twins in one of her portraits.

297

TOP ROCK GIRLY JOCK

St. Luke's Medical Center in Milwaukee, Wisconsin, has the largest display of my portraits of donors in their main lobby, and in The Karen Yontz Women's Cardiac Awareness Center where Dr. Nancy Snyderman, of ABC-TV's *Good Morning America*, was the honored guest at the grand opening/dedication ceremony.

Above and Right—
St. Luke's Medical Center, Milwaukee, WI

Right—
Dr. Nancy Snyderman of ABC's *Good Morning America* attended the dedication of the Karen Yontz Women's Cardiac Awareness Center, Milwaukee, WI

Alone Again, Naturally

Above—Kimberly Brown Moore—Oconomowoc Hospital, WI

Right—
In Chicagoland—
One of the founders of
the Inverness Golf Club,
Illinois

The Village of Roselle, IL—6-Foot Oil Hangs in the Village Hall

Alone Again, Naturally

Holy Family Catholic Community, Inverness, IL

Fr. Med Laz, Pastor   Fr. Pat Brennan, Pastor

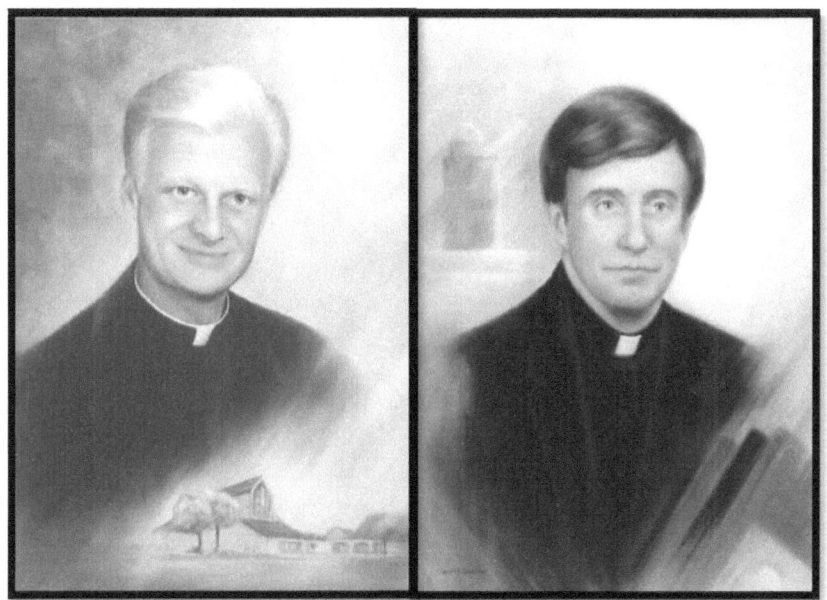

St. Mary's, Huntley, IL— Fr. Bob Garrity, Pastor

TOP ROCK GIRLY JOCK

My oil portrait of the foundress received a blessing
St. Mary of Nazareth Hospital, Chicago

Clients also include USG and numerous corporate
as well as private commissions

Marta—Pastel

Siblings—Pastel

Alone Again, Naturally

Above—Michael & Pal
Oil

Right—Sister & Brother
(Oil painting from family
black & white photo
when they sat on steps
of their childhood home)

There is something ethereal about doing portraits. Some of the people I've painted have already died. It's like I can almost *feel* how they'd like me to paint them, to look their best while still being truthful to their image. It's a gift. Sometimes I'll reach for a color, not even thinking about it. It's as if I'm being guided to use the right colors in the right places to create the best likeness. I've heard other artists say the same thing. And so I continue to keep this gift in my life. Because I believe that if you do not use what is given to you, it could be lost. And gifts from God should never be lost. The stardust within us was meant to be shared with the world.

TOP ROCK GIRLY JOCK

Left—
Pastel—
Won award in
THE
ARTIST'S
MAGAZINE

*Above & Right—*Pastels
*Below—*Watercolor

(View art in full color—www.PortraitArtChicago.com)

FIFTEEN

Ring My Bell

In September of 2002, I had just finished a painting—a commemorative oil for a family who had lost a child to cancer and ran a charitable fund-raising event in her honor. The Corinne Kreissl Memorial Foundation held an annual road rally around Lake Geneva, Wisconsin. The portrait was to be unveiled at the dinner dance at the historical Riviera Ballroom on the lake, where I'd heard Sinatra had once performed.

It was late in the day and I was just ready to run out the door, when the phone rang.

"Hi—this is Jim Smith—Program Director at WJMK. Is this Connie Szerszen?"

WJMK was the hot Chicago oldies station. (Uh-oh—I can hear this coming. I cringed.)

"I was wondering if you had ever thought of returning to radio."

I almost dropped the phone! Was this really happening! And did I even *want* it to happen? Earlier that year, around springtime, I'd met a girl at a church social function who had once worked for WJMK. We talked about radio and all the people we knew in the business and she suggested I call them to see if they had any openings. I thought back to many years ago, when Robert Feder, TV/radio columnist for the *Chicago Sun-Times*, had suggested the same thing to me.

"You'd be perfect there, Connie—give them a call!"

Robert Feder is the "crème de la crème" of TV/radio columnists, and coming from him, this was no casual comment. His words gripped me and hung on for over fifteen years. But I never did anything about it.

Sometimes I thought back to those great days in radio and felt as if I had thrown away something dear to my heart. Then I remembered the crushing responsibility to perform—to try and please your boss, while you were also trying to please the public in the best way you knew—and oftentimes you couldn't please both.

Many in management were once disc jockeys themselves. And there were two distinct groups—those who *chose* to abandon the performance side of radio to enter the slightly more stable management end of the business. These were the ones who only did air shifts to fully acquaint themselves with the business of radio. But there were also those who were not successful as disc jockeys, and *defaulted* into management. And if they had not been successful DJs themselves, was it really a good idea for me to take direction from them? To perform as they thought I should? I didn't want to end up in management; I wanted to entertain. So you always had to take a good look at your leader.

After many years in the business, I have come to see the difference. A truly gifted manager or program director allows the air personality to be true to their own individuality. They guide you only in matters of format and execution, but rarely your *humanity,* your *persona.* And when you have great guidance, you can grow to be an even better disc jockey than you were before. One doesn't always *hear* themselves as others do; and we're never that objective about ourselves. So great leadership can be invaluable!

But the old program director horror stories started replaying in my mind.

"Why did you say that?" one had asked, as we listened to one of my air-checks.

"I thought it was funny," I had answered in self-defense.

"Women can't be funny," he instructed.

"Oh, you mean, like Lucille Ball?" I'd snapped back.

(*Leave me alone!* My mind screamed out inside!) After several months of grueling critiques, he finally said (although befuddled),

"I don't exactly know what it is you're doing, but keep doing it—the ratings are up."

I had sighed with relief. But somehow I had known that all along. It's an instinct. A woman knows when something is working or not—just like she knows when a guy's cheating on her.

Again, I remembered Ricky Nelson's advice—"You can't please everyone, so you got to please yourself." And by pleasing yourself, you usually *are* pleasing someone else. I've always believed that each one of us has inclinations similar to many others. If you think something is funny or interesting, then "Chances Are" a good portion of the listening audience is thinking that too. Even though no two of us are exactly alike, we all do share the same humanity.

SIXTEEN

Heaven Knows

And so I said to Jim Smith, "Yes, I have often thought of returning to radio—but when I thought of the crazy hours, the low pay, and the instability of the business, I thought—*WHY*?"

So, laughingly, we continued to talk and he asked if I'd meet him for lunch where we could discuss the situation. The deal was not that great. Well, scale was only $220 per show, but there would be personal appearances that paid $500. But since it was an AFTRA union station, and I was already vested from previous radio work, my hours would add credits to my pension. Plus, I might even qualify for health insurance, which had been getting expensive in my self-employed state.

Although, I had no idea if I would really get *into it* again—that *fire in the belly* that former WCFL morning DJ, Bob Dearborn, once pointed out. Of course, I loved music. Music had pretty much been a part of my work life in the mobile DJ business, even when I wasn't on the air. In fact, wedding guests would often come up to me and ask where they'd heard my voice before—sometimes asking if I were that DJ they used to hear on WIND. I was always amazed at the way they picked up on this, because I barely talked when DJ'g weddings, other than introducing the bride and groom, and announcing the bouquet and garter toss.

So when Jim extended this invitation to come out of *radio retirement*, as he called it, I sort of said "Ye-es." (Even though I wasn't sure I really meant it.) It wasn't as quick a *"Sure"* as in my early days, that's for sure!

I called my brother Jerry. There are only the two of us left now. When I would've run to call Mom, I now called Jerry. And Jerry's great with advice. He can look at my confusion, and give me a non-emotional solution. Besides that, he's also very funny and sees the humor in things way before I do. But this time, he sounded so serious when he said,

"I think it's what God wants you to do."

That made me think. I thought about how I got into this line of work in the first place—through people pushing me and calling me. When I took my first radio job at WCFL as talent coordinator, which paid less money than I had been earning, it was my high-school friend, Sharon, who encouraged me to take the job.

"It'll be such fun—you'll get to meet all the disc jockeys. Take it!"

Then, after I took the job at WCFL, it was Penny Lane who had called the station for info, and soon was coaxing me to come in and audition for WSDM. (I hadn't even ever met her.)

It was WIND morning DJ, Ron Britain, who told me to keep trying at WIND and even put in a good word for me to management.

Another former co-worker-DJ had suggested I apply at WJJD. It was DJ Tony Russell who lured me to WUSN (US-99).

Now, here it was so many years later, after walking away from radio, Program Director, Jim Smith, was inviting me back. I felt a bit like a *cicada*—resurfacing after seventeen years.

So maybe Jerry was right. Maybe this was what God wanted me to do. I was making a living with the mobile DJ gigs on week-ends—

painting portraits during the week—and doing some real estate management. Was there really any room for more work? I was so overloaded already and, after all these years, hadn't even unpacked Mom and Dad's stuff that was moved from our house in Norridge.

Little did I know, when I said *"Yes"* to Jim, with his caution for me to not say a word to anyone, that it would be reported in Robert Feder's TV/Radio column in the *Chicago Sun-Times* just a couple of days later. I was thrilled to read what he wrote that October 9, 2002—

Dialing: 'Magic' brings back Connie Szerszen

Credit Jim Smith, program director of oldies WJMK-FM (104.3), with luring another legendary Chicago radio veteran back on the air. Connie Szerszen, who was a bonafide star of WIND AM (560) in the 1970s (and also was known as "Denpal Dawn" on the old WSDM), will sign on at "Magic 104.3" later this month as a part-time and fill-in personality. She'll join a stellar lineup that includes such greats as Dick Biondi, John Landecker, Greg Brown, Fred Winston, and Bob Dearborn. "I think it's important not only to give our audience the favorite songs that they grew up with, but also the radio names they remember." Smith said.

#

TOP ROCK GIRLY JOCK

MEDIA MIX

Wednesday, October 9, 2002

Halloween radio treat: 'Twilight Zone' to debut

With or without a Chicago radio outlet, a locally produced radio drama series based on "The Twilight Zone" is set to debut in national syndication on Halloween.

About 100 radio stations are expected to be onboard in time for the launch of the adaptation of Rod Serling's classic science-fiction series. The show also will air worldwide via the American Forces Radio and Television Service.

Hosted by Stacy Keach and featuring a distinguished lineup of guest stars, each hourlong drama will be adapted from Serling's original 150 television scripts.

With Serling as host, producer and, in many cases, writer, "The Twilight Zone" originally aired on CBS from 1959 to 1965. Serling's widow, Carol Serling, praised the radio adaptations, calling them "truly astounding."

Executive producer of the radio series is Carl Amari, chairman of northwest suburban Schaumburg-based Falcon Pictures Group and producer of the syndicated old-time radio series "When Radio Was." The entire production will be based in Chicago, under the supervision of veteran producer and sound engineer Roger Wolski.

Amari has been in talks about airing the series with two Chicago stations—WBBM-AM (780) and WLS-AM (890)—but no deal has been finalized. WBBM already airs "When Radio Was" at midnight Monday through Friday.

Dialing: 'Magic' brings back Connie Szerszen

■ Credit **Jim Smith**, program director of oldies WJMK-FM (104.3), with luring another legendary Chicago radio veteran back on the air. **Connie Szerszen**, who was a bona fide star of WIND-AM (560) in the 1970s (and also was known as "Denpal Dawn" on the old WSDM), will sign on at "Magic 104.3" later this month as a part-time and fill-in personality.

She'll join a stellar lineup that includes such greats as **Dick Biondi, John Landecker, Greg Brown, Fred Winston** and **Bob Dearborn**. "I think it's important not only to give our audience the favorite songs that they grew up with, but also the radio names they remember," Smith said.

And then there was my longtime listener, and by now, good friend, Mark Wilows. Mark had been a fan of the shows at WIND, and had toured the station back in the '70s. He talked of his dreams of one day becoming a journalist—(which he has successfully done).

Mark once invited me to the Radio Hall of Fame at the Museum of Broadcast Communications ceremony at the Chicago Cultural Center where they were honoring "The Men Who Made Radio." We got to meet the legendary Paul Harvey—whose "Rest of the Story" I always loved!

Right—Paul Harvey and me—1992

Many years after, I accidentally bumped into Mark, while dropping off a resume at Fox-TV's Channel 32. The station had been looking for a personality for the new evening show. He got the job instead of me and one day invited me to sit in. The guests that day were comedienne Phyllis Diller (a *Moonchild* like me), and the legendary DJ Wolfman Jack! It was exciting to meet such celebrities!

Phyllis was gracious and funny. And the Wolfman was as sweet as could be in his gravelly, low-pitched voice. When his bit on the air was over, he came and sat right behind me in the small studio as we watched the rest of the show.

Mark currently reports on soap stars on *www.Soapdom.com*, but at the time I was headed back to radio, he was a correspondent for the *Indiana Times*; and on Nov. 30, 2002, he spread the news in Indiana!

Heaven Knows

When the papers hit the stands, some friends got extremely upset.

"Why *didn't* you *tell* me?!"

"Well, I was told not to say a word to anyone," I explained.

"Well, I'm not just *anyone!*"

And I could see this coming around all over again. The same folks who never kept me updated on *their* jobs or life events suddenly expected all that from me; while I never even thought they'd care. And just as before, some who were close to me would now get green-eyed over my new *success*, as they saw it, and would no longer want to have much to do with me. Others who never wanted to have much to do with me would start crawling out of the woodwork. And I, myself, still didn't even know if I was even really going to go through with it. For the moment, I was just going through the motions.

So Jim Smith asked me to start listening to the station to get a feel for what they were doing. It struck me funny in a way—because for my first big radio job at WIND, I had to listen and listen. Although I loved music, I hadn't paid that much attention to some of the oldies they were playing (except for Elvis!)—and had to learn all about the other artists. Now, here it was, thirty years later, and I was doing it again, but this time I remembered them from the '70s! ("Seems to me, I've heard that song before.")

Next, he asked me to come in for training! Ah, the technical nightmare begins. In the late '60s, my radio days had begun with huge reels of tape and a semi-automated format; then on to an engineer-run board, where all I did was cue and talk. Later, I had to run the board myself again, this time with cartridges that looked sort of like 8-tracks, but with only one song on each. We used to stack them into bunches of twenty or thirty and carry them into the studio from the rack room. I once saw WIND's "Larry the Legend" stack so many, the topmost one under his chin and as far down as his hands could reach—and then he dropped them all! It was hysterical (in a mean-spirited sort of way). But I heard such colorful language—it was like a verbal Picasso—in his "blue period!"

During my years away from radio, I had heard the jocks were no longer playing cartridges. They played CD's. Easier to stack, I thought. But by the time I was called back to the airwaves, the CD era was about over. I had missed an entire era in radio. Imagine that!

And so, my training days were scheduled. Since I had known Dick Biondi back when I was the talent coordinator/secretary at WCFL, where he was the overnight jock, Jim had planned for Dick to show me the board. I was in Jim's office, going over some paperwork, when Biondi popped in.

"What are *you* doing here?" he looked at me quizzically.

"Good question!" I answered.

Dick seemed quite surprised to see me at the station. I thought for a split second that maybe *he* had referred me to Jim, but when I asked Jim Smith how he found me, he said,

"The internet—isn't that where we find everything!"

Jim has a great sense of humor!

Long ago, I briefly ran into Biondi at a restaurant in Northbrook; he had just moved back to Chicago, after years in one of the Carolinas. A few days later, he had called to ask if he could store some of his albums in my basement. I had to turn him down, since I barely had room for my own.

The last time I saw Dick was a month earlier at a remote broadcast at Holy Family Catholic Community's summerfest. I had just finished a portrait of Fr. Pat Brennan, the pastor. I'd heard that WJMK was one of Father Pat's favorite stations, and thought it'd be great if Dick could present the portrait to Fr. Pat! So I went up to him while he was broadcasting on the church grounds.

"Hi Dick! Remember me?—your secretary from WCFL!"

Dick introduced me to the radio staff that was there with him, along with some of his regular troupe. Ronnie Rice of the New Colony Six (and now a great solo act) was there, and several other community dignitaries. Dick said if there was time, he'd put me on the air to talk about the portrait. But it seemed there was no time. So he presented Fr. Pat with the portrait, and mentioned my name, telling the listeners how I used to be his secretary and now had become a popular Midwest portrait artist. (I guess he never knew I had also been the "Top Rock Girly Jock." I think he was still working out of town during that period. Anyway, at the time it really didn't matter, because that day I was a portrait artist, not a DJ.)

So, in October of 2002, I had my first training day at WJMK. The studio was beautiful. Some jocks have said the "most beautiful studio they'd ever worked in!" A corner room with L-shaped wall to wall windows. You could see down along Lake Street to Michigan Avenue. You could look out the other window and see Navy Pier and the gigantic ferris wheel that is one of Chicago's fave tourist attractions. It was just off "The Magnificent Mile" in the new "Prudential Plaza Two" building on the ninth floor.

Then it hit me—that a dream I'd been having lately—was of *this place!* There were the same gray, glassed doors; the same atmosphere—where I would turn around and see people I knew from my radio past. I'd be in a studio, broadcasting, and then wandering the halls as in the regular confusion of dreams. What did that mean? (Too much chili the night before?) *But this was the same studio that I had seen in those dreams!*

Biondi was on the air. I took one long look at the control board in front of him, the three computers beyond that, with keyboards on the left and right, the phone, the tape decks, CD decks. It was like the console of a jet airplane, I thought. My mind was made up immediately. There was *no way* I was ever gonna do this. First of all, I couldn't even read the titles on the computers, they were so far away. And the board—with all those sliders, red lights, white lights, yellow lights. (Where was *"Green for Go, Red for Stop"?*)

But I was here. Jim Smith had asked me to be a part of their station. The least I could do was try. I thought of how General

Manager, Mike Fowler, said that Jim Smith was jumping up and down when I agreed to work for them. I didn't want to let anyone down. Biondi started showing me the controls. He told me I only had to be concerned with a part of this set-up—not all of it. That was comforting, but I still wasn't sure I was going to do this.

Jim scheduled me to come and sit in with each of the DJs so I could gain some insight on their different techniques. There was quite an impressive line-up of jocks. John "Records" Landecker was the morning guy at that time. He had been my competition in the 6-10 PM slot at WLS in the '70s while I was at WIND. Greg Brown was the mid-day guy and he'd had spectacular ratings in the market for years as well. The week-end staff included such heavyweights as Bob Dearborn and Fred Winston—both of whom had been morning men at the AM powerhouses, WCFL and WLS. Bob Dearborn oozed creativity and was so helpful and encouraging. I felt at home again.

It was a little strange to see all these guys who used to have black hair, now with white hair (is this what radio did to them?) Hah!—but as I caught my reflection in the window, I noticed how well I fit in—my slim body had thrown a few extra curves of its own during my radio retirement—and who knew what was really underneath all that Clairol (does she or doesn't she?) Secretly, I had to laugh! Yeah! We were perfect for the *oldies* station. Fred laughed too, "Who else would want us?" he'd say. I really started enjoying the company of radio folks again. They are definitely an interesting breed. Almost like circus performers in a way. They could make me laugh in ways I had forgotten. I loved being back in this environment, surrounded by folks who shared one of my passions.

By November of that year, for my first on-air stint, Jim asked me to co-host a show with the Sunday evening jock, Jeff Laird. This was momentous! Jeff introduced me as a voice *"from the past"*—and then it was my turn to talk.

I said, "Hi! Nice to be here," or "Something Stupid" like that. (I think I might only be able to remember my exact words under anesthesia.) A friend ran a tape of that debut show, so I could play it later and cringe. (I never listened to it.)

My own first show at WJMK followed soon after. It was similar to my very first show at WIND, when the assistant program director encouraged me to say more than just my name and the call letters. And speaking of assistant program directors, Bob Lawson (who was very funny and created great promos for the station) had been a teeny-bopper listening to my shows at WIND; and he was now the assistant P.D. at WJMK, and I'd be taking some direction from him!

(*Hmmmm*—hope he hadn't learned radio by listening to me back then—Hah!—everyone assumes what you're doing is correct—because you're on the radio—kinda like reading something in print—or on the internet—so it *must be true*—yeah, right. But I had a *lot* of creative freedom at WIND—so I got to do things most stations would squelch today.)

I remember the agony the night before my first show. I sniffed my lavender-stuffed teddy bear to help me calm down. I just couldn't sleep. Why was I even doing this? It would just be the same thing all over again—weird hours—low pay, but high expectations from management—and eventually a format change or re-grouping of staff that would just leave you out of a job overnight. And some of that happened real soon.

Within six months, Infinity Radio brought in a new general manager, Dave Robbins; and a new program director, Charley Lake. Some jocks were let go and new ones put in their place. Paul Perry was the new morning man, charmingly entertaining (also a *Moonchild*). Greg Brown, was kept on mid-days and was a hit with his Brown Bag Lunch all-request hour. Chicago icon, Fred Winston, became the new afternoon man and had me laughing out loud—whether I heard him on the air, or just talked to him in person!

I remember when I first started and had to follow Fred on the air. I'd be driving in to the studio, listening to the station, and Fred would just be hilarious! His humor was infectious. When I got to the station,

TOP ROCK GIRLY JOCK

I'd stop in Jim Smith's office and say,
"You expect *me* to follow *him*?"

His was a hard act to follow! I have come to know Fred and am still in awe of his talent, quick wit and humor, along with his dedication. He's also a gifted photographer! And since I would usually pack my Sony digital, he was always ready with great advice. Besides that, he's just an all around nice guy. Everybody likes him and he speaks kindly of everyone. That's hard to find in a land of 1,000 egos.

Dick Biondi did the evening shift. The week-ends rotated with part-timers, such as myself, Ken Cocker (whom I had worked with at WUSN, US-99), John Calhoun, and our other girly jock, Lisa Greene.

So, as sorry as we were to have the old management leave, we crossed our fingers and held our breath. When the new team came to town, we all wondered who would stay—who would go.

Dave Robbins was chosen by Infinity to head WJMK because of his terrific accomplishments for the Infinity Group. Besides WJMK, he also ran WBBM-FM, WUSN-FM, and WCKG-FM. Dave was a sincere, hard-working guy, who was very encouraging to the staff. Not only were we all relieved that we'd be staying on board, but we were happy to be working with someone who was also a nice guy.

And Charley Lake, who became the new program director, had an incredible history with Infinity as well. He'd also worked with major music companies, and rock stars all over the country (*and had even met Paul McCartney!*) He, too, was very supportive of all the jocks, and some veteran jocks said they liked him best of all the program directors they'd ever worked for.

This is what drives you to do your very best—when everyone works together—to try and provide the best entertainment possible! It's a rare blessing to work for management that's at the top of their game and nice guys too! (Sometimes, they can be either one or the other.)

Heaven Knows

There was a wonderful team spirit at WJMK. Dave and Charley kept things fresh and exciting for the listening audience. We played oldies—the oldies had become *magic*—*"Magic 104.3"*—and now we played the *"Best of the '60s and '70s."* I loved being back in the radio game.

Did I make tons of money? No. In fact, it was a laughable incident at the last Infinity Radio meeting, when all of the CBS-owned stations in Chicago convened for a recap of our progress. I was saying hello to the highly successful, highly-paid, radio team of one of our stations, WBBM-FM (the most listened-to radio station between New York and L.A.)—Eddie and JoBo. Eddie is the son of Harry Volkman, the legendary Chicago weatherman. I was telling Eddie how sweet it was of his dad to treat us, when a friend and I ran into him at a malt shop, and how his dad had told me long ago that Eddie was DJ'g out of town, honing his craft, hoping to someday make it to Chicago.

Suddenly, a young guy rushed up, and interrupted us.

"Excuse me, but I just have to say hello to Connie Szerszen!"

He reached out to shake my hand.

I said, rather awkwardly, "And—who are you?"

Bernie Tafoya! My former engineer, way back from the '70s, at WIND! He'd gone on to become an award-winning journalist with our news station, WBBM-AM.

After a few words, I started to leave, when JoBo, who had overheard my name, reached for my hand.

"What a pleasure it is to meet you!" he said.

What?—I thought—a pleasure to meet *me*, who after all these years is still working for scale, while I read that he was earning over a million bucks a year? (What's wrong with this picture?) But he was so sweet.

I smiled and just said, "Thank you."

TOP ROCK GIRLY JOCK

So not everyone finds their fortune in radio. But radio is truly an art form—a much more immediate art form than painting portraits. And it's that immediacy that I love about radio—the thrill of the moment—when the listener doesn't know what you're gonna say next—and oftentimes, neither do you. Such fun!

# SEVENTEEN

Ball of Confusion

But while you may enjoy this art form, you also put up with a lot. Many jocks are never paid very much. The big dollars usually go to the morning or afternoon *man*, or someone lucky enough to become syndicated and played in many markets. I never did know much about the *business* end of this business. I've never had an agent. When a contract was offered me, I usually just accepted it on their terms—a pushover for the company, I know. So, primarily, you do this job for your own fulfillment rather than livelihood, and are often hassled along the way.

They're still in corners of my mind, from years in radio—like other jocks' insecurities. One legendary jock angrily accused me; he came up to my face, inches from my nose, and demanded I look straight into his eyes, and, as his eyes bored into mine, he quizzed me.

"Now, tell me the truth—are you back-stabbing me? My fans are telling me how much they like you on the air. You're after my job, aren't you?"

He had me in tears as I explained I just wanted to do my best work—*and* keep *my* job. This DJ had also ordered me off the air at remote broadcasts, and pulled me away from listeners when he noticed them surrounding me. They asked why he was so mean to me, shouting at me; I made excuses for him, but deep down I worried he might do something to make me lose my job. Some listeners thought he was such a sweetheart; but not to me, nor to other DJs whom he feared were better than him. Several jocks knew of his horror stories (which even included a knife-wielding incident). He had no radio friends at all—he was only nice to those who could do something for him. A DJ like this is very rare, and possibly even sick; so while it's frightening, you have to also feel sorry for such an animal.

Then, there's the hate mail. Of course, you get many great fan letters, but there are also *hate-mail* campaigns. This is when a co-worker is afraid that you're doing too well; so with the help of friends, letters are written to the station, tearing you down. Some jocks also do this in reverse, asking you to write to management for them, saying how great they'd be in a better time slot (with more money). *I've* even written letters for a legendary jock after being badgered enough, even tho I didn't agree, but to get him off my back.

All this is so silly because management isn't that easily fooled. Anyone on the radio can create a great mail-in campaign—but it doesn't truly depict who is listening. A disc jockey's performance should be analyzed by audience volume or time spent listening—not by how many letters they can get friends to send in. In the end, the ratings tell the true story of popularity—of success or failure.

Once while I was "live" on the air, another DJ ran into the studio, and yelled at me for playing a *drop-in*, since we were not allowed to do that! (This usually only happens with less experienced DJs.)

Surprised, I said I hadn't heard. And the jock went on to tell me how the program director specifically said that part-timers were not allowed to do drop-ins. (A *drop-in* is a pre-recorded sound-effect or voice track used to punch a line you're doing, or interact with your comment.) I didn't use them often, because I never liked to do anything very often, as it can become trite or predictable, which I think lessens the entertainment value for the listener. But at that moment, I was being accused and I could see a big confrontation headed to the

Ball of Confusion

P.D.'s office. Time for a little psychology, here, I thought—even though, I'd rather have kept my focus on my show. Thinking that the P.D. had told *that* DJ not to use drop-ins, but had not said that to *me*, might cause a problem for him, so I naively begged—to please not tell that I did that, or I'd get in trouble. The jock looked at me rather dumbfounded and left the studio. Mission accomplished.

I have never confronted, accused, nor threatened another DJ. Most jocks don't; most are fun, creative folks. When it happened to me, I found it all so hard to deal with. Disc jockeys should answer to management—not other DJs. But it seemed radio had gotten more cut-throat than I remembered.

Infinity did try to instill good work ethics regarding *hanky-panky*, though. In the old days, it could get a little awkward, when some *available* co-workers made moves. Now I truly *did* love everyone I worked with—I just couldn't take them all home with me.

And the other thing that goes on in radio probably goes on everywhere. Secrets.

"Ssssshhhhh, don't tell. She's only a fan, and my wife is very jealous." (My next book—*just kidding*—put down that knife.) (I don't squeal—after all, this is Chicago—having air let out of my tires by a real estate mogul once, was enough.)

But sometimes secrecy even applied to me—Hah!

"Let's meet after my show—" the other DJ suggested.

"That'll work," I said, "I'll pick you up in my little white Triumph Spitfire."

That day, we were two Chicago DJs *parked* on the top level of a downtown garage—"Paradise By the Dashboard Lights!" (It was just a harmless, but wild and crazy, rendezvous—I must've played too many love songs that day.)

The other DJ burden is that, no matter how great *your* work is, if you're a DJ at a music station, listeners have to like the music first. However, if the ratings don't look good, the DJ usually gets the blame. (Even though, in an hour of program time, most of the show is music, the second big chunk is made of up commercials, promos and jingles, and the smallest segment is the DJ.) Still, the DJ is very instrumental in presenting this package. So if the ratings slide, you have to be prepared to hear things like—

"Why *did* you say that?"—"Why *didn't* you say that!"

"Women can't be funny!"

"Laugh like I laugh—don't giggle!"

"More energy!"—"Less energy"—"More conversational!"

"Talk faster!"—"Slower!"

"Inside, Outside, Upside Down." It can all get to be a little confusing. I've heard more than one veteran jock say—"just say *Yeah* to the program director, and then keep doing whatever you were doing."

You may also finally hear, "You're doing great!" And, although you're somewhat relieved after all those directives in memos and critiques, you're not exactly sure what it is you're doing now that's so great. But jocks have to realize that it is management's responsibility to make things work, and if it worked before, but not now, they've got to find the reason. And, sometimes, it might just be the jock's fault.

So, as a DJ, you have to learn to brace up. Let the insecure jocks confront and threaten you. Many jocks and entertainers are insecure, so nothing new about that. Cream always rises to the top, they say. Ignore bad management. In the long run, you'll find that you last longer than they do. But you want to always try and do your best work, because you owe it to the listeners who have chosen your show above all the others on the dial. And you also owe it to your bosses who have entrusted you with a part of their livelihood. If you don't do well, they don't do well. After all, they hired you and are counting on you to help pull ratings with your end of the job.

Sometimes you have to struggle with the mechanics of it all. When I came out of *radio retirement*, a lot of things were not second nature. I remember starting my show one night; I opened the mic and hit the song. The song started to play (I could see it on the computer)

Ball of Confusion

but I didn't *hear* anything! I panicked. (I do that a lot.) I knew that if the song was playing, I should be talking, because there are only so many seconds before the vocal starts. So I did my bit. I had no idea how I was doing on this intro, because I couldn't hear a thing. After I shut the mic, I could hear the song just fine. I was ready to run out to tell an engineer that something was broken—when I realized I hadn't put on my headphones. *Duhhh.* (Hey, but my lipstick was on just perfect.)

Once, in the middle of a song intro, I was so *into it*, that, when I got off the stool, I stepped right onto the cord of my headphones, which yanked them off my head and almost onto the control board. Had they landed there, listeners might have heard a cacophony of sound, with all those buttons triggering *all* the songs at the same time.

Then there was the EAS test (Emergency Alert System) required by the FCC. Can't fool around with this. In the middle of a stop set, as commercials were running, I noticed there were only minutes before an EAS test was scheduled. Having done this just once in two years, I panicked. I searched for the memo on the wall—it was gone. Racking my brain, I tried to remember which buttons to push, and the password to activate the test. I realized I had to *wing it*, but as I looked to find those *magic* buttons, I saw a gaping hole where the cart machine used to be. It was totally gone! Maybe it had been moved—I bent down, looked under the control board, and all around, but saw nothing. I thought it must be out for repairs. No cart machine—no sound effect; and now, with only seconds left, no time to call for answers. So I did it—*my way.* On the computer, I hit the recorded *Open* message; waited a bit—and played the *Close.* Sounded good to me, except for that silence in between, where the tone used to be.

Later, I asked some friends if they happened to hear it. The wife said, "Yeah, but wasn't there supposed to be some kind of tone there?—my husband said, 'It was so annoying, they probably found another way to do it.'" Ahhh—you can fool some of the people some of the time. How's that go?

TOP ROCK GIRLY JOCK

The nice part is that when you've been in radio for any length of time, many listeners remain loyal for years—especially true in Chicago radio; it's akin to that of country fans for their entertainers. A loyal listener, Kathy, wrote a "Letter to the Editor" of the *Chicago Sun-Times* when the paper named "Chicago's Top 100 Women"—claiming that they had missed including me in that list. They captioned her letter—"Szerszen Deserves Mention."

Cara Jepsen, *Illinois Entertainer* Media Editor, pointed out in the 30th Anniversary issue, how opportunities for women in radio were no better now than they were 30 years ago. (She sure nailed that one!)

Ball of Confusion

And then there were those kids who had pretended to be me when they *played radio*. I also heard some grown women impersonated me. How flattering! (I think.) Becoming acquainted with sweet people like this are some of the rewards of working in radio.

But along with all this sweetness also comes the wackiness. It's frightening when you find that a listener has been calling you to chit-chat, then logging your comments and life events in a diary—for years and years, all dated and timed. My own diary isn't that detailed. Or when they claim you are their *true friend* and without you in their life, they will be back in the depths of depression. That they depend on you for their emotional well-being is an overwhelming responsibility I never expected from working in radio. It was just supposed to be entertainment—just a sharing of fun.

The music also often held sweet memories for me and would flash back to special times in my life. "When Will I See You Again" reminded me of a boyfriend who said that to me at the end of a date and then never called again. "I'd Really Love to See You Tonight" reminded me of another boyfriend who loved to see me—and *her*—and *her*. "I'm Not in Love" was a special favorite of the old boyfriend who I thought was "Mr. Right," but I was just his "Ms. Right Now."

I remember back when "Daniel" was playing as my mom's plane took off for a vacation in Poland. Since we were so close, that had been a worrisome time for me. I knew I'd really miss her, but I also knew it'd be fun for her—because she was going with her sister and they hadn't seen some family or friends for years. I couldn't go along because of station commitments. Call it woman's instinct, but something bothered me while she was away. It was during that week that I went into the talk studio at the station, where a guest psychic was taking calls from listeners. During a break, I asked him if my mom was OK on her trip—(in those days, it was difficult to call home from Poland). He looked at me, concerned, and just said,

"She's OK. She had a little accident—hurt her knee. But she's alright."

Well, now I was really worried. So when I finally went to pick up my mom at the airport, I looked at her swollen ankles (which I assumed were from the long flight) and asked the burning question on my mind—

"Mom, how's your leg?"

She was stunned.

"Who told you?" she wanted to know, looking at me curiously.

Since there had been no communication—how could I have possibly known anything. I hesitated to say *a psychic*. So I just answered,

"Why? What happened to your leg?"

And then she told me. How the car they were driving in had overturned on a dried, mud-rutted road. Her sister, Helen, had been thrown out of the car. Everyone was unconscious, but when they came to, my mom had a big gash on her leg. Then I told her about the psychic.

So, yes, the music spoke to me and brought back memories just it they did for the listeners. Music speaks to your soul. I was always *involved* with my shows. It was more than just a job to me. And, as in every other line of work, if you truly love what you do, you usually do your best. Personally, I always rely on the help of the Holy Spirit in any work I do. I believe that God works through each of us for the good of all. Yeah, so I never made any money to speak of. But hopefully, I brought some fun to someone who might have needed it that day, as well as to myself. Life is too short not to try and be happy and not to try and share some fun. As for money, God sends it in His Own way. My bills get paid somehow. Thank God we have God!

Right before a show, I'd laugh as I told the other jocks I was doing my *show prep*. And then seriously, I'd make the Sign of the Cross, and ask the Holy Spirit to help me do the best show I could. And the radio miracles would always happen.

As I'd drive home from the station, I'd listen to air-checks of the show I just did. I'd do my own critiques. Did someone laugh at that?

I'd wonder—did anyone find this interesting? Did they *feel* the music as I had at that moment?

And then, I'd smile—when I'd hear an intro and suddenly there was a quip—that for the life of me, I couldn't figure out where it came from—but I knew it didn't come from me. It was my voice—but it was not something that I was consciously aware of before I said it. It was just too spontaneous and delivered just right with the beat of the music. At times like that, I'd just look up and say, *"Thank You!"* Not that the *intro* was that important, but that God was there with me, working through me—helping me share some stardust. *That's* what was important! And so, I'd thank the Holy Spirit.

Actually, I'm always curious to hear tapes of my show, because they were often as much a surprise to me as they were to the listener. *Sssssshhhh!*—something you should never tell the boss.

EIGHTEEN

Rock On

As for Top Rock Girly Jock's return to radio—my regular shows were scheduled for either Saturday nights or Sunday afternoon or evening. I was also often scheduled to fill in for vacationing DJs, like Fred Winston and Dick Biondi. The personal appearances (paying $500 each) that I had been lured back to radio with, never amounted to much. Since they were based on seniority, and since I was the newest jock, I only got two of them in the four years that I worked at WJMK. But I loved being back in radio.

In 2004, our Program Director, Charley Lake, created a new show to replace the syndicated show that was losing ratings on Saturday night. He chose me to host *'70s Saturday Night!* We played rock and disco from the '70s—very rhythmic—I loved it! I had finally reached that radio pinnacle in my life—from the early days of playing jazz at WSDM (and listening to rock and roll on my transistor radio, while I did my jazz show)—to actually becoming a real rock jock myself. On June 3, 2004, I was honored to headline Robert Feder's column in the *Chicago Sun-Times* as he announced the show.

TOP ROCK GIRLY JOCK

It was the "third of June—another sleepy, dusty, *downtown* day—" (Ode to Connie Szerszen—Billie Joe had her own thing goin' in the *delta.*)

'Top Rock Girly Jock' comes home to the '70s

Chicago's premier oldies station is turning to radio's self-styled "Top Rock Girly Jock" to host a new Saturday showcase for the music of the '70s. Starting this week-end, Connie Szerszen will host "'70s Saturday Night" from 6 p.m. to midnight Saturdays on WJMK-FM (104.3). The show replaces Dick Bartley's syndicated "Rock n' Roll's Greatest Hits" on the Infinity Broadcasting station.

For Szerszen, a lifelong Chicagoan and pioneering female rock jock on WIND-AM (560) and the former WSDM (where she was known as "Den Pal Dawn,") it's a perfect fit.

"Doing a '70s show will be 'bringing it home' for me," said Szerszen, who's been working as a part-time jock at Oldies 104.3 since 2002. "We'll be playing the music that will take us back to a time when we laughed and got silly together, when our hearts were torn together, and when we shared those special events in musical history." Szerszen still recalls meeting Elvis Presley as he stepped off a freight elevator at the Arlington Park Hilton, having a date with Neil Diamond, and emceeing shows with Wayne Newton, Tom Jones and Bobby Vinton.

"Music in the '70s was more diverse than it is today," she said. "There was something for everyone….Now young people are hearing the music of Elvis and the Beatles for the first time and making them hits all over again."

#

Rock On

NEWS 61

MEDIA MIX

ComEd ads focus on workers' reliability

LEWIS LAZARE

e-mail:
llazare@suntimes.com

Leo Burnett put some of its most cutting-edge creative talent on the ComEd business when the city's largest agency handled the account not that long ago. And not surprisingly, Burnett and its talent delivered some pretty way-out-there advertising for a relatively conservative client. Remember, for instance, all those plastic snowmen or off-key factory workers warbling that "Winter Wonderland" ditty?

Well, the Burnett work may have been attention-grabbing stuff. But in the end, maybe too much attention was paid to the grabbing and not enough to the content.

Instead of wacky plastic snowmen or off-key factory workers making like Placido Domingo, the considerably more subdued new print work breaking this month from ComEd's new agency of record — Tierney/Philadelphia — focuses on ComEd employees and their supposedly unwavering commitment to superb service. The campaign's tagline is "That's My Promise. That's Our Way." Each simple print execution features an image of a ComEd employee — some named and some not — and a second shot related to the ad copy.

In one ad featuring ComEd employee James Pitchford and a photo of a large fan, for instance, the copy states: "I promise to work in the heat so you can stay where it's cool. I promise to outlast the hottest days of summer when the sun's in my eyes and sweat's dripping off my nose."

In another execution with an

I promise to get drenched so your clothes can get dry.

flashy in any of this work from Tierney — just neatly organized advertising about ComEd employees' dedication to getting the job done. Some might say Tierney's take on ComEd is a step backward for advertising, because the work is so subdued and — well — so basic, just like you would expect a utility company to be.

But we think Tierney deserves points for coming up with work that has a clearly delineated mes-

ROBERT FEDER

e-mail:
feder@suntimes.com

'Top Rock Girly Jock' comes home to the '70s

Chicago's premier oldies station is turning to radio's self-styled "Top Rock Girly Jock" to host a new Saturday showcase for the music of the '70s.

Starting this weekend, Connie Szerszen will host "'70s Saturday Night" from 6 p.m. to midnight Saturdays on WJMK-FM (104.3). The show replaces Dick Bartley's syndicated "Rock 'n' Roll's Greatest Hits" on the Infinity Broadcasting station.

For Szerszen, a lifelong Chicagoan and pioneering female rock jock on WIND AM (560) and the former WSDM (where she was known as "Den-Pal Dawn,") it's a perfect fit.

"Doing a '70s show will be 'bringing it home' for me," said Szerszen,

Connie Szerszen

who's been working as a part-time jock at Oldies 104.3 since 2002. "We'll be playing the music that will take us back to a time when we laughed and got silly together, when our hearts were torn together, and when we shared those special events in musical history."

Szerszen still recalls meeting Elvis Presley as he stepped off a freight elevator at the Arlington Park Hilton, having a date with Neil Diamond, and emceeing shows with Wayne Newton, Tom Jones and Bobby Vinton.

"Music in the '70s was more diverse than it is today," she said. "There was something for everyone. Now young people are hearing the music of Elvis and the Beatles for the first time and making them hits all over again."

Taking over Szerszen's former Sunday night shift on Oldies 104.3 will be Lisa Greene. Fans can check out her Web site at: www.LisaGreene.net.

Dialing: 'Soul 106.3' all-stars

♦ Crawford Broadcasting is

Were the Days" old-time radio showcase from 1 to 5 p.m. Saturday on WDCB-FM (90.9).

Schaden will serve up "audio snapshots" of the news coverage and the response of network radio to the Allied invasion that led to the liberation of Europe. Listeners will hear how virtually every program airing on June 6, 1944, dropped or modified its planned programming to reflect the nation's concern for its armed forces and their mission.

♦ **Jill Egan**, former morning co-host at WZZN-FM (94.7), has landed as weekend and fill-in jock at WLUP-FM (97.9).

♦ **Mancow Muller's** WKQX-FM (101.1) morning show will pay the bill for everyone who pumps gas from 7 to 8 a.m. today at the Marathon station at 373 W. Main St. in south suburban Glenwood.

♦ WGCI-FM (107.5) will be "Stoppin' the Hits" at 7 a.m. Friday — long enough for morning host **"Crazy" Howard McGee** to interview Gov. **Blagojevich** about health care for children.

July 3rd is my birthday. And that year, the Village of Palatine Jaycees asked me to be the Grand Marshall at their 4th of July Parade. People lined the streets, shouting, *"Connie—we love you! We love your show!"* My neighbor, Chris, drove the parade car, as I sat on the back of the convertible, and tossed candy to the kids along the way. What a wonderful birthday present from God!

So this was how we felt God's love—not love from a prince charming (I'm still just wearing one glass slipper)—not only from your family, whose love will always be most special—but through *everyone*—people who know you better than you will ever know them. They love you because they *feel* your love for them—when you go on the air and laugh, tease, inform, or *play* with them, and are there to just share some fun. So this must have been what God wanted me to do. My brother, Jerry, had been right—he just *knew* it.

We drove on through the parade route—the streets were blocked to normal traffic. For other cars, it was *"Red for Stop,"* but for us, it was *"Green for Go"* all the way! Huge signs on the sides of our car announced—

CONNIE SZERSZEN
2004 - 4th OF JULY GRAND MARSHALL
OLDIES 104.3 WJMK RADIO

Our radio was tuned to WJMK—the volume was cranked! Suddenly, Grand Funk's "American Band" started playing—

> "We're an American Band—
> Sweet sweet Connie was doin' her act
> She had the whole show and that's a natural fact
> Feelin' good, feelin' right, it's Saturday night!"

Again, credit the Holy Spirit for the timing—*exactly* as I was leading the parade—and even plugging my Saturday night show! Hah! (And, yeah, I'm sure the *Connie* in the song had a whole different act.)

Rock On

From left—Dick Biondi, me, Fred Winston—A DJ Sandwich!
(DJ's I filled in for at WJMK)

Connie Szerszen

TOP ROCK GIRLY JOCK

WJMK Studios—Two Prudential Plaza, Chicago

Rock On

Fun Times When I Wasn't Playing Radio

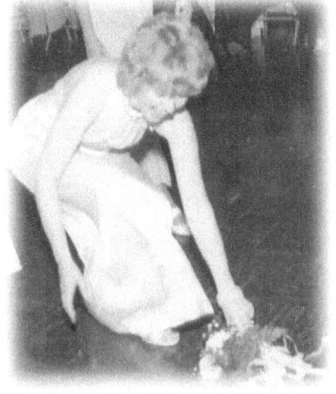

Left—As DJ for weddings, I caught lots of bouquets— but no prince!

Below—Love to sail— but only in shallow lakes

Above—Can't swim, but loved floating in the Dead Sea

Above—Horseback in Poland Camelback in the Holy Land

Above—Sun Studios & Elvis' 1st microphone Memphis, TN

TOP ROCK GIRLY JOCK

Some Dear Photos of My Family

Mom and Dad at our first new home in Norridge

340

Rock On

My brother Jerry—
When he isn't engineering
video games like *Pac Man*,
naming *"Inky & Blinky,"*
he's out for the big catch—

Right—
Just warming up

IT'S A STAGE I'M GOING THROUGH

Left—
The trophy fish!
(as opposed to trophy wife)

4-Foot Muskie
Lake of the Woods,
Canada

NINETEEN

Hit the Road Jack!

In its first ratings book, according to Arbitron, ***'70s Saturday Night* was the #1 show in Chicago** (excluding urban stations) in the highly desired 25-54 demographics. On June 4, 2005, on the eve of the first anniversary of the show, I was looking forward to thanking our listeners who helped make us such a success. I thought about this as I headed for a shower, listening to WJMK. When I stepped out of the shower, something strange was playing on the radio. I'd never heard this before, and listened to see if it was a new promo for something or other—but it was so long—longer than a promo would be—it went on and on.

And then I realized what it was. We had changed formats. Just like that. WJMK was *Oldies* when I stepped in to the shower—and *Jack* when I came out. And I don't take long showers.

Naked, and dripping wet, I ran to the phone and called Charley, our P.D. It was true. The station, as we knew it, was gone.

Infinity in New York decided on it and made the change in New York and Chicago at the exact same time. But Charley assured me none of us would lose our jobs.

TOP ROCK GIRLY JOCK

So in the following days, the jocks worked their shifts and ran the board for the new *Jack* format. We were not allowed to talk—but we kept our jobs. Dave Robbins, Vice President and General Manager, tried to save us. He created WJMK 104.3 HD2 and made us the "first all-digital radio station in America to broadcast with live air personalities."

And so, once again, I became *"the first woman."* In the '70s at WIND, I had always felt honored to be the ***"first female on AM radio to have her own show in prime time in a major market."*** Now, in 2005, at WJMK-104.3 HD2, I was honored again to be ***"the first female in America to broadcast 'live' on an all-digital radio station!"***

ALL_ACCESS.COM -

NET NEWS as of FRIDAY, AUGUST 12, 2005
Updated at 9:14a (PT)

    INFINITY Oldies WJMK-HD2/CHICAGO made history this morning by becoming the first HD Radio station to broadcast with a live airstaff. GREG BROWN kicked off the historic event at 10a and welcomed in the new age of digital broadcasting on WJMK 104.3 HD2. He becomes AMERICA's first DJ to broadcast on a fully digital station with a live airstaff. Legendary air personalities FRED WINSTON and DICK BIONDI will follow this afternoon and tonight in their regular shifts. PAUL PERRY will be on heard in mornings beginning MONDAY (8/15), while CONNIE SZERZEN will do "70's Saturday Night" live on SATURDAY nights beginning tomorrow (8/13).

Of the occasion, Variety Hits WJMK (JACK-FM), Country WUSN, and Oldies WJMK-HD2 VP/GM DAVE ROBBINS said, "Today is an historic day for radio, as we welcome the era of Live Digital Broadcasting on supplemental channels. Unique content will drive the digital broadcast age." If you would like to hear the new HD2 station, it is currently being simulcast online at www.wjmk.com.

(Mis-spelled again! It's ***S-Z-E-R-S-Z-E-N***. Sounds like "Ser-zen")

Hit the Road, Jack!

Wow! I was amazed that I had this honor—the first woman in America! For this historic event, I brought in my camcorder and video-taped the opening moments; it's now shared with the world on YouTube—*http://www.youtube.com/watch?v=tCcw3vAOLrg*—and documented in Wikipedia.

And so we did our radio shows—my *'70s Saturday Night* was now on the HD2 channel and streaming on-line. I enjoyed streaming because now I heard from former '70s listeners who had since relocated to different cities all across the country. It was nostalgia to the extreme—for them and for me—bringing back so many fun memories. WJMK 104.3 HD2 made the *All Access Net News* and, just as FM radio, with its stereo capabilities had once overtaken AM radio, HD, digital radio, would now challenge analog radio.

But just about a year later, in July of 2006, CBS made another top-secret move. They decided to automate the new, all-digital station. In the middle of the week, the news hit the jocks hard and fast; we were all let go—there went my $220 salary! We read about it in The *Chicago Sun-Times*— Robert Feder headlined it, "Black Wednesday."

I realized then that my last show there may have been my last show—*ever!* My usual sign-off was "Jezcze Polska Nie Zginęła—see you next week" or something like that. But that last time, something inside made me suddenly change my sign-off. I said—

"Jezcze Polska Nie Zginęła! I'll be looking for you next *'70s Saturday Night*—unless, of course, I meet *Mr. Right* between now and then and become a trophy wife, in which case I may have to travel the world in search of rare 'Objay D'Ar' (in English, that's 'Objects Dart') and then I'd have to throw lavish parties—but if all that doesn't happen, I'll be looking for you right here—WJMK104.3 HD2."

Of course none of that ever happened, but I wouldn't be back anyway. Little did I know.

The song started—Thelma Houston's, "Don't Leave Me This Way." So coincidental—that last song. *Hmmmmmmm—*

TOP ROCK GIRLY JOCK

Some of the jocks have found other radio homes. Some are writing a book. (*Hellllooooo—*) I continue to paint portraits of people, houses, towns, pets, and other commissioned works. *(www.portraitartchicago.com)* I still take my music on the road—entertaining at parties and special events. (*www.toprockgirlyjock.com*)

As for radio—my former shows are riding those airwaves in the cosmos. And I'm always on the look-out for a new radio home—to bring me into *your* home. There's more music and fun to share. So stay tuned—but you're probably gonna have to change that dial!

Thank you dear listeners—A big air-kiss to you!
Jeszcze Polska Nie Zginęła!

There's a bit of Stardust in everyone—

So we may *sparkle* for each other!

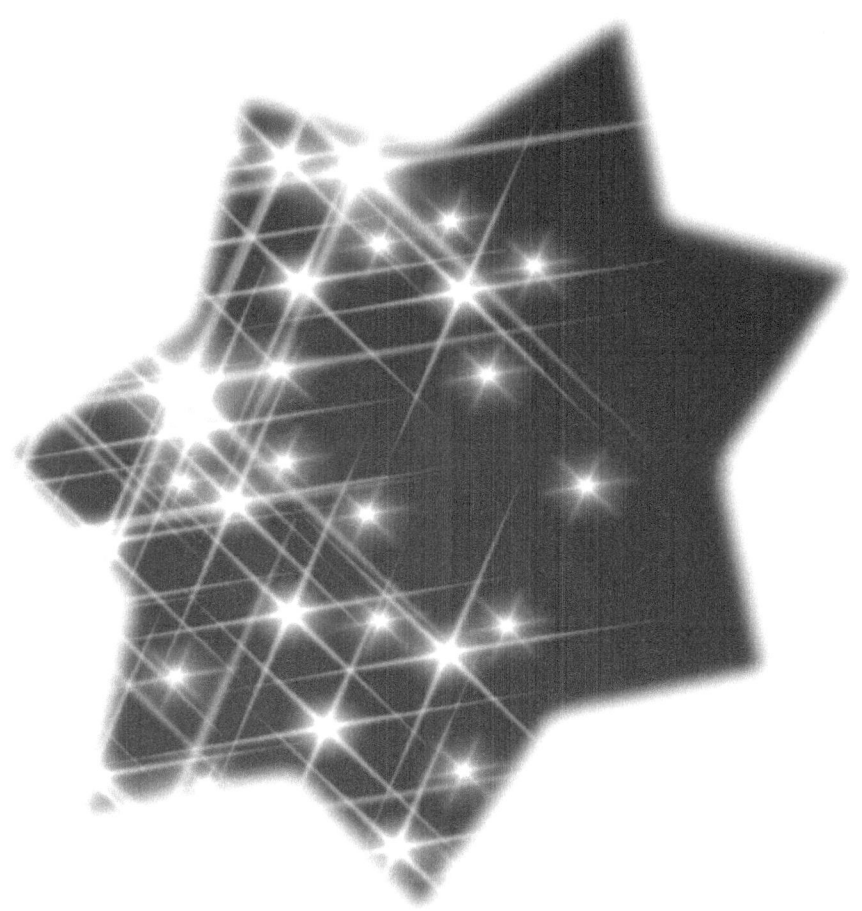

Thank you dear readers—
A big book-kiss for you!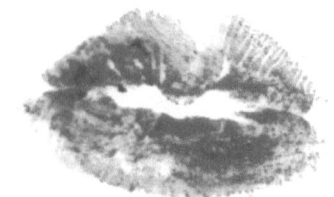

(Where's that Chapstick?!)

Photo Credits

Grateful thanks to all for permission to reproduce the photographs in this book. Every reasonable attempt has been made to obtain permission on copyrighted material used here. Any errors or omissions brought to attention will be corrected in future editions.

All photos from the personal collection of Connie Szerszen, except for the following—
Pp. **29**, **30**, **31**, **32**, **33**-The Chicago American; Pp. **35**, **36**, **37**, **38**-The New World; Pg. **52**-Courtesy of The Jolly Roger; Pg. **53** (Top)-Doris M. Barnes/Betty J. Beardemphl; Pg. **58**-U of I Medical Center Campus; Pp. **65**, **66**-L.A. Herald-Examiner; Pp. **76** (Top), **86** (Top), **218**-WCFL; Pg. **79**-Joe Gino, United Photographers; Pg. **85**-Chicago's American; Pp. **93**, **94**, **95**, **96**, **112**-WSDM; Pg. **104**-Northwestern News, NWU; Pp. **127**, **129**, **140**, **146**, **155**, **156**, **159**, **160**, **168**, **169**, **170**, **174**, **175**, **178**, **189** (Bottom), **213**, **214**, **220**, **221**, **222**, **223**, **224**, **252**-WIND; Pg. **129**-Chicago Daily News; Pp. **133**, **134**, **135**-Mademoiselle; Pg. **145**-U.S.Congressional Record; Pg. **148**-United Photographers; Pg. **152**-Playboy Clubs, Int.; Pg. **153**-FACES; Pg. **154**-George Tebbens Photography; Pg. **157**-La Grange High School; Pg. **158**-Hillside Merchants Center Assoc.; Pp. **162** (Top, left), **200** (Right), **251** (Bottom)-Chicago Tribune; Pp. **163**, **164**-Jim Feeley Enterprises; Pg. **180**-Suburban Trib; Pg. **183**-Dorothy and Vince Mayer; Pg. **185**-American Cancer Society; Pg. **186**-(Top) Chicago Today-(Bottom) Lions Club; Pg. **187**-Easter Seals; Pg. **188** (Top)-United Cerebral Palsy Foundation; Pp. **188** (Bottom), **195**, **217**, **219**, **248** (Bottom), **257**, **270**, **312**, **335**-The Chicago Sun-Times; Pg. **189** (Top)-Jerry Lewis Telethon; Pg. **199**-Dziennik Zwiazkowy; Pg. **201**-Polish American Police Association; Pp. **200** (Left), **202**-Heritage Club of Polish Americans; Pg. **204**-NBC, Ch. 5, Jim Tilmon; Pg. 205-Arlene Kero; Pg. **206**-The Herald Press; Pg. **208**-Francis Grabowski; Pg. **209**-Bill Donovan; Pg. **242**-Women in Motion Picture Industry; Pp. **248** (Top), **249**, **250**-WJJD/WJEZ; Pg. **251**-(Top) The Jeannie C. Riley Fan Club; Pg. **264**-Kathy Bassett; Pg. **272**-Lerner Papers; Pg. **278**-Terry's Photography; Pg. **296**-Crain's Chicago Business; Pg. **297**-Daily Herald; Pg. **302**-St. Mary of Nazareth Hospital; Pg. **313**-Mark Wilows; Pg. **314**-The N.W. Indiana Times; Pg. **328**-The Illinois Entertainer; Pp. **337**, **344**-(Bottom) WJMK; Pg. **346**-Michael G. Bush;
Front Cover-And Frontispiece before Table of Contents—
Gerry Dunn/Jack O'Grady Photo Prod., Inc.,
Back Cover-Jim Feeley Enterprises, Michael G. Bush, WIND

www.ingramcontent.com/pod-product-compliance
Lightning Source LLC
Chambersburg PA
CBHW031544300426
44111CB00006BA/163